Heads above Water

Heads above Water

*Gender, Class, and Family
in the Grand Forks Flood*

Alice Fothergill

State University of New York Press

Cover photo courtesy of FEMA (website).

Published by
State University of New York Press, Albany

For information, contact State University of New York Press, Albany, NY
www.sunypress.edu

Production by Judith Block
Marketing by Michael Campochiaro

Library of Congress Cataloging-in-Publication Data

Fothergill, Alice.
    Heads above water : gender, class, and family in the Grand Forks flood /
Alice Fothergill.
        p. cm.
    Includes bibliographical references and index.
    ISBN-13: 978-0-7914-6157-0 (hardcover : alk. paper) —
978-0-7914-6158-7 (pbk. : alk. paper)
    ISBN 0-7914-6157-2 (alk. paper) — 0-7914-6158-0 (pbk. : alk. paper)
    1. Floods—Social aspects—North Dakota—Grand Forks.   2. Floods—
Red River Valley (Minn. and N.D.-Man.)   3. Women disaster victims—North
Dakota—Grand Forks.   4. Women—North Dakota—Grand Forks—Social
conditions.   5. Sex role—North Dakota—Grand Forks.   I. Title.

    HV6101997.N9 68 2004
    978.4'16—dc22
                                                        2003058781

10 9 8 7 6 5 4 3 2 1

Dedicated to my parents

Priscilla Royce Fothergill
and
William Rolston Fothergill

Contents

Acknowledgments

M any individuals helped me to produce this book. I would like
to begin by thanking the forty women in Grand Forks, North
Dakota, who shared their stories, their time, energy, and emotions
with me. Having promised to keep their names confidential, I cannot thank them personally for having confided in me. They were
open, generous, and kind.

I would like to thank Professor Dennis Mileti and the entire
staff at the Natural Hazards Center at the University of Colorado,
where I worked from 1994 to 2001. In my first year of graduate
school, Dennis recruited me to work on a large National Science
Foundation (NSF) research grant documenting issues of inequality,
including gender, class, and race, in the disaster context. That project planted the seed for this dissertation. Dennis provided generous
material support and strategic career guidance, as well as never-
ending confidence in my work. Mary Fran Myers, a North Dakota
native, was the seed for my "snowball" sampling, so without her, I
would not have known where to start. Dave Morton, now retired,
was the best librarian one could have hoped for while working on
such a large undertaking. He always found exactly what I was looking for, even when I did not know exactly what it was. Gilbert
White provided valuable weekly advice: "The best dissertation is a
finished dissertation." All the rest of the staff and graduate students
at the Hazard Center—Janet Kroeckel, Dave Butler, Sylvia Dane,
Diane Smith, Fay Tracy, Wanda Headley, Jackie Monday, Lori Peek,
Eve Passerini, and Len Wright—provided a wonderful home base
during graduate school, full of good humor, computer assistance,
potlucks, and support. Thanks also to Steve Graham in the sociology department for his friendship and assistance.

Thanks are also due to the NSF (Grant Number CMS-9312647), which funded me for many years. Their funding got me to Grand Forks six times in thirteen months and paid for lodging at the lovely C'mon Inn; that, of course, helped to make the research project possible. I am indebted to NSF, and to Bill Anderson in particular, for believing in the importance of graduate student research in the natural disaster field and especially for prioritizing the topic of inequality in disasters. Financial assistance was also provided by the University of Colorado's Beverly Sears Dean's Small Grant Award, which is gratefully acknowledged.

The members of my dissertation committee, my mentors, also deserve heartfelt thanks. Patti Adler introduced me to the field of ethnography and worked closely with me to conceptualize the chapters. Her guidance and insights made the whole project come together. Martha Gimenez provided, over tea and scones, much support and always pushed me to consider the structural issues at play. Joyce Nielsen, the first feminist scholar ever to write about gender and disasters, introduced me to feminist theory, and convinced me to pursue a dissertation on gender and disasters. Janet Jacobs spent hours with me at her kitchen table sorting through the ideas of my work and helping me to connect them to feminist literature. She was incredibly generous with her time and insights, and helped smooth over some rough spots in the analysis. Dennis Mileti, the chair of the committee, was instrumental in making sure I did not get carried away in the disaster field, and stayed grounded in the discipline of sociology. The help of mentors Elaine Enarson, Brenda Phillips, and Betty Hearn Morrow, three inspiring scholars in the area of inequality, gender, and disaster, was also greatly appreciated. I am grateful to Joanne Belknap for her help with chapter 8.

Thanks also to my fellow graduate students and friends who helped me complete this project. Joanna Higginson, Jen Lois, Dana Johnson, and Seana Lowe were helpful in the early years of this project, as I began to formulate my prospectus and draft outlines. Our monthly meetings to prepare for preliminary exams, comprehensive exams, and then dissertation proposal defenses will never be forgotten. In my last years of graduate school, my main intellectual and emotional support for this project came from two wonderful individuals, Adina Nack and Katy Irwin. They read every word of this document during our Saturday meetings at Vic's, helping me to make sense of it all. Their intellect and good-naturedness were invaluable.

Several individuals in North Dakota were also extremely helpful. Professors Cliff Staples and Kathy Tiemann in the Department of Sociology at the University of North Dakota were incredibly generous, offering office space, securing my research appointment at UND, providing me with housing, sharing their flood research results, and fielding my phone calls from prospective research participants. Thanks to UND President Kendall Baker and Dean John Ettling for appointing me as a visiting research scientist at the university while I was conducting my study. Grand Forks residents Janet Rex, Jenny Ettling, and Karen Davis also took time out of their busy lives to help me get my research project off the ground—and to make me dinner. Thanks to the staff members of the Community Violence Intervention Center in Grand Forks who helped me gather vital information.

Thanks also to the faculty and staff in the Department of Sociology at the University of Akron, my collegial home during the years when I turned the dissertation into a book. Special thanks to Andre Christie-Mizell, Jeff Lucas, Kathy Feltey, and Becky Erickson (and their families) for their support and friendship during that time. Thanks to Lane Magnuson at the Grand Forks Planning and Zoning Department and Ann Donkin at the University of Akron for help with the maps, and to Pattijean Hooper, Jeri Jewett, and Meridee Danks for their help with photographs.

I also owe a great deal to several individuals who over the last few years have taken care of my children so that I could work on this project. In Colorado, thanks to Robin Gray, Andrea Jones, and Larissa Sandri. In Ohio, thanks to Emily Chilbert, Ann Taddeo, Katherine Kormos, and Michelle Bemiller. Thanks to Joe's wonderful teachers at ECEC: Dorothy Harris, Shalimar Colbert, Marina Duvall, Kelly Carroll, Sheila Mahrer, Halle Garber, Michelle Woodbridge, and Carolyn Biro. And thanks to Maggie's kind caregivers at Childtime: Barbara Heard, Jennifer Heard, M. J. Reiter, and Francine Wahome. I knew my children were in good hands and that was critical for getting this project finished.

I would like to thank the publishers of several journals who gave me permission to reprint my articles. Chapters 3, 5, and 8 are based on journal articles that were previously published. I would like to thank the following: Sage Publishers for permission to use "Women's Roles in a Disaster," 1999, *Applied Behavioral Science Review* 7(2):125–143, which appears in revised form as chapter 3; to the University of California Press for permission to use "The

Stigma of Charity: Gender, Class, and Disaster Assistance," 2003, *Sociological Quarterly* 44(4):659–680 which appears in revised form as chapter 5; and to the Research Committee on Disasters for permission to use "An Exploratory Study of Woman Battering in the Grand Forks Flood Disaster: Implications for Community Responses and Policies," 1999, *International Journal of Mass Emergencies and Disasters* 17(1):79–98, which appears in revised form as chapter 8.

Finally, I would like to thank several family members and friends for their help. Catherine Teare, friend since age twelve, read more than three-hundred pages in a few days and edited the entire manuscript for grammar, punctuation, and clarity—for free. I cannot thank her enough for that gift. Gratitude also goes to my generous in-laws, Janet and Buzz, who helped in a myriad of ways during the many years that I worked on this project. My parents, Bill and Priscilla, and my sisters, Kate and Anne, have always been the ones who gave me the support and confidence to pursue a Ph.D., as well as providing me with much-needed breaks along the way. They also provided valuable editorial assistance in the final hours. My mother, especially, deserves thanks for watching my children while I finished key parts of the project and thanks to my father for coming up with the book's title. Most of all, I want to thank my husband Jeff, my son Joe, and my daughter Maggie. Jeff was by my side from the very beginning of this project, providing encouragement and good humor. Joe, now an energetic and curious preschooler, made his debut between the data collection and the final phases of the dissertation, and Maggie joined us several years later when I was turning the dissertation into a book. They made me smile at the end of each day of writing and researching.

Chapter 1

Introduction: Red River Rising

Elaine was cold, hungry, and exhausted. She sat down on the pile of sandbags and put her face in her hands. She tried not to cry, but she could feel the tears fill her eyes. She let herself sit like that for a few minutes, resting, thinking, and then she knew she had to keep moving. She had been up for thirty hours, and her hands and back ached. It was frigid outside, and even though it was April, it felt like winter. Spring was often a little slow to arrive in North Dakota. She moved her toes in her boots, hoping to warm them a little. Looking out at all the volunteers, Elaine felt both profound warmth toward her fellow neighbors, as well as the hopelessness of a situation out of their control. *What else can we do?* she thought to herself.

A few older women had just arrived at the sandbagging site and were handing out sandwiches and cookies to sandbaggers. Elaine accepted one and ate the butter and ham sandwich on white bread—not her favorite, but under the circumstances, it was fine. She got back in the sandbagging line, knowing that the work must continue if they were going to save the neighborhood. The man to her right, a retired teacher, was cold and tired, too, but he offered a smile as she joined back in the line. The sandbags started coming and he turned and handed Elaine a bag. He managed to somewhat roll it into her arms, and she used both arms to cradle the bag and turn in one motion to pass it to the teenager on her left. Then she turned back to the right, received another bag, and continued. Elaine didn't talk much in line, but she listened while others chatted as they tried to pass the time and keep positive attitudes. She tried to think only of the task at hand, focus on the sandbags, and not think about the possibility of disaster. *Take the bag, pass it along,*

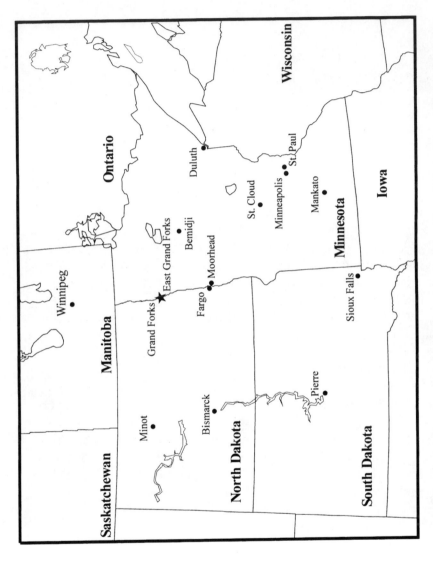

Regional Map. *Map courtesy of the Grand Forks–East Grand Forks Metropolitan Planning Organization.*

take the bag, pass it along, she said to herself. *Don't think about what might happen.*

After another hour, they ran out of sandbags and had to wait for a delivery from "sandbag central." Elaine decided to head home and finish moving her belongings to the top floor. Ed, her husband, thought it wasn't necessary, but she felt that it was something she wanted—and needed—to do. The night before, she had moved clothes and boxes from the basement to the first floor and stacked them in the living room. They had accepted that the basement would probably get a little water. Now she stood in the doorway, ran her fingers through her hair, and considered the situation. *The first floor is not high enough*, she thought. Moving quickly, but not panicked, Elaine started putting photo albums in a laundry basket to carry upstairs. She couldn't help but peek in one older album, and seeing a photo of her children as toddlers smiling in the backyard of their home, she felt a rush of emotion, and the tears returned to her eyes. She had been in this house for twenty-one years, and it was the only home her children had ever known. Looking around the room, she felt an attachment to the house that she could not describe, but it was potent.

Several helicopters flew overhead and the house seemed to shake. The sound of them made her feel unnerved. Quickly, Elaine closed the album, placed it in the basket, and began moving everything to the bedrooms upstairs. She carried afghans from the couch, the quilt hanging on the wall that her aunt had made for her wedding, and the ashtray her daughter had made when she was five. On her third trip upstairs, she piled her son's baseball card collection and some coats on her bed, then turned to head back downstairs. It was at that moment that she heard the siren. She stood perfectly still and listened. *This cannot be happening*, she thought, but there was no doubt that it was the flood sirens. The city was flooding.

Elaine ran downstairs and picked up the phone to call her husband. Her children, now teenagers, were at her sister's house across town. Suddenly there was the sound of someone yelling through a blowhorn on her street. It was some men from the fire station, and one was yelling, "Evacuate now!" as the truck rolled through the neighborhood. Elaine moved quickly from room to room, not sure what to take, not sure what to do. The phone rang. It was her husband. "The dikes have been breached," he said. "You have to get out immediately. I'll meet you at Susie's." Fortunately, her sister's house was on the west side of town, farther from the river. Her husband, who worked at a construction company, was at his office. *He's calm, I will be calm*, she said to herself as she corralled the dog outside and into the family van. She left their cat, Lucky, because her sister was allergic to cats, and Lucky would be fine upstairs for a night or two. Her neighborhood felt like a war zone, with helicopters overhead and Humvees rolling down the streets. She ran back inside and grabbed her purse and a basket of dirty laundry. Not believing that they would really have to leave, Elaine had not packed bags, but she thought the clothes in the basket would tide them over for a night or two until they came home again. *This won't be so bad*, she reasoned, as she pulled out of her driveway; *we'll stay with Susie for a night and it'll be fine. Maybe Susie will make her baked chicken for dinner.* But when Elaine got to the end of her block, and started to make a left turn, she looked to her right and stopped. She saw the water. Her neighborhood was filling up like a bathtub, slowly but steadily.

Elaine headed west, driving through some streets where the water was halfway up her van's tires. *Please don't stall, please don't stall*, she repeated under her breath, knowing that she probably couldn't carry her ninety-pound dog out of the van to safety. She arrived safely at her sister's house, only to learn that her neighborhood was also being evacuated. Her sister's face looked strained, nervous, but she didn't acknowledge her fear and worry. "Okay, let's think about what we should all do," she said positively, as if they had arrived at the beach and had to decide between volleyball and swimming. The family was stuck. They could not stay at the shelter set up at the airbase because it did not take dogs. They could not get to their parents in Minnesota; all the roads going east were closed because the bridges over the river into East Grand Forks, Minnesota, were out. After deciding that a motel was probably their best bet, they loaded into their cars and headed out of town.

Elaine and her family joined in as the entire city of Grand Forks, North Dakota, evacuated its city limits. Seeing the steady stream of cars, knowing that everyone was leaving, made Elaine feel somewhat stunned, as if this was too surreal to even talk about with her family. Her family members must have felt the same way, for no one spoke as they drove slowly away from their home. They listened to the radio announcers, who surprisingly were still broadcasting from their Grand Forks studio, discuss the details of the water influx. Looking out their window, the announcers could see couches and portable toilets floating down the street, and they made jokes about this to their audience. Elaine's daughter laughed from the backseat. Elaine smiled at her in the rearview mirror, happy to hear the sound of her laugh. The radio announcers continued with listing the offers of families to take in evacuees: "The Millers of Bemidgi can take two adults, but no pets. Joan Larson of Grand Lake has offered to take in a family; cats are okay. Mike Cooper of Manvel can take one adult, no children." Suddenly, the radio announcers stopped the list of names and offers. At that very moment, Ed gasped. Behind them, he could see in the rearview mirror, was thick, black smoke rising from the city. "I think the city's on fire," Ed said as everyone in the car whipped their heads around to see. Indeed, the city *was* on fire. There was nothing Elaine and her family, or any of the other residents, could do except to continue driving as their home went both underwater and down in flames at the same time. Elaine ached with fatigue, worry, and fear as she stared out ahead onto the highway. *What is going to happen to all of us?* she thought.

Suddenly, her son sat up straight in the backseat and cried out, "Lucky!" They had forgotten about their beloved cat, still in their house. The thought of her drowning there was too much for all of them, and they felt an overwhelming feeling of despair and sorrow. Her daughter began to cry, and her son pulled his baseball cap low over his face. They could not go back now; it would be impossible to drive into the city. They drove on in silence. The last few weeks had been unimaginably difficult and stressful, but their ordeal was really just beginning.

Their evacuation would be for not only a day or two, as Elaine had thought, but for two and a half months. They stayed in a motel, then in the home of strangers, then with a family friend, and then finally moved into a Federal Emergency Management Agency (FEMA) trailer. They felt unmoored and nomadic. They felt homeless, and they were: their home was completely destroyed by the flood. The night they evacuated, they watched on television as the city burned and the water went up to the rooftops. Photographers went down streets in boats, filming house by house, and eventually Elaine and her family saw the roof of their home. They recognized the big oak tree in their front yard, the one they had hung a swing on when the children were little. At that moment, Elaine felt almost as if she was having an out-of-body experience: *None of this is really happening, is it?*

In many ways, Elaine felt fortunate. They were all safe, they were able to evacuate together, and volunteers had rescued their cat. She worked hard to count her blessings, to take one day at a time, and to feel thankful for what she had. Yet, when the moment came, months later, to go back into her home, she felt it was the worst moment in her life. She stood on the sidewalk and looked up at their sweet two-story home. It had been perfect. Her feet felt like lead, and then she felt faint. She took Ed's hand, and they walked slowly up the front walk and up the stairs to the front door. "I'm not sure I can do this," she whispered to Ed. "You don't have to," he reassured her, but she knew it was time for her to go inside. Her neighbor, an elderly woman, had decided that she could not go back in her house, so she let relatives report the damage to her and volunteers cleaned up the wreckage. Elaine wanted to be strong and see it for herself.

The first thing they noticed was that the deck Ed had built was in the side yard, detached from the back of the house. The front screen door was hanging on one hinge, and there were several water lines on the house: the first from the initial level above the bedroom windows, and the second one, where the water had sat for weeks, about four feet up on the first floor. Inside, the house was dark and cold and smelled awful—a mixture of sewage, mold, and oil. Elaine's heart skipped a beat as she scanned the room: furniture overturned, dark mud covering the walls, a living room chair on top of the dining room table. Black slime covered every item. They slowly walked from room to room, commenting in low, somber voices on the damage. For some reason, they felt they needed to talk softly, as if someone was sleeping—or dying—in the house. Elaine thought that the kitchen was the hardest sight, until she got upstairs and looked in the bedrooms. The slime was on their beds, in their sheets, on their clothes. She put her hands over her mouth, feeling violated by the sight. Then she noticed the albums. The photo albums, which she had worked so hard to place in high spots on the second floor, were scattered about their bedroom, soaked with water and mud. The faces of her toddlers smiling in the backyard were behind a layer of mud, and the photo curled at the edges.

In the weeks and months that followed, Elaine worked tirelessly. She helped to gut her house and washed any salvageable items and furniture. She lugged water-soaked clothes and toys to the berm for trash pickup.[1] She dealt with the enormous amount of paperwork necessary for postflood life, and she stood in lines for donations that had been given to the city. Elaine, like many residents in her town, was surprised by how long it took for life to feel normal again. Even years later she thought it did not feel like it did before—before the flood. *I am so grateful that no lives were lost in the flood,* she often thought to herself. Yet, as she threw away the handmade afghans, her son's baseball collection, and the quilt made by her aunt for their wedding, Elaine would think to herself, *but I feel like a lot of my life was lost.* She pushed aside those thoughts, finished washing the footstool her grandfather made her, and admired her work. *It looks wonderful,* she bragged to herself, *no sign of mold or slime.* Elaine stood up, peeled off her rubber gloves, and inspected her flood tan: brown arms from her shirt sleeves down to the top of the rubber gloves. The sun was out and Grand Forks looked beautiful with the green of summer. Suddenly, she heard the sound of the Red Cross food truck and realized that she was hungry. Her neighbor waved and Elaine, smiling and waving back, ran up to the truck for a free sandwich and pop. She would need the nourishment for energy to tackle all the work that still lay ahead of her.

This book is about women's experiences in a natural disaster. It is the story of what happened to women like Elaine. Based on ethnographic research on women from Grand Forks, North Dakota, and East Grand Forks, Minnesota, two adjoining towns on the Red River that experienced widespread flooding, evacuation, and destruction in the spring of 1997, this book tells the story of their everyday lives in extraordinary times. The women in my study, such as Elaine, shared their stories with me, and I sought to make sense of what happened to them in one of the worst natural disasters ever in the United States.[2] They relayed the challenges they faced, including coping with loss and emotional trauma, managing the stigma of charity, and keeping their families together. Many of them lost their homes, their sense of stability, and many of their familial artifacts in the flood. They worked hard to rebuild their everyday lives, maintain some control over their emotional and physical health, and negotiate the demands of the public and private spheres of life. The goal of this study is to capture and make sense of these stories, to understand how women re-create their daily lives in a way that is meaningful for them. While this study focuses on a natural disaster, it is applicable to other crises—financial, emotional, familial, or environmental—that women endure every day. It is a story about overcoming and managing a crisis situation; it is about family; it is about social roles and identity; it is about gender; and it is about social-class standing and the trauma of downward mobility. It is a story about continuity and change.

Gender and Disasters

Interestingly, little is known about women's experiences in disasters. Prior to the late 1990s, women's perspectives on their disaster experiences had not been included in the fairly extensive sociological research on disasters. In 1984, sociologist Joyce Nielsen pointed out that gender was an important dimension of the social structure that was critically underdeveloped in disaster scholarship. By the 1990s, both disaster scholars and national experts, in their commitment to reduce the vulnerability of more marginalized groups, recognized a need to focus on women. The knowledge base on women and disasters is derived largely from surveys that included gender as a demographic variable and provided only basic information on gender differences. These studies did not engage in any thorough explanation or analysis of women's experiences or perspectives in a disaster. Many earlier disaster studies focused largely on male-dominated settings, such as emergency operations centers, and search and rescue teams.[3]

Several studies since the 1990s have found that women are more vulnerable in a disaster. Due to their structural location, the devaluation of their work, and their caregiving responsibilities, women are more likely to be at risk in disasters and to have a harder time recovering. This is true in developed countries, and even more so in developing ones. Yet, despite these studies and the recognition that more research is needed on women and disaster, the knowledge base on this issue is still remarkably weak and underdeveloped. Thus, women's voices and experiences in a disaster have not been explored. My study is designed to address this knowledge gap by investigating and analyzing women's experiences in a disaster and placing women's everyday lives at the center of the analysis.

As I studied the women of Grand Forks, it became clear that several underlying themes and tensions marked their experiences.[4]

These themes and tensions will unfold throughout the book. The first theme incorporates the tension between women's commonalities and women's differences. Historically, the fields of sociology and gender studies have debated and detailed the arguments around the problematic nature of the concept of "woman." Gender scholars face a dilemma of wanting to give significance to the differences among women, while still recognizing the importance of what women have in common. Many contemporary gender theorists criticize the dominant Western feminist thought that speaks of an essential "womanness" that all women have, with no consideration of differences in social and demographic characteristics. According to Judith Grant (1993, p. 20), the category "woman" is one of the "most foundational if contentious ones in contemporary feminist theory" because it derives from the belief that women are oppressed not by their class or race, but by their womanhood. It was important to see women as a collectivity for political purposes. By focusing on commonalities, the feminist theorists overlooked women's specific experiences and knowledge that resulted from the material division of labor and the racial stratification system.

In the past twenty years, feminist theories have acknowledged and included the different life experiences of women based on their race, ethnicity, social class status, disability, and sexual orientation. Feminist thought is shifting away from the view of a shared female identity, and toward an understanding of difference. For example, some sociologists have researched and written about how the lives of poor African American women are markedly different from upper- and middle-class white American women (hooks 1981; Collins 1990). Ruth Frankenberg (1993), in her book on women and race, argued that "whiteness" is a location of structural advantage, a "standpoint," and a set of cultural practices. Feminist theorists agree that the differences among women are immense. At the same time, some scholars are reluctant to give up the notion that women living in a patriarchal system have more in common than not. Research has shown that gender is a central organizing principle of social life and that being a male or a female affects almost every aspect of one's life. For example, there is much evidence that women of many backgrounds share the burden of the housework and childcare, and women of all backgrounds are also victimized by sexual assault and domestic violence. As Barbara Risman (1998) noted, women in all classes and races have lower status than men in those same categories.

Thus, feminist theorists strive for a balance between the view of women having common experiences and acknowledging the very real differences in life chances for women of various backgrounds. Theorist Nancy Tuana (1993) argued for this balance of common interests and observable differences. In exploring women's lives, she stated, "We are less likely to find a common core of shared experiences . . . than a family of resemblances with a continuum of similarities" (p. 83). Today, it is common to see this discussion center around a conceptualization of race, class, and gender as "interlocking systems of oppression" that have interacting, simultaneous, and complex effects on women's lives (Spelman 1988; Collins 1990). In this perspective, no factor or system of stratification—race, class, or gender—is considered the primary or most determining one.

The women whose stories I share in this book did not have the same experiences in the disaster. Their differences were significant. Class mattered, race mattered, disability mattered, and sexual orientation mattered. It also made a difference if a woman's family was functional and tight-knit, if she had self-confidence, if she had a reliable job, and if she had good health on her side. It will be clear, as their complex and compelling stories unfold, that the material, social, cultural, and emotional conditions made a difference in how the women experienced the disaster. However, there were also commonalities in their experiences, because being a woman shapes a great deal of one's experience in the social world. The tension between commonalities and differences can be seen in many aspects of the women's stories and will continue to be seen as their experiences are revealed in the book.

A second theme that underlies the women's stories concerns the way in which women negotiate the public, private, and communal spheres of social life. Past research has examined the way that women handle and negotiate the distinct roles associated with the two designated spheres of life: the family role in the domestic sphere and the work role in the public sphere. Yet, interestingly, many social theorists, gender theorists in particular, criticize the two-sphere model of public and private domains. They argue that the public/private dichotomy is inadequate for understanding women's lives (Rosaldo 1980; Lamphere 1993). Nevertheless, despite the criticism, it has remained the predominant framework used in research to examine women's work, roles, and lives.[6] Several alternative frameworks have been proposed that take into account a third sphere in the public/private model. Hansen (1987), building on the work of Hannah Arendt (1958), proposes a social sphere, which includes activities and behaviors such as visiting neighbors, going to church, and other types of interaction within a community among nonfamily members

Related to the idea of a social sphere is a third sphere based on women's community work. Milroy and Wismer (1994) define community work as work that is done outside of home and work. They explain their concept of this third sphere: "It can be political or publicly directed, yet often appears to be maintenance work—part of the "social glue" which holds a community together. While it may include personal or family benefits, it is always intended to provide goods and services to a broader group of people than solely oneself or one's household's members. . . . It is also more inclusive than the formally organised voluntary sector, because it includes small and informal neighbourly care-giving actions by individuals or organisations. Although it is not paid work, it is also not "voluntary" in the sense that it is not discretionary. . . . Its spatial location is neither home nor work place, primarily, but community" (p. 72). According to Milroy and Wismer, community work by women has long been overlooked and needs to be more visible in order for women's lives to be understood in full. For example, they continue their argument on the importance of recognizing community work: "Our working premise is that if domestic work is building homes, families and households, and traded work is building companies and economies, then community work is building communities and should properly be identified as a separate nucleus of productive effort" (p. 82).

Taking this premise into account, I examined all three spheres of women's lives in order to understand the scope of women's social roles, activities, and experiences in the flood. Their stories showed that they employed various and strategic tactics so they could move from one sphere to another, or suspend duties in one when another became more demanding. One of the most important findings is that the women in Grand Forks experienced "role accumulation," (Sieber 1974), meaning that they were committed to their multiple roles and were able to negotiate and fulfill them. Helena Lopata (1994), in her book *Circles and Settings,* discusses how women's roles and work are devalued in a gender-stratified society and how most often the societal panic over women's role conflict is due to the cultural expectations for the role of motherhood. In Grand Forks, I found that the "greedy role" (Coser 1974) for women was their family role, especially if they had young children. Yet, as will be seen as the stories unfold, the women were able to meet the responsibilities of many demanding roles, including the greedy family role, in a competent and uncompromising manner.

The third theme that emerges in the stories of women's experiences in the flood is how women cope with downward mobility in a culture that embraces the ideology of achievement. The ideology of achievement is the prevalent social perspective which pronounces that "any child can grow up to be president" because the United States is full of opportunity for those who are willing to work hard. Thus, as Jay MacLeod (1995) argues in his classic study of class and race, *Ain't No Makin' It,* the achievement ideology posits that success is based on merit, and a lack of ambition or ability is the root of economic failure. As a result, when individuals are poor, the blame is put on them rather than on a capitalist system that perpetuates poverty. As Katherine Newman (1999) describes, thousands of Americans plunge down America's social ladder every year, feeling powerless. After this "fall from grace" many individuals have to turn to others—church, government, community—for help. Unfortunately, receiving such assistance is fraught with problems, often due to the belief in and the internalization of the achievement ideology.

A natural disaster provides an interesting context for a test case of attitudes toward and perceptions of poverty and welfare. A natural disaster and its destruction are not usually blamed on individual victims—it is not seen as a result of their laziness, their weak wills, or defects in their characters. Natural disasters are mostly seen as random, often indiscriminate acts of God over which individuals have little control. Some disasters may be seen as the fault of those in decision-making positions. In other cases, blame is directed at those who choose to live in high-risk areas such as California (earthquakes), Florida (hurricanes), or Oklahoma (tornadoes), or at those who do not take appropriate precautionary measures, such as purchasing insurance. Most often, however, there is a public outpouring of sympathy for those who are affected by a disaster, and criticism of the victims is considered socially unacceptable.

What are women's experiences with downward mobility and the reception of assistance in a disaster? Do such experiences lead to any shifts in ideology about poverty and welfare? Disasters often throw individuals and families into downward mobility. While there have been studies that touch on economic losses to communities and businesses in disasters, there are no studies that examine how downward mobility affects the victims of disaster, how they cope, who they blame, and how, or if, they recover. Downward mobility is also a gendered experience. Economic inequality, divorce, and the growing number of female-headed households in the last three decades have led to the feminization of poverty, as thousands of women and children have plunged into poverty and onto welfare rolls. Thus, the experience of downward mobility, the stigma of charity, and the ideology of achievement have to be examined with a gendered lens.

The women of Grand Forks greatly appreciated the generosity of others after the flood but profoundly disliked the feeling of accepting charity, whether from public or private sources. They felt humiliated and stigmatized, and they believed that other people thought they were taking advantage of the system. The women felt humbled and embarrassed by needing help; they experienced the stigma of charity. Lewis Coser (1965), expanding on Georg Simmel's ideas on poverty, argued that the poor are viewed "not by virtue of what they do, but by virtue of what is done to them."[7] Simmel declared that when people were classified as the poor, they lost their previous status—they went through a "formal declassification"—and their private troubles became a public issue. According to Coser, being poor meant people lost a right to privacy and their behaviors were open to public observation and scrutiny. Thus, the more public the charity—standing in lines for food or staying at a large public shelter—the more difficult it was for the Grand Forks women. Public exposure meant that the women lost their middle-class status. In Grand Forks, the receivers of charity often were women. Women, more often than men, went to stand in line for food, clothing, shelter, cleaning supplies, and gas vouchers. Perhaps how men and women have fulfilled their social roles historically can help to make sense of this phenomenon. While it was a violation of the women's caregiving role—which involves giving to and taking care of others—to accept charity, it would have been an even greater violation of men's provider role, which was to take care of their families financially, and would have contradicted the general cultural expectations that men be self-sufficient, independent, and stoic. Historically, women's family role has included being the link between their families and community services and agencies. Accepting charity during the disaster was an extension of this role, but it was also "dirty work," which is often women's responsibility due to their lower status.

The women of Grand Forks had a difficult time being suddenly classified as poor because it went against the norms and expectations of their traditional middle-class, female role of giving and making contributions to society. The poor, Simmel (1965) theorized, are no longer expected to make a social contribution. Coser (1965) added that the poor have a low status specifically because they cannot contribute to society, and they fall into a "condition of unilateral receivers" (p. 147). The poor, according to Coser, can be "fully integrated into the social fabric only if they are offered the opportunity to give" (p. 147), an idea that explains why the women were determined to find ways to give to others in the midst of receiving assistance: they were resisting the "unilateral receiver" role. The women felt virtuous when they had given, shame when they received. Coser supported this assertion by claiming that the price of accepting assistance is the degradation of the individual and that receiving assistance "means to be stigmatized and to be removed from the ordinary run of men" (p. 144). The experience of downward mobility and the stigmatized nature of receiving charity led some of the women to rethink their views about poverty, welfare, and the ideology of achievement. "It's easier to work than to be on welfare," as one woman told me, surprised by the amount of red tape, humiliation, and time involved in receiving assistance from a public source.

The fourth and final theme that emerged in the research was the notion of the "self" and how women's identities were altered or solidified based on their everyday actions in the disaster. According to Mead (1934), we have no self at birth, but through interaction we learn to stand outside of ourselves and develop an ability to self-reflect. This sense of self, which is a sense of having a distinct identity, arises through social activity and social relationships. The conception of self, or the taking of self as an object, arises out of a human reflexive process. Individuals actively construct a sense of self through their interactions with others. Turner (1976) explains that the self-conception "refers to the continuity—however imperfect— of an individual's experience of himself in a variety of situations"

(p. 990). However, even though there is some constancy of personal identity, the self can change with time through the course of one's life, especially under the impact of "disjunctive experiences" (Lindesmith, Strauss, and Denzin 1975, p.10). Traditionally, the self is seen as the core conception of the real person, no matter the various roles that one occupies; the self is the thinking, feeling being that links the various roles and identities that people put forth in various situations." In other words, an identity that is tied to a role has implica tions for one's real self, although some roles are more salient to an individual's self than others, and some roles are so important that they merge with the self (Stryker 1968; Turner 1978).

The self is a gendered concept. Gender scholars have shown that gender is an achieved identity and that being a woman is what Hughes (1945) called a "master status," meaning that one characteristic of an individual becomes that person's identity. A woman's self, therefore, is her core identity. A gendered self is formed early in life, as society communicates its views and expectations of gender when individuals are very young. Gender theorists believe that gender is one of the most significant categories of identity in our society. In other words, it is a major focus of how others perceive us and how we view ourselves. Individuals are rarely able to imagine themselves as the other sex because being male or female is central to their sense of who they are.

According to some gender theories, a gender identity implies that maleness and femaleness are properties of individuals, created by early childhood socialization and fully solidified as different personalities for men and women by adulthood. Women have been socialized to be nurturing and family oriented; men are competitive and work oriented. This is the creation of a "gendered self" (Risman 1998). This gendered self, or self-identity, provides the motivations to individuals to fill their socially appropriate roles. Others do not see gender identity as so fixed and static, but rather a product of interactions—in other words, men and women "do" gender (West and Zimmerman 1987). According to Kimmel (2000), gender identity is socially constructed, meaning that "our identities are a fluid assemblage of the meanings and behaviors that we construct from the values, images, and prescriptions we find in the world around us" (p. 87). Our gender identities are voluntary, but also coerced—we do not get to make the rules, but "nor do we glide perfectly and effortlessly into preassigned roles" (p. 87). There are elements of both structure and agency in the formation of our selves and identities.

This book is concerned with the tension between structure and agency, and the relationship between self, identity, and roles. It examines how women construct a sense of self and how they feel about themselves, as individuals, women, family members, and community members, as well as how external forces, such as cultural expectations or institutional opportunities or constraints, help shape those feelings of self. In other words, I believe that each woman's sense of self develops in a dynamic process within a culture and social structure that often devalues women and relegates them to the domestic sphere.

In this book, the women's stories show how they perceive themselves, what they see themselves as capable of achieving or coping with under circumstances of distress, and how they maintain or construct their self-conception. Their stories illustrate that they experience both shifts and continuities in their roles and identities: some stay the same and some are altered by the flood experiences. One important finding is how identity is tied to the conception of "home" (Sarup 1994) and interpretations of self engender a sense of being "at home" (Cuba and Hummon 1993). In the Grand Forks flood the women lost the cornerstone of their selves—their homes. Unlike those who give up their everyday routines and homes voluntarily to travel and for the discovery of self, the women in a disaster do not have the same "liberating experiences" (Hatty 1996). Instead, women affected by a disaster, either a flood or homelessness, are thrust involuntarily into situations where they must construct identity in the absence of the defining framework of home. Furthermore, because of this profound alteration of identity and self, disaster survivors have to rebuild their homes and also their "sense of reality" (Smith and Belgrave 1995, p. 265). To do so, many women reaffirmed their selves as intimately tied to home and family. Yet, women's identities shifted with the expansion of their nondomestic roles. It is indeed a paradox—how women embrace stereotypical roles that reflect and perpetuate gender inequality at the same time they emerge from the disaster with new skills and confidences to challenge the status quo.

Chapter 2

Disaster Strikes

O n April 11, 1997, the residents of Grand Forks woke up and opened their copies of the *Grand Forks Herald*. There, to their horror, was the tragic and ominous story of a woman named Pamela Jean Wagner. Pamela was driving at night with her three-year-old daughter, Victoria, on a country road south of Fargo when she lost control of her car on the icy road and it slid into a half-frozen creek. She and her daughter were able to escape through the driver's window and get out of the creek and onto dry land. It was a rural area, with no lights on the horizon. It was only eight degrees outside, and their clothes were soaked with freezing water, but Pamela and her daughter were able to walk for over three hours in the dark searching for help. Pamela, three months pregnant, carried her daughter some of the way, talking to her and trying to keep her warm. They finally got close to a farmhouse, but they were blocked by a different section of the same creek and there was no way to get through it safely. They died there in the field—lost, frozen, and so close to safety. Residents of Grand Forks retold this story many times and mourned for Pamela Jean and her daughter, even though they did not know them. For many of them, these tragic and avoidable deaths seemed to be a sign of what a difficult year for the region it had been—as well as what was in store for them. The deaths of the mother and child signified just how battered they felt by the brutal winter and served as a sign that the cruelty of the winter was not over for them. That winter, symbolized by Pamela Jean Wagner's story, was characterized by destruction and adversity.

This study took place in Grand Forks, North Dakota, and East Grand Forks, Minnesota, two adjoining towns on the Red River, which flows north along the North Dakota-Minnesota border into

Canada.[1] Grand Forks, the larger of the two municipalities, is a university town with approximately fifty-two-thousand residents, and East Grand Forks, with only nine-thousand residents, is part of the larger Grand Forks community. The towns together cover ten square miles. The residents are predominantly white, working and middle class, and from fairly conservative, rural backgrounds. The economy centers around the University of North Dakota in Grand Forks and the large sugar beet industry in the region. The weather conditions in the region are rough, but the residents do not mind the Red River Valley winters because, as they say proudly, "40 below keeps the riffraff out" (Tiemann and Staples 1999). Because of the low relief of the region, the valley often floods a little every spring as the southern part of the river melts and the northern part remains frozen, thereby spreading the water over the river banks. The highest flood on record in Grand Forks occurred in 1897 (International Red River Basin Task Force 1999).

The Red River Valley region had one of its worst winters in 1996–1997, with eight major blizzards and an ice storm that wiped out power for several days. Blizzard "Hannah" in April, 1997, produced more than twenty inches of snow and winds of over sixty miles per hour. Hannah was the most severe blizzard in the area since 1941. Most residents knew by witnessing the volume of snow outside their homes that there would be some flooding, although few anticipated the magnitude. During this time, flood insurance advertisements began to run on television, and some residents began talking with each other about the flood risk. By mid-April the threat was real, and the National Weather Service (NWS) issued a flood forecast of forty-nine feet above the river level. Grand Forks officials began to hold town meetings to brief residents, and the community organized an enormous sandbagging and dike patrol effort. During the week of April 13–18, workplaces and schools encouraged employees and students to participate in the sandbag lines. The two towns had never been better prepared for a flood. Yet the river continued to rise and threaten the stability of the sandbag dikes protecting the city.

On April 18, 1997, the dikes were breached, and Grand Forks experienced the worst flood in over one-hundred years. The river crested at 54.11 feet on April 21, 1997 (International Joint Committee 1999). Despite the residents' efforts, the sandbag dikes did not hold, and the flood water broke through and filled the streets.

The record flooding put 1.7 million acres under water. Within a matter of hours, on a day bright with sunshine, the entire community of approximately sixty-thousand residents was evacuated from the two towns. This was the first time in American history that the entire population of a city was evacuated from its city limits. The majority of homes in both towns were damaged, and hundreds were destroyed. Indeed, in the entire town of East Grand Forks (pop. 9,000), only twenty-seven homes escaped damage. One participant in my study said that looking out at the river was like "looking across the ocean—it was water as far as you could see." Indeed, the entire region was affected, including some flooding in Fargo, North Dakota to the south, and Winnipeg, Manitoba, to the north, although nothing compared to what happened in Grand Forks and East Grand Forks.

In addition to the flood damage, there was fire destruction. On Saturday, April 18, the day the dikes broke and the city was evacuated, a fire started in an old downtown building. The accidental fire was started by an electrical short circuit caused by flood waters. Fire fighters were not able to move their trucks through the water to get to the blaze. The fire spread to other buildings and a total of eleven historic downtown buildings, housing offices and apartments, were destroyed. As found in other disaster research, the fire and flood did not cause panic among the residents, and the evacuation of the residents was smooth and safe.[2] Of course, this does not mean that there was not a sense of urgency in the days and hours at the height of the crisis. Jennifer, a twenty-six-year-old single homeowner, explained how quickly she had to identify her most important possessions when she needed to evacuate immediately:

> My mom grabs me by the shoulders and says, "What are the ten things you cannot live without? Ten things that you could never replace no matter what?" I'm, like, "Videos, photo albums, get them out!" And there was my jewelry box from my grandparents, too.

In the days that followed the evacuation, residents watched the local news continuously from their evacuation sites to stay abreast of the flood and fire. Some, like Elaine in the opening chapter, found out their homes were lost by watching the flood coverage on television and recognizing the roofs of their homes. Despite the seriousness of the reporting, residents told me that they always

After a severe winter of blizzards and record snowfall, the twin cities of Grand Forks and East Grand Forks experienced a flood of historic proportions in the spring of 1997. This photo shows downtown Grand Forks after a fire broke out in the Security Building at the height of the flood. Before fireflighters could work on the blaze, they had to finish evacuating residents. Eleven historic downtown buildings, including the home of the *Grand Forks Herald,* were lost. *Photo by Meridee Green Danks.*

smiled when they saw their familiar newscasters—not just because they were familiar faces, but also because the newscasters, still at their stations, were not able to shower and thus with each day they looked dirtier and more disheveled. I was told that they resembled the scene out of the movie *Batman* where the Gothic City newscasters appear unshowered, with hair askew and no makeup.

After the mandatory evacuation, residents were not allowed back into the community for several weeks. For many weeks after that, there was neither water nor electricity, making it difficult for most families to return for several months. During the evacuation period, many residents tried to take breaks for their emotional health. Marilyn, who, like many, had evacuated to "the Cities" (Minneapolis/St. Paul), took her teenaged daughter to the Great Mall of America, an outing she described as necessary:

> She's a sensible kid, and a strong kid, but still, you know. I wanted to take her to the Cities and take her away and do things that she likes to do, see people she likes, and shop and so on. So we could pretend that things were okay. Well, not really pretend, but at least be distracted from it and cheer her up a little bit.

Almost all homes in both towns were damaged, with hundreds beyond repair and later demolished. Most of the residents had no flood insurance. Some residents did not purchase insurance because they were in denial that their homes would be touched by the flood waters. In the days before the flood, a common expression around town was "If my house goes, then the whole town goes." The assumption was that neither their homes nor the town would be hit by water. A second reason that many residents did not purchase flood insurance was because they were discouraged from buying it by their local flood insurance agents. The agents, acting on what they felt was good information, believed their clients were not at risk and that they were saving them money. Finally, and perhaps most important, the National Weather Service prediction that the flood water would crest at forty-nine feet reassured the residents that their homes would be fine as the community had sandbagged to that level. In a survey in Grand Forks after the flood, 95 percent of respondents said they were aware of flood insurance, but approximately 80 percent reported that the National Weather Service forecasts made them believe that flood insurance was not necessary, which was not the message the NWS was trying to send.[3]

When they were allowed back inside the city weeks later, residents were horrified to see mud, silt, oil, and sewer residue in the streets, picnic tables in trees, a family's deck on a garage roof, homes off their foundations, cars upside down, and lines on every house showing the ultimate water level. The mud and silt had worked their way into every crevasse and corner of their homes. Women were surprised to find mud inside of sealed canning jars, and heartbroken when they found the silt in their boxes of Christmas decorations. Cecilia, a nurse and mother of four young children, talked to me about this loss while stroking the hair of her three-year-old who had climbed up into her mother's lap during the interview:

> All of the children's things, and all of the Christmas decorations were lost. Every year I've made us an ornament, and I've made the children each an ornament, and all of those went. And my mother has made us stuff for Christmas for years. All that stuff went. My mom has made us a quilt every year for Christmas. I don't know what she thinks we'll do with all of them [she laughs briefly, then starts crying]. I tried to save those but couldn't.

The clean-up work ahead of the residents was overwhelming, and the total destruction and the size of their losses—physical, emotional, financial—were immense. Carol, a forty-three-year-old mother of a teenage son, spoke about how that difficult time affected her as a mother and a neighbor:

> I think what is hard is when you're a homemaker and you get involved with volunteer activities, your nature somehow becomes more and more nurturing. And you want to be able to get things in order, and you want to help, and you can't do that because you are so overwhelmed yourself. . . . If there is a death in the family, or when there's been an accident, you run over with food, or you watch somebody's kids or you haul that person back and forth to rehab or whatever you do. You couldn't do that for other people anymore.

The residents of Grand Forks felt proud of their community for having fought so hard, sandbagging around the clock in the days before the dikes broke, but they felt dejected that all their work was for naught and overwhelmed by the destruction.

The Grand Forks residents suffered both individual and collective trauma. The disaster, which cost hundreds of residents their homes and belongings, also left many of them without adequate child care, physically and emotionally exhausted, homeless, jobless, separated from family members, and uncertain about their futures. Sandy's story, for example, illuminates some of the challenges and stresses in the disaster aftermath. Sandy, who had divorced an abusive husband several years before the flood, lost her new job at a local business when it was destroyed in the flood. After a short stint at a temporary FEMA job, she spent months trying to find a job so that she could support herself:

> I decided to go to the job service and get job counseling because I didn't know what to do. The wages in Grand Forks are $5.50 an hour and I was distraught, and said, "I can't live on that." [After several more temporary jobs], now I am in my fifth week of being unemployed, and I haven't found anything. I have interviews, but I never get called back. This is a tough year because my alimony ends. I'm kind of scared. I've never been unemployed. I did borrow money from my retirement fund to pay for my car. [Before the divorce] I never had to work full-time, and when we divorced, everything was paid for, our home was paid for, our vehicles, financially we were doing well. I now have $20 in my checkbook.

The city also experienced a permanent loss of schools and housing, and some neighborhoods had to be completely demolished. According to official statistics, no deaths or serious injuries were attributed to the flood, a fact that made city officials and residents grateful. However, many residents spoke of elderly residents who passed away and of younger residents who committed suicide in the weeks following the flood. Residents believed that both types of tragedy resulted from the stress of the flood and the anguish over losses. Research has shown that suicide rates usually increase slightly after a disastrous flood and stay higher than normal for four years.[4]

Blame is not considered a common or typical natural disaster phenomenon, although researchers admit that research on blame in disasters is lacking.[5] In Grand Forks, residents did express some anger and blame after the flood. Similarly to the reaction of other disaster victims, many Grand Forks residents blamed the National

Weather Service for the poor prediction.[6] As graffiti on one destroyed house in Grand Forks said, "49 Feet, My Ass!" The National
Weather Service felt that residents misinterpreted their flood "nu-
merical outlook," which is not an exact science. Other residents
blamed the City of Grand Forks for turning off power and issuing a
mandatory evacuation, which prevented residents from staying in
their houses and continuing to operate sump pumps, an action that
might have saved their homes and belongings. One of this study's
participants, a city employee, noted that everyone badmouthed "the
city," and asked, "Who exactly do they think 'the city' is? It is people, people like me." Other residents, however, refused to blame
others for the disaster. Cindy, who lost her daycare business in the
flood, described her feelings concerning blame after the flood:

> I never felt anger toward that river. I have never felt that. It's na-
> ture. It happens. That makes as much sense as screaming into the
> wind. I never felt any anger towards the city officials, the Weather
> Service. It's a sense of fatalism, I guess. It's nature; it happens. We
> certainly aren't the first people that it's happened to.

In the years since the city was flooded, the community and the
residents have continued to heal. One participant in my study,
Louise, wrote me a letter three years after the flood and said that
the past year was the first year that felt somewhat normal since the
flood. Even six years after the disaster some survivors adamantly
refuse to open any of the flood photo books or watch any flood
videos, unwilling to relive the experience. Some neighborhoods
near the river are now parks, and many residents have left town for
good, although the figures vary as to the extent of the exodus. Estimates put the financial damages to the area at one to two billion
dollars. One social worker told me that there were increased reports
of violence in the high schools a year after the flood. In one instance, a school had a fire approximately eight months after the
flood; when a psychologist came to talk with the students about
how the fire destroyed their cafeteria, they wanted only to talk
about the flood. The city, in an effort to put a positive spin on recovery, ran a "Miracle in Progress!" campaign. They also spent
thousands of dollars to install a festive ice rink and lights in the winter of 1997, a controversial move angering some residents who
thought the money could have been better spent on flood recovery

projects but pleasing others who believed the town needed more enjoyable things to do and on which to focus.

The disaster was a national media story. The image of the burning downtown buildings amidst a sea of water became a symbol of the disaster. Northwest Airlines, as part of a campaign to raise money for the area, featured Grand Forks in their in-flight magazines and in-flight videos, reaching twelve million passengers. In addition, the Grand Forks newspaper won the Pulitzer Prize for its coverage of the flood, an honor bringing more national attention to the disaster and the community. While most Americans will not remember the disaster ten or twenty years later—chiefly because there are so many disasters each year across the country—the residents of the Red River Valley will never forget the flood of 1997. Six years after the disaster, in fact, many of them refer to their lives in two time frames: *BF*, before the flood, and *AF*, after the flood.

Disasters as Important Research Sites

The Red River Flood of 1997 was just one of thousands of natural disasters that occur every year, and Grand Forks's losses are only a minute portion of the total disaster losses around the globe. Disaster losses worldwide increased considerably in the late twentieth century (Alexander 1997). While most of the deaths from disasters occurred in developing countries, the United States has also suffered staggering social and economic losses. In fact, between 1975 and 1994, natural hazards killed twenty-four thousand and injured one-hundred-thousand people in the United States. According to Mileti (1999), the conservative estimate of the actual average dollar losses from natural hazards and disasters during those years was $500 billion. These loss estimates for the United States have not included indirect losses, such as lost employment, impacts on the environment, emotional effects on victims, and down time for businesses. Floods, in particular, are a destructive and common hazard to Americans. Floods were the most costly natural disaster in terms of deaths and dollar losses from 1975 to 1994 in the United States. Estimates of deaths from disastrous floods from 1975 to 1994 are unclear, but some estimates range from 1,600 to 2,310. Annual property losses from floods were approximately $70 billion in the 1975 to 1994 period, and during this time many regions of the United States were flooded more than once. The percentage of repetitive claims is highest in North Dakota, the lower Mississippi Valley, and the mid-Atlantic states. While these regions have recurring floods, flooding is a disaster that affects all regions of the United States (Mileti 1999).

Disasters do not affect everyone in the same way, as they are not equal opportunity events. Indeed, disasters disproportionately affect more marginalized groups, such as the poor, people of color, and women. Less access to resources leads to increased vulnerability.[7] Women are often considered the population most at risk from hazardous events (especially in developing countries) because of their lack of social and economic resources. Indeed, disasters reveal power relations in intimate relationships, as well as in community and global structures. Disaster management organizations and federal agencies in the United States have recently acknowledged that they must understand more about differential vulnerability in order to be successful in their mitigation efforts (Anderson 1996). In addition, many in the disaster field have called for more in-depth social science scholarship because physical mitigation measures, such as dams and levees, are no longer considered the sole solution to decrease losses.[8] Recently, disaster researchers have called for more disaster research on vulnerable populations, such as the poor, people of color, and women in the United States in order to reduce disaster losses.

Over the last five decades, sociologists who study disasters have made important and extensive contributions to our understanding of the social world. The disaster setting is considered a unique laboratory or strategic site in which to learn about social phenomena, examine social relationships, and reveal social problems because disasters strip away the veil that usually obscures or disguises many social conditions.[9] Social processes, some sociologists contend, are more visible in times of a disaster as they are compressed in a very dramatic and short time span, and disasters "break the cake of custom" of the predisaster form of life (Fritz 1961). A natural disaster has been found to be a realistic laboratory for studying social phenomena and relationships because disasters give social scientists advantages that cannot be matched during stable times (Fritz 1961). Merton (1969) explained that collective stress situations reveal aspects of the social systems that are not visible during the "less stressful conditions of everyday life" (p. xii).

Despite this recognition that the noneveryday qualities of disasters make them important research settings, disaster scholars are not arguing that the disaster process is separate from the social structures of the everyday. Disaster researchers have fully accepted disasters as social phenomena, not "natural" ones. Indeed, the fundamental notions of the current disaster paradigm are that disasters are inherently social phenomena and have their foundation in the social system or social structure. In other words, disasters are social and political events linked to who we are, how we live, and how we structure and maintain our society. Disaster research is not a separate substantive area of sociology for several reasons. There is no "disasterology" (Nigg 1994) because sociologists have long used the theoretical perspectives of collective behavior and social psychology as their frameworks for study.[10] Sociologists in this field study core concepts of sociology: collective behavior, social order, social change, inequality and marginalization, community structures, and social roles. What happens in a disaster has larger implications for our understanding of the social world and social interactions.

Goals and Methods

With this in mind, I sought to listen to women's voices in this study. I believe that women's lives can be better understood by studying a collective stress event, such as a flood, which disrupts the social order and allows us to see their experiences and perspectives more clearly. Thus, examining the nature of women's lives in a disaster, when taken-for-granted and unquestioned arrangements are disrupted, provides an opportunity to learn how women construct and make sense of their everyday lives in both crisis and noncrisis periods.

The Grand Forks disaster was an optimal research site, as it could be classified as a "catastrophe," not merely a "disaster," for several reasons: all of the residential community was affected; emergency organizations and operational bases were themselves impacted; most local officials were unable to take on their work roles throughout the emergency and recovery periods; and most community functions were sharply and simultaneously interrupted across the board (Quarantelli 2000). Few disasters had affected such a large percentage of the community, residential houses, and geographic boundaries. For these reasons, Grand Forks was a unique and special setting for research as it could provide important practical, theoretical, and empirical information.

I traveled to Grand Forks several weeks after the flood waters inundated the city and collected data there during six site visits. I used three data collection methods: in-depth interviews, observation, and document analysis. I interviewed forty women, twenty of them twice, for a total of sixty interviews. The women were contacted through snowball sampling and from women calling in to be interviewed after reading in a newspaper article that I needed volunteers for my project. The sample was diverse in terms of age, marital status, amount of damage to their homes, and family composition. Most of the women were white and identified as middle class. Most interviews were conducted in their homes and lasted several hours. Observations were conducted in various locations throughout the community, at churches, diners, Fourth of July celebrations, and family picnics. Document analysis included a wide range of items such as personal diaries and journals, calendars, the local newspaper, graffiti, and data from the local battered women's organization. I collected data for two years, continuing with letters, e-mails, and phone calls with some informants even five and six years after the flood.[11]

Selected Portraits

This section features a few selected portraits of some of the women I interviewed in order to present the range and scope of their disaster experiences and to help personalize their stories. I will briefly tell the stories of Dana, Beth, Tina, and Peggy.[12] All four women are natives of Grand Forks and have extended family in the area. Their experiences, however, were very different.

Dana is a twenty-five-year-old mother of two small children, a four-year-old daughter, Jenna, and a son, Jack, who is six. Private and soft spoken, Dana is slow to smile but gentle in her manner. As we sit at the picnic table behind her destroyed house, I can see the pain and sadness in her face. She and her husband, both natives of Grand Forks, met in high school and married shortly after their high school graduation. Both of their extended families have been in Grand Forks for as long as Dana can remember. Her husband, Gary, works doing manual labor at the potato processing plant. Dana works as a waitress at a restaurant not far from her home.

Dana and Gary owned their small, wood-framed home on a tree-lined street in the Lincoln Park neighborhood in central Grand Forks. The house had a small front porch, a modest living room, dining room, and kitchen on the first floor, and three bedrooms on the second floor. Their house had a large back yard, with a detached garage adjacent to the alley, where Gary used to work on cars and neighbors would stop by to chat on warm evenings. They had a swing set and a picnic table on the lawn in the back yard. Lincoln Park was a beautiful, old, working and middle-class neighborhood that bordered the Red River. The river curves widely to the east and then sweeps back to the west, creating a small isthmus, which was the Lincoln Park neighborhood.

Gary and Dana, and all the residents of Lincoln Park, loved the neighborhood's peacefulness and quiet and the shade of its one-hundred-year-old trees. Because the neighborhood was surrounded by the river on three sides, there was no outside traffic; driving through the neighborhood did not lead anywhere. Residents said that the neighborhood was safe and friendly. Dana felt that the house, the neighborhood, the neighbors, and schools were exactly what she and Gary wanted for their family, and they hoped to raise their children and grow old there.

The flood destroyed their house and devastated Dana and her family. Because their home had over 50 percent damage, it could not be repaired and reinhabited, although this is what Dana and her husband wished to do. Dana was lost without her home, and she never quite felt at ease in the more middle-class suburban neighborhood they moved to but could not quite afford. Ten months after the flood, Dana's mother died suddenly and unexpectedly, sending Dana into a sea of grief. Dana felt distraught emotionally by her losses and worried about her family's financial future.

Beth is a thirty-year-old single mother of a five-year-old son. She has lived in and out of poverty since she was a child. She and her son, Eli, are on their own—Eli's father left the family shortly after Eli was born and has never provided any child support. Beth worked hard over the years, as the manager of a restaurant, a black-jack dealer, and in sales, but she never became established in one profession and never had the opportunity to advance. Beth and Eli had never had health insurance. Before the flood, she was earning minimum wage working as a cashier at a store in Grand Forks.

The Red River Flood did not hit Beth's apartment, even though it was basement level, because it was located on the far western part of the city. The day the city evacuated, Beth received a call from her father, who was volunteering in the city's Emergency

Operations Center (EOC). He wanted her to join him, as they needed available people to help run the EOC, and they needed people who were quick on their feet and sharp. Beth was able to rely on her mother and sister, who were temporarily unemployed because of the flood, to take care of Eli for what she thought would be several days, but what turned into several weeks.

Beth excelled in her emergency position. She worked long, hard hours, and she maintained good humor and sound judgment despite the exhaustion and stress of the situation. Beth had never been in a position of authority before and found herself with an immense amount of responsibility and decision-making power. She thrived under the pressure and was efficient when faced with multiple tasks, skills that city officials noticed. When the crisis period was coming to an end, and residents were returning to town, the EOC shut down. The city, however, offered Beth a job in one of its departments, a position that paid well and provided health benefits for both Beth and Eli.

Beth felt that the flood was the best thing that ever happened to her. She felt more confident and more optimistic about her future and Eli's future than she had ever before. Six months after the flood, Beth's boyfriend, Lance, moved in with her. They had become very close during the flood, as he also worked in the EOC. A year after that, Beth and Lance were able to buy a home, and Beth gave birth to their daughter, Moira. In the birth announcement, Beth wrote of her joy and contentment with her life now.

Tina is a nurse from East Grand Forks. She is the mother of two young children and married to Frank, who owns his own plumbing business. Tina and Frank believed they were comfortably in the middle class with her education and profession and with his successful business. Their daughter and son went to private school, and they owned a beautiful Victorian house with five bedrooms. Tina loved to garden and can her own vegetables and preserves. Her kitchen was sunny and warm and overlooked their backyard, vegetable garden, and flowers. Her siblings and her mother lived within blocks of her in East Grand Forks.

The flood hit East Grand Forks hard, and Tina's house had water up to the roof. On the day before the whole city evacuated, water ran through the streets in Tina's neighborhood after one of the dikes in East Grand Forks was breached. There was only one bridge between Tina's house and her children's school, and while she was packing, Tina heard that this bridge was being closed because the water was too high. Panicked, Tina called the school bus operator, who informed her that they could not help her get her children, but that the children could walk across the bridge.[13] Tina refused to have her children walk alone across the bridge. With no other options, Tina and her husband walked across a potentially dangerous bridge and walked back with their children. About an hour later, a military truck picked them up and took them all to an evacuation center.

Tina lost her home and all of her belongings in the flood. She and her husband had painstakingly moved many items to the second floor, assuming that if they were flooded, it would be only in the basement, and, in the absolute worst case scenario, there would be some water on the first floor. Financially, Tina's biggest losses were the tools and equipment from her husband's business. Her mother and her sister and her family also lost their homes. Immediately after evacuation, Tina and her family lived for several months with two other families, fourteen people in total, in her mother's unheated summer trailer by a lake. During that time, Tina's mother, who had been sick for a long time, died.[14] Tina wished that her mother had been spared the sight of the flood's destruction of her home and her children's homes.

Eventually, Tina and her family were assigned a FEMA trailer in a large temporary trailer park on the outskirts of town, in a field that was unmanageably muddy no matter what the season. They set up the trailer and made it livable for a year, with temporary furniture and donated clothes to wear. After a year, they purchased a home which they were excited about, and moved in, happy but in severe debt. They transplanted flowers and blueberry bushes from their old yard to their new one. As she and I walked around her new yard, admiring the flowers in bloom, she talked about the pain of the flood. To help herself cope emotionally, Tina produced this imagery to help make sense of the physical and emotional pain of the flood:

> I think of it kind of like childbirth. You have this intense pain, and then you kind of forget about how it was until you rekindle some of the stuff. So for me it is like childbirth. That's what I equate it to. I hope it will progress like the childbirth cycle. So you will have this pain, and you feel the pain, and then just remember the

pain, and then you get to a point where it is only good that you remember. You know, you just remember the birth. We aren't there yet, but it would be nice.

It is clear that Tina still mourns heavily for the loss of her home and her previous life. In the years since the flood, Tina has frequently visited the site of her mother's house to admire the only thing left on the plot, a beautiful, enormous tree planted by her parents fifty years earlier.

Peggy is a forty-five-year-old homemaker, with two teenage children and a husband who owns his own supply business. They had another child who died as an infant. Peggy and her family lived in a house in the Riverside Park neighborhood. Peggy's family had lived in Grand Forks for many generations, and she loved her neighbors and her house. She never liked the North Dakota winters, and while she was tan from being outside in the summer, she hibernated every winter, wishing that she lived in a warmer climate. Just before the flood, Peggy's teenaged daughter, Erin, gave birth to her own daughter. Erin was still in high school, and the father of her daughter had made it clear that he had no intention of helping with their child or being involved in her life in any way. Peggy took an active role in helping her daughter with the new baby, such as watching her while Erin finished her high school classes.

Like almost all the other residents of Lincoln Park and Riverside Park, Peggy and her family lost their home. The damage was extensive, but because they had built some of the house themselves, they considered moving it to another location. This idea turned out to be financially unfeasible. Peggy spoke about how she felt leaving the home where she raised her children:

> We've been married and in that home for twenty-three years. It was a hundred-year-old home. In 1995, we finally completed our work on it, and it was just the way we wanted it. We did all of the work ourselves. For twenty years we worked on that house, and we finished it the night before my son's sixteenth birthday party. We've been out of our home for eighty-two days now, and I just feel lost. . . . My kids never wanted to leave that house. My daughter wanted the house willed to her because she wanted to raise her kids in that house. A very safe and nice neighborhood. It was just a nice, beautiful area of town with the great hundred-year-old trees. I just can't picture myself *not* living there. I just

can't picture anything else than getting back into my house that we designed and worked on and built.

Peggy and her husband's relationship did not fare well during the flood, as they could not find ways to communicate or to support each other. During the evacuation period, they decided to separate. Her husband, Lou, stayed at his business office, and Peggy and her two children and her granddaughter lived in a small two-bedroom apartment.

Peggy found herself at a crossroads after the flood. Because she had long considered moving to a warmer climate, she felt that it was time to go. She was getting a divorce, and no longer had a home or any clothes, furniture, or other household items. She was free. She and a divorced friend started to look into moving to South Carolina, investigating jobs and housing. Ultimately, however, Peggy decided not to leave, as she felt responsible for her elderly parents in Grand Forks. She had two brothers in Grand Forks, but she was the only daughter and knew that she would be her parents' primary caretaker as they got older. She also felt attached to her new granddaughter and knew that her daughter needed her help if she was going to finish high school with a baby. Peggy took her maiden name again, bought a small townhouse with a Small Business Association (SBA) loan,[15] and sent her son to college. Her daughter and granddaughter moved out on their own after a year with the help of low-income housing assistance. Four years after the flood, Peggy, single, in a new home with furniture from garage sales, felt like she was starting over.

In the stories of Dana, Peggy, Tina, and Beth, some of the themes presented earlier become apparent. Clearly, there were some commonalities in their stories but also differences, based on available resources, family dynamics, and amount of loss incurred. There is evidence of role conflict and role accumulation, as well as the devastation of downward mobility for some and the opportunities presented in the crisis for others. Tina plunged down the social and economic ladder, seeing what she worked for disappear, while Beth actually found herself better off economically—and with increased feelings of self-efficacy—due to a crisis-related job. Beth also found that her romantic relationship was strengthened and solidified because of the flood, while Peggy's marriage could not withstand the undeniable stress and the profound losses of the disaster. Dana's sense of self felt shaken, as she felt that her world was turned upside down and she no longer knew who she was or where she belonged. For Peggy, Dana, and Tina, the loss of their homes meant not only a loss of status but also a loss of identity. For almost all of the women in this book, the flood was a crucial, turning point moment in their lives.

Chapter 3

Women's Roles

———————

Women's roles have changed considerably since the 1960s. Sociologists have conducted extensive research on women's new and changing roles, both in the public and private spheres, and examined what these changes mean to women and to families. There has been research, for example, in the area of women's role in the modern workplace, and as homemaker, as mother, and as family caregiver (Oakley 1975; Kanter 1977; Lopata 1994; Hays 1996; Hochschild 1997). Most recently, as more women have entered the paid workforce, research has focused on the conflicts between women's roles in the workplace and their family roles at home. Notably, research finds that due to women's workload in both spheres, many working women experience a "second shift" when they return home after a first shift at their paid job (Hochschild 1989). As discussed in chapter 1, in this work I examine three areas of the women's lives: work, family, and community.

One way to understand women's roles in all three spheres of social life—the domestic arena, the workplace, and the community—is to examine a disruption of their daily routines and explore the work and roles they take on when the social world is in crisis. What are women's roles in a disaster? Disaster scholars disagree about the nature of traditional gender roles in a disaster.[1] Some researchers have found that traditional gender roles are suspended during times of natural disasters, as the circumstances demand that individuals take on new roles (Taylor 1972). Others argue that there is "role carryover" during such crises and that traditional gender roles and expectations are maintained (Forrest 1978). Finally, some find that men and women in less traditional, more egalitarian relationships actually revert to traditional roles in a disaster (Hoffman

1998). Yet no research has thoroughly addressed women's roles in a disaster, whether they break out of traditional division of labor arrangements, and how they maintain or construct their roles during the rebuilding of their everyday lives.

The women who experienced the Grand Forks flood negotiated both traditional and nontraditional roles throughout the crisis. Social roles are most often defined as the behavior attached to a status or position, such as mother, but also may be conceptualized as a set of relations between a social person and a social circle, "involving negotiated duties and personal rights" (Lopata 1994, p. 4). The women in Grand Forks articulated that the process of taking on new roles and shedding established ones was a significant aspect of what the disaster meant to them and how it affected them. Not only were their homes and neighborhoods changed forever, the women themselves felt different—they performed different tasks or the same tasks in a new context and even felt for the first time how their old roles confined them. Their roles in the community, at home, and at their places of work were all affected by the disaster event, and the obligations and expectations of each role produced some role expansion, role strain, and role conflict.

The Community Role

Disasters have been found to increase one's identification with the community (Dynes and Quarantelli 1976), and in Grand Forks this appeared to the case. Women found that their community role, being involved in work for the good of their immediate neighborhood or the larger city, was an important one during the disaster. As the river was rising, the role of sandbagger was the quintessential community role in Grand Forks. Participating in sandbagging was important for one to feel like, and to be seen as, a member of the community. As Billie, a social worker in her thirties, put it:

> The community was really helping each other out. Everyone was out sandbagging. If you weren't out sandbagging, *you were not a member of our society.* We were all out there. Everybody was out there doing their part, whether it was making sandwiches for the Red Cross or whether it was sandbagging. Whatever people could do, they were out there doing it.

Sandbagging was a significant and well-respected part of community work prior to the flood. Indeed, after the flood, children in town proclaimed that they wanted to grow up to be sandbaggers. The town residents stacked two million sandbags on top of the dikes in the days before the river crested. The sandbags, which weighed from twenty to ninety pounds each, were passed from person to person, and each individual had to be able to receive the bag, hold it, and pass it on without dropping it or stopping the line's flow. Many women expressed amazement that they participated in such difficult physical labor, saying, as one woman did, that she was proud she worked until it felt as if her "arms were going to fall off."

In addition to the heavy weight of the sandbags, the sandbagging line was somewhat problematic for women because they felt it was a masculine environment. Diana, a forty-nine-year-old resident, explained how it felt to be a woman—and particularly a small one—in a sandbagging line, a predominantly male group:

> There were eight men and two women on my team. The men who were already there were *really* uncomfortable to have these women in the sandbag line. That made it hard for me and I also realize now, because I'm short. Because it isn't fun to stand next to somebody who is short when you're sandbagging. So, the worst thing when you're doing this is not being physically able to do it. I remember at one point I just thought of sayings, "Look, guys, I'm not a fireplace ornament. I'm not a mantelpiece ornament. Let me in." They were closing me out. So I had to completely assert myself to get a place in the line.

Diana tried to justify the men's behavior by acknowledging that her height made things difficult, and she refused to let what she perceived as a "this-is-men's-work" attitude deter her. Like other women in the study, Diana was pleased that she could be so assertive, determined, and, ultimately, useful to the effort. In addition, Diana was redefining her self to the men in the sandbag line: by asserting that she was not an ornament, Diana refused to be defined as fragile or delicate and rebuffed the feminine identity that she felt the male sandbaggers were assigning to her.

As is the case with many other women entering blue-collar, male-dominated work environments, these women experienced high job satisfaction in these community roles. The women in Grand Forks spoke proudly of their ability to participate in the sandbagging efforts, despite, or perhaps because of, its difficulties. Lisa, a fifty-six-year-old teacher with three grown children, was proud of her sandbagging efforts. She told me how she felt when she participated in sandbagging lines:

> Then we started sandbagging houses. It took a lot of physical strength. You feel like you're kind of a little bit the grandmother and the mother with the gray hair. At the sandbagging areas, you don't really get invited to do a certain job. But I went over and joined in. There was a bunch of sand, and then people would fill those bags, and then those bags had to be lifted and carried over to where the start of the line was. But I couldn't. It was *awful*. I kind of felt like I was *old*. But I ended up, for awhile, holding the bag. And then on the line, you don't have to be so strong because you don't have to bend over and pick it up. You just pass it. So there you do kind of get into a swing, and you forget that you're tired. Lots of Advil. A four-Advil night.

Lisa was determined to participate, despite feeling as if she did not belong in a sandbag line and observing that many men were not comfortable working side by side with women in an environment of physical labor. Some women did not perceive sandbagging as a masculine environment, and some even described the sandbag lines as "egalitarian." Most, however, did perceive them as gendered work sites. Rachel, a thirty-eight-year-old single mother, observed, "When there was a stall in the sandbag line, women would rock sandbags like babies, so all these women would be on the dike, kind of rocking back and forth." In addition, there were stories of "love among the sandbags," as people met and began romances during sandbagging.

Other women considered the sandbagging line a masculine environment but expressed no hesitation or humiliation about participating in it. Piper, a teenager, expressed that sandbagging with her high school class was "cool," and Teresa, a sixty-six-year-old grandmother and store clerk, told her story of sandbagging with nonchalance, explaining that throughout several cold nights she sandbagged until four o'clock in the morning. Amy Sue, a thirty-nine-year-old separated woman, described her days sandbagging with her former sorority sisters as "a lot of fun." Other women also discussed their community sandbagging role without noting the enormity of the physical labor, only the pride of taking on the role and the necessity of such work for the community.

Another component of women's community role was more traditionally feminine, such as preparing and serving food to the sandbaggers. Some women chose the sandbag support role without question, while others fulfilled it by default because they lacked the physical strength to work in the line itself. Other types of support work women did included preparing food at the Red Cross, sorting donated clothes at a shelter, or staffing evacuation centers, which sometimes entailed giving emotional support to evacuees, particularly the elderly there on their own. Other research has found that women are expected to fill—and do fill—similar support roles in nondisaster times. Kanter (1977) found women are stereotyped as emotional support givers, and Hochschild (1983) demonstrated that there are expectations for women to perform "emotional labor" and that women do carry out this role. In Grand Forks, the women found the community role of supporting the sandbaggers, especially serving food at the sandbag lines, very satisfying. The work, which was similar to work they do in their own homes, was very rewarding in a more public setting largely because it was more visible, more recognized, and less isolating than work performed at home. In this way, when women fulfilled the traditionally female role out in the community, it had the distinct advantages that come with work performed in the public sphere.

A third aspect of women's community role was providing assistance to neighbors and other nonfamily members. One way they assisted was by taking care of neighborhood children or their children's friends. Women also assisted neighbors by loaning items needed during the crisis, such as food or tools; helping them prepare their homes, as by bringing up furniture from the basement; giving emotional support; and opening up their homes to one another. Pat, a nurse with three adult children, explained how this assistance changed the nature of relationships in her rural neighborhood:

> We didn't know our neighbors real well. We've been there five years, but it's a private area. A lot of people live there because they want privacy. But during sandbagging we all became real close; we walked into each other's houses. We all said to each other, "Our door is open, go in and take what you need." So that was breaking all the privacy issues. In rural Scandinavian culture, you are there to help each other, but you don't interfere in each other's lives. So, during sandbagging we were all helping, going in each other's houses, and doing things together.

Like Pat, many of the women felt more connected to their neighborhoods and neighbors as a result of their expanded community roles.
Genie, a homemaker in her thirties who had moved to Grand Forks
several months before the flood, had not felt at home in her new city
and had wanted to move back to her hometown in the South. Yet,
after her community role expanded and she met new people during
the flood efforts, she reported feeling connected to and even missing
Grand Forks during the evacuation. Lydia felt that she and her neighbors got reconnected during the flood because "togetherness had
gone by the wayside" over the previous ten years. In addition, as Pat
described above, the boundaries between the public, private, and
community spheres of life were not as rigid during the disaster, a finding made by other disaster researchers (Fritz 1961).

Women in Grand Forks experienced conflict between the three
demanding roles—community, family, and work—they performed
throughout the flood. Many women spoke of not sleeping at all
during the week prior to the flood because they were working
around the clock on their jobs, community work, and homes. Many
of them found ways to deal with the conflicting time demands and
expectations in an attempt to resolve the role conflict.[2] The
women's community role and their work role had perhaps the
fewest conflicts. Prior to the flood, most employers gave employees
time off to sandbag in the community. Those women who did have
to continue at their jobs during the community preparation stage,
when most community roles were enacted, would patrol the dikes,
sandbag, or do sandbag support work at night.

Women experienced substantial role conflict between their
community and family roles, however. Many women were not
able to take on time-demanding community roles due to their
domestic obligations and responsibilities. Decades ago, a study
found that in disasters, men with children were the most likely to
participate in public activities, while women with children were
the least likely to help outside the home (Barton 1969). My data
support this finding. Women's family role demanded that they
often put the role of mother ahead of their community role. As a
result, men were often more available for the community work.
In Grand Forks, a common situation was women staying home
with children while husbands sandbagged. Even when the disaster provided the opportunity for change, couples maintained the
traditionally gendered work arrangement. Leslie, a part-time sci-

ence teacher in her thirties, could not participate in the community effort because she was taking care of her two-year-old daughter. She felt frustrated that she was confined to the private sphere while knowing that most of her community was in the public sphere working together. Leslie could have worked in the community and her husband could have stayed home with their child, but when I asked about this possibility, Leslie replied that it would have worked, but that she had never thought of that option. An article titled "A Flood is a Guy Thing" in the April 27, 1997, *Grand Forks Herald* made light of the gendered division of labor: "They [guys] get to use big trucks, earth-moving machines, build dikes, get and stay dirty, use military language, etc. . . . [T]his flood allows guys to be guys like guys have never been before. The flood. . . . seemed to trigger the testosterone level in every guy in town. . . . Women have fallen into their traditional roles, too. Mostly, they are making sure that we absolutely never are without food in our mouths."

Overall, the community role was important and meaningful to women. Some women took on nontraditional roles, such as sandbagging, and expanded their definitions of self by seeing themselves as physically competent, as well as assertive and civic minded. Others adopted more traditionally feminine roles, performing support work, but felt more rewarded and less isolated than when they performed this work in the private sphere during nondisaster times. The community role of assisting neighbors encompassed both traditional and nontraditional work, while increasing bonds between neighbors and decreasing some privacy boundaries. These roles, as well, encouraged women to shift their views of themselves as they gained new skills, received recognition for their efforts, and found their sense of what they were capable of had expanded with their roles.

The Family Role

The second significant role that women performed in the disaster was the family role. While most domestic responsibilities fell on women prior to the disaster, their family role shifted and expanded during the crisis. Many interviewees felt that women were still primarily responsible for the domestic domain and family caregiving. As Pat remarked, "The flood did not change *who did what*." In other words, the disaster did not alter preestablished role expectations in the context of home and family. If they had children, women's family role involved, foremost, the work of childcare. The caregiving role was continuous, as taking care of dependent-age children was a significant responsibility women faced before, during, and after the crisis. In particular, women with small children did the majority of the childcare work in their households. The situation was made more difficult when residents returned from evacuation to find that they faced severe daycare shortages. For example, in June, two months after the evacuation, there were daycare spots for 495 children, when there had been 4,000 children in daycare prior to the flood, a fact reported in the *Grand Forks Herald*. Thus, daycare was a significant problem for women, as has been found in other disaster research (Alway, Belgrave, and Smith 1998).

While families prepared for the impending flood, the women kept the children occupied, entertained, and safe. They packed the suitcases for the children's evacuation, made sure they had their favorite clothes and books, and worked to keep the children, especially young ones, safe and busy at all times. Women with older children also felt responsible for caring for and protecting their children. Roseanne, a forty-six-year-old working-class mother of a nineteen-year-old, lamented, "I wanted to mother and to provide a safe environment, but I failed. My son loves the house, and I failed him. He has no house." Roseanne felt that as the caregiver it was her job to protect her son and his house, and that by failing at this role, her identity as a mother was challenged. In this situation, Roseanne's self was based on the role of mother, and as she felt unable to fulfill that role adequately, her definition of self was questioned.

Most women, as part of their family role, were concerned about their children's physical safety. Julie relayed that the tensest time for her was one night when her teenage children had been out sandbagging but had not returned as planned. She did not know what had delayed them, and while Julie was waiting for them, the flood waters had risen into the streets in her neighborhood. She explained how she felt that night:

> During that time they were late, I was in shock. All I could do was continue emptying the basement, so I was doing that by myself, but I was crying, and I was swearing, and I was almost hysterical. On the radio they were saying: "Evacuate the town. Your area.

Mandatory. You should be going before all the dikes start breaking." In the meantime, these sirens are going constantly. All I
could hear were helicopters flying over the town. By the time they
came home, I was crying, and I was mad, but I was hugging them
'cause I was so happy to see them.

Most of the women fulfilled the caregiving duties as part of their
family role without much thought or consideration. Crystal, a
thirty-nine-year-old married social worker, explained that her husband went sandbagging and "*someone* had to watch the kids." As
Hochschild (1989) found, even when women embrace an egalitarian ideology regarding childcare work in the home, their family role
includes childcare work more often than it does for their spouse.
Some of the women in Grand Forks held egalitarian ideologies and
believed that their husbands should take an active role with the children. However, most women typically took on more of this role before the crisis and did not renegotiate or alter this role in the crisis;
their childcare responsibilities carried over into the disaster period.

Women's family role also included preparing the home for the
flood and gutting and cleaning it afterwards because their families
saw that as part of the women's family role. They brought belongings up from the basement while their husbands were either working at their paid jobs, doing community work, or not helping
because they believed the disaster was not really going to happen.
As Louise, a forty-two-year-old homemaker, brought things up
from the basement and placed them in the living room, her husband got frustrated. "I would bring things up . . . but Rodney was,
he did not believe it. He's, like [sigh], he did *not* want to be walking around this stuff." The women of Grand Forks often reported
perceiving the flood as more of a threat than their husbands did and
taking precautionary measures more often than their husbands did,
which is a pattern found in other disaster research as well.[3] I believe
that the reason women took the threat more seriously and engaged
in more preparation activities in the home was due to social location: women have less control over their lives, have less power in the
world, and therefore must take risks more seriously than men do.
Most women felt that during the preparation and evacuation stages,
the household work fell along fairly traditional gender lines.

However, for some women, there was one period when the
family roles did not follow traditional gender lines. Women whose

As it became clear that the Red River of the North and the Red Lake River were going to overflow their dikes, even after weeks of sandbagging by volunteers, all residents had to evacuate. Shelters were set up at various sites, including churches, schools, and the Grand Forks Air Force Base. The residents, who mistakenly believed their evacuation would only last a few days, preferred to be called "evacuees" rather than "refugees." *Photo courtesy of FEMA (website).*

homes had only basement damage experienced an unusual amount of teamwork and egalitarianism with spouses, siblings, parents, and older children during the clean-up stage of this particular part of the house. Many of the married women in the study recalled that teamwork with their spouses was unusual in that they had never worked on housework projects together before. In their study of Hurricane Andrew, Alway et al. (1998) found that some tasks, such as boarding up windows, were two person tasks, thereby facilitating teamwork among married couples. In Grand Forks, the cleaning of basements also required two people—one to haul the gutted materials to the window and one to drag them to the sidewalk—and thus encouraged teamwork that had never occurred before in many marriages. The teamwork may have also been facilitated by the fact that the basement was the first area to be cleaned and men were not back at work yet, or because the basement fell into a somewhat ambiguously gendered domain. Jean Marie, a recently engaged woman in her fifties, told me that she and her fiancé, both of whom were embarking on a second marriage, were "laughing and chatting and listening to music" while they worked together on the basement.

Although the family roles changed during the gutting of the basement, this situation was temporary. After the basements were stripped of debris, women and men returned to their gendered domains, with women doing work in the kitchen and men working on the garage or the yard. Fran explained how they returned to their separate spheres:

> We pretty much did the basement together. Got on our rubber boots and down we went. So that was pretty much shared. But then once we got that cleaned up, then we split in terms of what we were working on. Phil pretty much did the garage on his own. I guess I worked more around [inside]. I spent probably several days in the kitchen. I cleaned out the refrigerator. I spent almost three days just on the cupboards, and then I was doing that while he was doing the garage basically. And now we're pretty well back to normal.

For some women, the end of the teamwork phase was upsetting and isolating. Louise recalled how things changed when her husband went back to his paid job while she stayed at home cleaning:

> At that point, it started getting more stressful. That one week when you first came in and were working together, it was kind of fun doing that. But once he went back to work, he just wasn't available for clean up. So I've been working on cleaning down there in the basement since he's been working. It's probably been helpful in some ways for him to be working. It was really hard for me though. All those days, all those afternoons, sitting and cleaning down there. It's, just, many afternoons I would just sit down there and be cleaning, and I would end up crying.

As other research on disasters has found, women clean up at home after a disaster, while men work on more visible town projects in the public sphere, such as search and rescue and debris removal.[4]

Family roles shifted in other ways as well. Jennifer, a twenty-six-year-old single professional woman, found that after the disaster she and her father divided work along a traditional gendered division of labor. Although she had purchased her own house and distanced herself somewhat from her parents, Jennifer's father felt that he should be in charge of her home's repairs because that work should be performed by men. Prior to the flood, she perceived her life as independent, but the outcome of her family role was traditional and dependent, a situation that was difficult for her to accept. Only one woman, Carol, made a point of saying that gendered division of work responsibilities was blurred during recovery (beyond the basement gutting tasks): "There was no 'this is your job and this one's yours.' I'm just as apt to carry up the big things and do the dirty work, and [my son and husband] are just as apt to do the laundry and dishes."

A third important facet of women's family role was serving as the link to community services. Historically, women's tasks have included connecting the family to the community agencies and services (Chafetz 1990), and this could be seen in Grand Forks. Women often stood in line for supplies or waited at home for repair people. Jane, a fifty-four-year-old teacher, summed up her family role of resource finder: "All I remember is *standing in line*." Women in Grand Forks also completed necessary paperwork, made phone calls to insurance and relief offices, and did numerous follow-up visits to assistance agencies.[5]

However, despite the women's family role of working with various service agencies and repair people, their husbands' public role facilitated some of the repair work. For example, sometimes the women's husbands' ties to the public sphere were crucial to their home recovery. Often they were part of a professional network, enabling them to find scarce plumbers, electricians, and carpenters. In addition to such networks, men often had further connections because of their position of power in the community. Lisa explained how her husband, who held a prominent business position in Grand Forks, was able to use his authority and visibility in the recovery process.

> Oooh, this made me jealous. I was doing all the work, and Daniel would come home, and he was so proud that I was doing all the work, but then he would get everything done. I could call for a month for an electrician. And he arranged for an electrician because of course he knows them. It's not that I resent it; it's just that he knows those people, and I don't know those people, and they'll do him favors because he's a big shot. I called the insurance company and they never called back. I called again. Finally, I say, "I'm Mrs. Daniel Richman," and she says, "Oh, all right." You know, I don't usually introduce myself as Mrs. Daniel Richman. I just am not that sort of person. So from then on, no matter what happened, I was Mrs. Daniel Richman. Then the furnace man came, then here's the hot water man.

Lisa realized that ultimately she had to use her identity as someone's wife in order to pull any weight in the public sphere. No matter how hard she worked, she had no control over those connections and networks. It was common knowledge that women were desperate for repair people. One popular postflood T-shirt worn around town showed a cartoon of a woman who had spent the night with an electrician in exchange for his electrical work on her house, only to find out in the morning that she had misunderstood. He was not an electrician; he was a mortician. While only a joke, the message illustrates how relatively powerless women were in their ability to hire people to restore their homes.

The family role was a significant one for women during the disaster. For most women a large part of their sense of self came from their family role performances. It was important for women in Grand Forks to make sure their children were safe, to prepare and clean up their homes, and to seek out the community services necessary for their families. They perceived themselves as the family caregivers. As

previously discussed, their family role conflicted with their community role, especially prior to the acute phase of the disaster, and it also
conflicted with their work role, especially after the flood waters had
receded and businesses were reopening. Women did not abandon any
of their roles but attempted to negotiate all three simultaneously.

The Work Role

The third role performed by women during the crisis was their
work role, their role as employees in their paid jobs or professions.
Some women's work role required that they continue working
throughout the crisis. They worked as nurses, hospital administra-
tors, public employees, and social workers, and their services were
needed throughout the flood. Many had no break whatsoever from
their jobs. Pat, for example, had to commute to her job as a nurse in
a boat, and Lorna, a hospital manager, was responsible for evacuating patients from the hospital and overseeing their care until they
could return to Grand Forks. Many women felt that it was important that they had worked continuously throughout the disaster.
Lorna noted a difference between those who worked continuously
and those who were absent during the disaster:

> People who weren't here will never understand what we had to do
> here. So I'm glad that I was here. One woman I work with
> couldn't get here, and I think it's harder for her to understand her
> staff and to help and support her staff. She just doesn't have much
> of an understanding. She is definitely supporting her staff, but in
> a different way than I'm helping mine, having been here.

Beth, a thirty-year-old, working class single mother, found
herself in a pivotal role in the middle of community response efforts
in one of the city's main emergency centers. Sitting at her kitchen
table one Saturday afternoon, she reflected with a relaxed manner
on her new work role:

> Well, I've had a whole lot of jobs. I've been a blackjack dealer,
> restaurant manager, radio sales. But this work, it was great. I
> worked hard, everyone knew me. I was completely in charge . . .
> and it was all on me. Everyone came to me. I even got thanked by
> the mayor.

Unlike the women who continued their regular work role, a number of women, like Beth, found their work role transformed into completely new jobs that emerged with the crisis. Many of these roles carried a great deal of responsibility and authority. As a result, for some women in the study, the disaster provided an opportunity to take on leadership roles in the community that would have been unattainable prior to the flood. As with community sandbagging and community support work, women in these temporary leadership positions were satisfied with their roles. Esther, who took on a leadership role at a different emergency center, was pleased by the responsibility and recognition she received. A low-ranking city employee, Esther found herself in charge of the emergency center because she happened to be the highest ranking official who was not flooded out of her home and was able to report to work. In her case, her existing work role expanded to include others' responsibilities:

> I have a real—I don't want to say a craving, but I thrive under crisis. I enjoyed it. I gained a lot of respect from the city employees during that time because, of course, they expected that I would be the person that they should all be taking care of, and instead, I was there helping them, organizing. We worked sixteen-hour days straight for over five weeks. But I enjoyed it. We have a good old boys system here, so afterwards this one guy didn't want me to attend the meetings anymore. I told him, "I have been here since day one, and I've had to make a lot of decisions; my signature is on everything, and you should back me." The city council completely supported me. And now, well, they all definitely listen when I say something.

Esther's work role during the crisis gave her the confidence to resist the "good old boys" who wanted her to step down after the flood.

Most of the women in my study held paying jobs prior to the flood, and most of them returned to these jobs after the flood, except those whose workplace was destroyed and not rebuilt. Some women were not happy when they were first called back to their jobs, and some went only out of fear of losing their jobs. Cecilia, for example, at first resented returning to her job in an insurance office but then found she was glad to be back at work. Most of the women reported that returning to work had positive consequences for them. Reestablishing this work role was important for the women's sense of self as a working person, as well as for establishing a sense of normalcy and routine in their lives, which is a pattern in the disaster recovery process found by other researchers (Alway et al. 1998). For example, Pat explained that she found herself "really wanting to throw myself into work, and I don't mind if I have to work late."

The inability to engage in their paid or professional work seemed to increase women's commitment to reconstructing that work, and thus, their public sphere roles. When women returned to their work role they found it very satisfying, even though they admitted there was still so much work to do at home. Diana explained her feelings about her work role:

> Within two weeks of evacuation, I was able to get into my office. They didn't open up the buildings right away, but my office was in a building that was relatively untouched by the flooding. So I was very lucky and at first spent a few hours a day there. And that was really wonderful.

While Diana returned to her job on her own volition, other women had employers who required that they return to work before most residents had returned to their homes. Lydia, a sixty-seven-year-old mental health counselor, was looking forward to going back to work, saying she was "lucky to be able to go to work and get away." She had a network of female friends at work, a "coffee group," that was very comforting and important to her. Carrie also found work to be supportive during this time: "There was a lot of closeness among the staff. Instant rapport. Add flood waters and stir, and you have an instant team."

Women continued to return to their work roles at various times throughout the summer months of 1997. Returning to their offices gave the women a break from the household recovery, which by this time was mostly left to them. Many of the women found that their spouses returned to their workplaces sooner than they did, leaving them to juggle home and work.[6] As Hochschild (1997) reported, many women find work to be less stressful and less difficult than the pressures and demands of home life. Such a situation is exacerbated when home includes disaster cleaning and rebuilding in addition to the usual tasks of cooking, shopping, cleaning, and taking care of children. As many women in the study admitted, it was good to go to work and not deal with flood clean-up for a period of time.

Still, women experienced a great deal of role conflict between their work role and family role. Those with small children found it especially difficult to return to work when there was no reliable day-care. Some women found that extended family and friends helped relieve this conflict somewhat. By receiving help from family and friends during the crisis, women gained some flexibility in meeting the demands of each role. Esther found that hosting evacuees, two other couples and their children, changed her family role and allowed her to pursue her new work role at the emergency center. She explained how one female evacuee, Cindy, took over many of Esther's family role responsibilities:

> Cindy's a wonderful cook, and she said, "I will just be the house-wife. You just let me cook and take care of the house, and you go to work." My sister came to visit and she was here about three or four days, and she said "You're just enjoying this." And I said, "How can I not?" I come home, and they're cooking, and the kids are happy and, you know, I think it's great, I loved it! Plus, I get to go to work all day every day. My sister was so shocked. She said, "How can you let someone else clean your house?"

Other women spoke of how the help they received from extended family members reduced their work/family role conflicts. Beth was able to send her young son to her mother's house for several weeks so that she could fulfill her emergency worker role. Lorna, the hospital manager, also used extended family so she could perform her work role; she sent her two small children to her mother's house outside of Grand Forks. As role expectations increased during this time, women found they had more flexibility in how they met the demands of each role, such as letting houseguests clean and having children stay with family for extended periods of time. However, these changes in how they met their role expectations did not mean that they gave up any of their roles or no longer identified with particular roles. Indeed, women continued to negotiate the demands of each role and to iden-tify and define themselves by all three roles.

In general, I found that women in Grand Forks experienced a type of "role accumulation" (Sieber 1974). They were committed to their multiple roles and were able to negotiate and fulfill them. Having multiple roles has usually been associated with role conflict, a situation that seems difficult for women and appears to have purely negative consequences. Indeed, the general cultural message is that women are stressed by the demands of too many roles and that they should therefore abandon their public roles, as their true and most important roles are the ones geared toward their families and domestic lives (Lopata 1994). In Grand Forks, it was clear that the family role was the "greediest" role, and at times, women experienced family role engulfment, which forced them to abandon their community and workplace roles temporarily.

Yet role accumulation, contrary to popular thinking and much current scholarship, has some advantages for women. For example, occupying these multidimensional life spaces can result in individual enrichment, autonomy, independence, psychological well-being, a mastery over one's life, and a strong sense of selfhood and self-worth (Lopata 1994, p. 259). Lopata explains that conventional wisdom holds that women's multiple roles drain them of energy and cause them great stress, but she argues that this view overlooks the fact that multiple activities and responsibilities also stimulate and energize. As Lopata notes, Durkheim first stated that complex social involvement is enriching and revitalizing. This is similar to Marks (1977), who critiqued the "scarcity" approach to human energy, positing that individuals, when confronted with multiple roles, are not drained of energy but rather find reservoirs of energy within themselves. Baruch, Barnett, and Rivers (1983) confirmed this notion, finding that women's multiple roles and their ability to coordinate all their obligations had an enormous positive impact on their well-being and self-worth. The women of Grand Forks spoke at length about the personal satisfaction and the feelings of accomplishment and pride of being heavily involved in their three roles, roles that were more demanding and important than usual due to the crisis. Fulfilling their roles made the women more valued in society because the completion of them suddenly became so much more important to the social order and the maintenance of societal stability. As a result of feeling valued in the public sphere, their sense of self shifted and they experienced improved self-concepts as a result of the disaster.

Chapter 4

Financial Fallout

_____

In her book, *Falling from Grace* (1989), anthropologist Katherine Newman describes the experience of the hundreds of thousands of Americans who experience a sudden drop in economic and social standing each year. The stories, heartwrenching, complex, and poignant, illustrate the hardships families face after downsizing, divorce, or other crises. The experiences of middle-class downward mobility are in need of analysis, and yet, she argues, the downward mobility of the middle class, a group she calls an "invisible minority" is a "hidden dimension of our society's experience" (pp. ix, 9)."[1]

The women of Grand Forks experienced a variety of economic consequences as a result of the flood. However, the most prevalent experience was one of sudden and severe downward mobility. The women of Grand Forks also recognized the importance of resources, including money and power, in recovering from a crisis. As discussed in earlier chapters, these women were mostly from working-class and middle-class backgrounds, while several were lower class and upper middle class. Most identified as middle class, which is consistent with how most Americans identify their class standing. Most of the women in Grand Forks owned their homes but did not have many financial resources beyond paychecks and home ownership. Yet, because of their class standing, many of the women enjoyed a certain amount of privilege and had, to a degree, a sense of entitlement.

There is very little research on the financial impact of disasters on families and individuals, although some research has looked at the overall costs of a disaster to communities. It is clear, however, that natural disasters can be financially devastating and logistically complicated, with SBA loans, insurance issues, and disaster grants.

It is also possible that disasters can have positive economic consequences in some cases. There is also very little research on what the downward mobility and other economic dilemmas families face actually mean to them, how individuals cope with these economic changes, and how they make sense of the financial fallout from the disaster. As Newman found, the middle class people who go through catastrophic losses have feelings of failure, loss of control, and social disorientation, and they must deal not only with the financial hardship but with the psychological, social, and practical consequences of "falling from grace" (p. 8). By examining the plight of the downwardly mobile, we learn what it means to be middle class in America.

Downward Mobility

The women and their families experienced severe and sudden downward mobility in the flood. Sociologists call this "intragenerational downward mobility." For some women, this was the first time in their lives that they experienced downward mobility and the feeling that they were poor. The women spoke of how unsettling and stressful it was not to have any money. Jean Marie, a secretary in her fifties, said it "was scary when we didn't have any money, and we didn't have any clothes." To deal with their tremendous downward mobility, Tina tried to place less emphasis on money and the things they no longer had: "Money is nice, but we certainly are not as driven by that as we were before the flood." Some women, during evacuation, enrolled their children in federal programs for free hot lunches at their new schools. They were grateful for these, but their participation in the programs made them feel poor.

The way the women and their families experienced poverty was a result of living in a consumer culture, which espouses values that people's worth can be measured by possessions. Carol's teenaged son felt the effects of their downward mobility and commented to his mother, "Mom, if we were measured by our possessions, I'm in trouble. Everything I own fits in these two boxes." Genie made similar comments: "Everything we owned was in that duffel bag. And our dog was in a little gym bag because we didn't have a pet carrier. And I felt *so poor*." Pat's family, with three drivers, had to learn to share one car. She said, "We were used to everyone having their own car." This feeling of poverty, of course, is relative;

many poor Americans survive with no car and would not find sharing one car with other family members to be a burden. Middle-class Americans, however, take it for granted, because cars are just a part of a larger standard of living they have come to expect.

Sabrina felt particularly nervous about her family's downward mobility because she and her husband were young and had a small child. Genie and her family, who ultimately experienced some upward mobility, did experience temporary downward mobility. In her situation, she could not pay for anything for months because "we have no money, we left our checkbook, and we didn't carry our credit cards. And so we had nothing, no cash, no credit cards, no checkbook. It was a sad, hopeless, helpless feeling."[2] Thus, while her anguish over being destitute was real, it was also temporary as it was only a matter of regaining her access to her finances. Most women, however, had to go several months with no paychecks and enormous bills, making them truly downwardly mobile. Peggy, for example, knew that her financial situation might be long- term, so during evacuation she went to work cleaning motel rooms for minimum wage.

For other women, this was not the first time in their lives that they experienced downward mobility and poverty. Rachel and her children had experienced downward mobility many years before the flood when she went through a divorce, lost her home, had three small children and no car, and received welfare benefits. Years later, when the flood hit, she was more economically stable but still living close to the edge of poverty. Rachel and her partner rented a small house that was lost in the flood, an event that triggered feelings of going backwards toward poverty again. As they could not afford to live anywhere in town after the flood, Rachel enrolled in school so that she could live in the University of North Dakota family housing with her partner and children. Julie, a thirty-eight-year-old social worker, also experienced downward mobility for the second time: "I went through a divorce ten years ago, and I lost everything. I was starting out with two kids and nothing. I feel like that again."

Grand Forks residents faced a dearth of affordable housing after the flood. Other research has found this to be a serious problem in the aftermath of a disaster, especially for low-income residents.[3] In Grand Forks, downward mobility increased because the housing market was skewed against buyers. Lydia, who was a part-time realtor, said that the prices for homes were unusually high after the flood, and there was "a captive market" because people needed a place to live immediately. Housing was also a problem for renters. Past research has found that renters, especially low-income ones, usually have more trouble finding housing after a disaster than homeowners.[4] Liz, who had a Section 8 housing voucher for her apartment, found out that her landlord raised the rent from $325 a month to $425 a month.[5] The federal government would only pay up to $364 a month for individuals with the Section 8 vouchers. Liz lived in fear during evacuation that she would be homeless when they finished rebuilding her apartment, and the landlord starting charging the new rent. Luckily, a housing worker was able to get a waiver from the federal government for Liz, and she was able to stay in the apartment.

In Grand Forks, the women who were homeowners found that there were restrictions on the types of houses that could be bought with government funds. Many families had restrictions on their SBA loans and various grants, in the same way that food stamp recipients are told how to spend the money they are given.[6] Cecilia, for example, wanted to buy an older home downtown, but the SBA financing prohibited her from taking a flood-damaged home, which most older homes downtown were. Cecilia and her family were forced to buy a home they did not really want, a newer suburban home. They did not have furniture in their new home for several months, and no beds for five months. Cecilia felt that they "had done with a lower style of living" but not anything "of real hardship." As Newman (1989) wrote about the downwardly mobile, they are not going hungry, but they are experiencing a lower standard of living. Women in Grand Forks were coping with a loss of economic privilege.

Many families were at risk of becoming "house poor" by having all their worth tied in their houses, with nothing left over for other expenses. For instance, Carol, a forty-three-year-old homemaker, knew they were in danger of falling in that category. When they finished their repairs on their flooded house, they decided to move to a new home but felt cautious about spending above their means:

> We had a cap on what we would spend, since we wanted to be able to travel and do stuff. I grew up in a family with seven children and no money. So we knew we didn't want everything sunk in a house.

Other women, despite their worries, did end up house poor after the disaster. Indeed, many experienced forced upward mobility by having to move to neighborhoods higher on the social and economic ladder. Dana and her husband moved to a middle-class neighborhood from a working-class neighborhood because that was the only housing they could find. They borrowed money to afford the new house in the wealthier neighborhood, but they still felt working class:

> My brother jokes that I moved out to the rich area. Actually, I feel like I really don't belong here because I'm not, you know what I mean, I'm not rich, so I don't belong here. But so far the people here don't seem to have that attitude of "I can't associate with you people because I'm not in the same tax bracket."

Cecilia and her family also moved from a working-class neighborhood, where their home was destroyed, to a newer, suburban, and more affluent neighborhood. She felt that "it is more affluent, and it's got more children, but it's not as friendly. Our other neighborhood had all these little old people that loved to see our kids, so they were out and about and coming to visit, or we were going to visit them." These women and their families, by moving to an affluent area where they felt that they didn't belong or the people were not as friendly, were experiencing social isolation and a loss of their community. Genie and her family also moved to a house and neighborhood above their price range after their original home was destroyed. She had actually looked to buy a house in this new neighborhood only months before the flood but could not afford it. For some of the women and their families going through this forced upward mobility, they often felt socially isolated and like outsiders in their new neighborhoods.[7]

Cindy, a warm, engaging woman in her late forties, ran a successful daycare business in her basement for seventeen years. Unfortunately, the entire business was lost in the flood. Her husband retained his job selling cars, but they needed two incomes. With no money to redo the basement, Cindy took a clerical job, which brought in less money for the family than the daycare. She explained how they handled the downward mobility:

> The regular clerical wages in Grand Forks are not very good. It is a step down from what I am used to making. My kids have had to

make some changes. They have had to change their expectations about how many pairs of jeans they can buy and what brand they are going to get. It seems really insignificant, but when you are a teenager, it's not. We've all had to tighten our belts somewhat, and that's not such a bad thing. Nothing wrong with that.

In her research, Newman found the same phenomenon with families experiencing downward mobility from the loss of a job. It was difficult for the teenagers to adjust to the lower standard of living and to be unable to buy the clothes and accessories that they had been accustomed to. White, middle-class teenagers, in Newman's study and in Grand Forks, had a sense of entitlement around consumer goods—they felt they were entitled to certain clothes and entertainment items. Overall, Cindy's story illustrates how employment troubles during the flood greatly contributed to the women's downward mobility.

Some women felt very fortunate to have job security throughout the crisis, especially those who were salaried and could continue to collect paychecks while they were not working. Pat and her husband, for example, were both paid their regular salaries throughout the crisis. This helped alleviate stress and lessened the degree to which they experienced downward mobility. Sabrina was also paid during the crisis through what her employer called the "Act of God" pay, which apparently was covered by the employer's insurance.

Women who were paid hourly before the flood typically received no paychecks or unemployment payments during the crisis. Lisa insisted on paying her cleaning woman, Catherine, during the flood, even though there was no house to clean. Lisa felt that because she was being paid her salary but not going to work, then she should pay Catherine even though she was not coming to work. Catherine, who had evacuated with her mentally disabled brother and her husband, who was a janitor, "had her hands full" and was "overwhelmed and thankful" for the payment, according to Lisa. Judith Rollins, in her book on domestic workers and their employers, *Between Women* (1985), posits that such benevolence and gift giving by employers to their domestic workers is really an expression of maternalism in a highly exploitative relationship. Thus, Catherine, by thanking Lisa profusely for the pay, could have been showing her deference to her employer, an action that is required in the relationship between employer and domestics. Other women, such as Kim and Teresa, who worked in service-oriented jobs, received no pay throughout the crisis.

Another employment problem was the very real fear of losing a job. Liz's daughter, who worked at a large supermarket and could barely afford rent every month, was told by her employer to return to work immediately or be fired. While she did not want to leave her disabled mother, Liz's daughter felt that she had no choice. As Liz described, "She said that she had to leave me to go to work, and we cried and fought, and it was terrible." Sabrina, who received the "Act of God" pay during the crisis, found that just a few weeks later, her employer "laid on the guilt" to come back to work, saying there would be repercussions if employees did not return. Amy Sue, a thirty-nine-year-old divorcee, lost her job of many years during the flood, although her employer claimed that the layoff had nothing to do with the flood. Amy Sue was livid about being fired, especially after having done flood-related work for the business throughout the crisis for no pay. She felt that it was unconscionable to fire someone in the midst of the flood, and she asked her employer, "How can you, knowing that I have no home, no means of support, do this at this time? How can you do this from a social, economic, and *moral* position?" Sandy also lost her new job as a secretary at a law firm when the office was destroyed in the downtown fire. She was scheduled to start at the job two days after the flood, so she was not paid at all during her time of unemployment.

Another consequence of downward mobility is putting future plans on hold. Jane and her husband had planned for years to remodel their lake home in the summer of 1997. After the flood, however, they had to abandon that plan because they were too financially strained. In addition, Jane took on extra work throughout the summer to earn extra money. As a result, they ended up with a summer they had never imagined: working all the time, on their home and at their jobs, and not only forgoing the remodeling but not going to their lake house at all.[8] Louise and her husband had to give up their dream of adopting a child when they realized that they did not have enough money after the flood for the adoption fees and for repairing their house to make space for a child. Because they were older, they felt that they lost their one window of opportunity to pursue adoption. It would be too late in five to ten years when they were back on their feet financially. Louise explained that it was "a dream that might have come true if the flood hadn't happened."

A more common dream that had to be abandoned was a simple one: a family vacation. Most families had to drop plans to leave Grand Forks for a getaway during the summer after the flood. The loss of these family vacations greatly contributed to increased stress levels and family conflicts.

Disasters do not take place in a social or economic vacuum, and many of the women already faced other financial challenges, such as going through a divorce or sending their children off to college. These women found themselves in particularly dire financial straits after the flood. Peggy, who started divorce proceedings during the flood aftermath, found that her financial situation was problematic and realized that she could no longer support her teenage daughter and her young granddaughter. Genie, who had to undergo carpal tunnel surgery after the flood, was overwhelmed by the medical expenses on top of the flood costs. "I have no money. I was just sitting looking at all of those bills, and I had the surgery, and the insurance pays 80 percent, but that 20 percent really adds up."

Undoubtedly, downward mobility was harder on those who were poor before the flood. Joanne felt that she was already only just getting by when the flood hit:

> I live on the poverty line. I made $16,000 this year and that's the most I've made in sixteen years. So it's a chronic kind of poverty. We just don't get any raises. Truly, and I'm not exaggerating this, I can't think of a year where I had enough money to buy the postage stamps that I need to. I mean, I budget that tight. That is one thing about the disaster, that is so amazing, is that I had to buy and replace so much. I think I spent something like $25,000 in four months.

Unfortunately, Joanne was not able to get any money from FEMA, because her home had too much damage, or from the SBA, because her income was too low to qualify her for a loan. Luckily, she received money from the Angel Fund,[9] a Minnesota Individual and Family Grant, and a loan from the city of East Grand Forks to help her repair her home. Joanne was also fortunate because her employer made it clear that her job would not be in jeopardy as a result of the flood. Liz was also poor before the flood but experienced further downward mobility due to the flood. She survived on $120 a month in food stamps before the flood, income that continued throughout the crisis, but she was overloaded with new expenses to replace what she had lost.

The flood was financially harder on the twelve women in the study who were single because they had to rely on only one income to get back on their feet. The flood was perhaps hardest of all for the four single mothers of young children, all of whom were lower or working class. For example, Rachel, being a single parent and trying to find new housing after the flood, wondered how she was going to make it financially.

Many of the women found themselves and their families incurring large amounts of debt.[10] Their losses had turned out to be much greater than they originally anticipated, as the loss of just a basement was often financially devastating.[11] Lorna, a married, middle-class mother of two, was overwhelmed by the large loan they had to take out to rebuild their house: "We took out a $45,000 home improvement loan from the SBA, and every month we'll be reminded of that as we make our payments for a long time. $45,000 is a *lot* of money. We'll be reminded of it for a *long* time." Carrie, a married professional in her forties, found that she needed to phone her friends long-distance for much-needed support, while at the same time recognizing that the phone bills were a source of stress for her and her husband:

> We were running up enormous credit card bills, and there was a lot of anxiety around this, a *lot* of anxiety. I constantly am calling my friends for support. We are having $800 phone bills month after month. And trying to keep track but not really having any idea of how badly off we are.

For those who owned their own businesses, there was an added anxiety over finances, as there was no employer during the crisis. Tina described her family's situation:

> Frank had to go back to work, so we did all his stuff first. All his supplies and equipment, we had to deal with that loss first. We got no support in that area. It's like people are unsympathetic when you have your own business. So there is no assistance there, from the city, from SBA, there was nothing.

Other women, like Cindy who owned her daycare, had to close their businesses because of the economic losses. Julie was worried about those individuals who owned appliance stores; they would have a boom when every resident replaced their washers, dryers, refrigerators, freezers, and hot water heaters, but then no one would need a replacement for twenty years.

Kimberlee, who lived in a trailer park on the west side of town and did not have any flood damage, was still affected financially by the flood. The daycare for her young daughter was destroyed, and she had to quit her job to stay home with her. Shortly thereafter, her husband was laid off from his job in a nursing home: "I quit my job, and then he lost his job. Then he worked in a warehouse, but then he was off for two more months. It was pretty stressful. It was hard." Ultimately, Kimberlee felt that their situation turned out well, as she was much happier being home with her daughter, Sophie, and they were doing "okay" financially. They tried to cut their expenses, and Kimberlee joked, "Sophie doesn't care what she wears!" Kimberlee's story raised issues of class differences in coping skills. Many women in the lower class and working class were more accustomed to struggling materially and having less power in their everyday lives. The coping skills they developed in everyday life were useful in getting through the disaster. Because they had less of a sense of entitlement, they coped better with the losses.

Middle-class women, however, had a slightly harder time coming to terms with their losses because they were accustomed to a certain lifestyle and a certain amount of economic fairness. Peggy, a forty-five-year-old homemaker, was overwhelmed by financial responsibilities for the year after the flood. Her house was destroyed, but because she and her husband still technically owned it, they were required to continue their house payments. Peggy was infuriated that she had to pay house payments on a destroyed house and also pay rent twice the amount of their house payment for an overpriced temporary apartment. Carol was taken aback by how much they had lost, acknowledging that their financial problems were going to be worse than originally expected. They took out a $5000 loan, thinking that they only needed to do a few repairs, but then they found out that the damage was much greater than they had realized. Carol felt that "it was absolutely devastating to find out the tens of thousands of dollars of stuff that we lost." They tallied up all their losses and Carol sighed, "This is going to hit us later." They applied for an SBA loan, but, of course, they will have to pay that back.

Others felt fortunate that they did not have to take on any debt. Fran, an elementary school teacher who had basement damage, felt that her financial resources made a large difference in the manner of her recovery:

> We qualified for more SBA than we needed. We just needed $10,000 because we had the resources. So we didn't have to take on more debt. So, we'll pay off the mortgage and the loan at the same time. If we had to take on a whole new debt, it would have been much different. The resources you draw from make a big difference. We were very grateful for our situation, that we were able to [fix the house] and still plan for retirement, and not have to readjust a whole bunch of future planning. That would be very stressful. We are looking at being eligible for retirement in six years. All of our planning has been to that point. Our mortgage and everything is set up for that point. If we had to take on a whole new debt, that would have changed things a lot. That would be an added stress.

Genie, who had such success "pounding the pavement" for her buyout check[12] and voucher money, was alarmed when the money disappeared so quickly:

> I worked hard to get the buyout check and the relocation voucher of $10,000. It sounds like a lot, but it went fast. A new roof, new garage door. That was pretty "spendy" as they say around here [she speaks in a put-on North Dakota accent]. Then one day it was all gone. And we still needed to do the basement.

Genie and her husband then had to find additional money to finish repairing their new home, which had been damaged but not destroyed. Dana, who moved to a suburban home and faced social isolation, as mentioned earlier, worried about how much they had to borrow from the bank to get the new house.

Louise also was concerned about money after the flood. During part of their evacuation out of state, her husband thought it would be fun to go gambling, which, Louise said, "did not prove to be a good idea." She felt that they did not know if they were losing their home or not, and were not in the right frame of mind to be gambling. Louise worried that her husband would lose all their money, and she spent the evening frantically trying to win back all the money he was losing. The outing, she said, "really stressed me out," even though they went home with a gain of $38. This scenario is similar to women's greater preparation of the home and greater likelihood of perceiving a disaster threat as serious and risky: unlike her husband, Louise did not feel invincible and in control of the situation. Instead, she felt as if she had no control over what was happening in her life and therefore was much more worried about losing money.

Upward Mobility

A very few women were able to experience some upward mobility as a result of the flood, as certain opportunities arose. In contrast to the forced upward mobility described earlier, this could be considered a welcome upward mobility. Other research has found that occasionally poor disaster survivors experience a slight increase in their standard of living after a disaster.[13] Like other research, my study showed that the few women who experienced some upward mobility were the exception to the rule.

Upward mobility was most frequently due to job opportunities. As discussed earlier, Beth, who took on a leadership role in the emergency operations, was offered a better job after the flood as a result of her emergency work. She described how this improved the financial situation for her and her young son:

> My highest paying job ever before the flood was $6.50 an hour, and the job that I was working for [when the flood hit] was $5.75 an hour. So the city paid $7 an hour, and then I got another job with the Disaster Assistance Program, and that bumped us up to $8 an hour. And then the funding was running out, and I got hired for the Special Needs Assessment. So we are now at $9.77 an hour, plus full benefits, which is forty hours of sick, forty hours of vacation, full medical insurance, with the total premium paid for me and Eli. I've *never* had health insurance for me and Eli before. All the bills are now paid, and I have $2,000 in the bank. I have *never* had money in the bank.

Genie and her family also experienced upward mobility due to employment opportunities. Her husband, a manager at a large company, was able to prove himself during the flood, by putting his work first, living in an old camper at his work site, and working

around the clock. Because Genie and their children evacuated out
of state, her husband had no family responsibilities. Genie said
that she and her husband "have both acknowledged that this flood
has been great for his career." He received a promotion, and they
were eventually transferred out of Grand Forks. Genie was thrilled
by their impending upward mobility, describing her conversations
at a business picnic for her husband's company the summer after
the flood:

> His boss's wife asked me what I liked about Grand Forks, and I
> said, "I love being a manager's wife. A lot better than being a
> truck driver's wife, or a courier's wife. I like being a manager's
> wife." One day I'm going to be a district director's wife! I didn't
> say that part, but I sure thought it!

In Grand Forks, some middle-class women perceived that the
poor and the homeless were doing better as a result of the flood.
Jean Marie, a divorced secretary in her fifties, saw the homeless residents from the Mission, the Grand Forks homeless shelter located
downtown, at the Air Force Base hangar: "They took the mission
people in, and they were having a ball. They got new clothing, free
food, and they were wandering around. It wasn't bad for them!"
Again, however, it should be pointed out that any type of economic
movement upward was the exception to the rule, as in the cases of
Beth and Genie—and in the case of the homeless from the mission,
it was also minimal, temporary, and superficial; they still were
homeless and poor after the disaster.

Financial Conflicts

Many of the women found themselves in conflicts over money
with the city, FEMA, various agencies, churches, and local government.[14] For many, this was the first time they were involved in such
contentious financial disputes. In almost all of these conflicts, the
women showed resolve, determination, anger, and strength, none
of which are typical "North Dakota nice"[15] or fit within the image
of the stereotypical, accommodating female. Women are socialized
to avoid conflict and to placate volatile situations, yet many women
described feeling so angry that they reached their breaking point.
These financial conflicts often brought about a shift in the women's

presentation of self and their self-perception, as they became more assertive and outspoken in the public sphere.

Financial conflicts with federal agencies, especially the Federal Emergency Management Agency (FEMA), were common. Cecilia, a mother of four in her late thirties, described her conflicts with FEMA:

> We had some ongoing struggles with FEMA. They asked us to send money back to them, so we sent them documentation that we had used it for rent. Then they sent us a letter saying, okay, you don't have to pay it. Then we got a letter saying they were turning us over to the collection agency and beginning judicial proceedings. I got tired of it all, and I got our congressman on it. Then we got letters of apology.

Cecilia, who is educated and middle class, called her congressional representative with ease. Despite her gender, and perhaps because of her class, Cecilia felt entitled to contact her representative and demand his time.

Related to the discussion on upward mobility, some women had conflicts with FEMA over the trailers. In one FEMA trailer park, residents received what they felt were harassing phone calls from FEMA just a month or two after they moved in, asking them when they were leaving; they had been told that they could live there for one year. Tina felt that the FEMA officials misunderstood the middle-class residents using the trailers:

> It was hard when they would continually call us and ask us when we were getting out of the wonderful FEMA trailer. They just think you will become so comfortable that you aren't going to want to get out of government housing. I hate to burst their bubble, but the accommodations are not quite that glorious. We knew some people who had rats in their trailer!

Tina felt insulted that the FEMA officials thought she wanted to live in a trailer, when she felt that such living conditions were beneath her standard of living.[16]

Some women felt that the city was receiving millions of dollars in disaster relief, but that the residents were not seeing any of it. Liz appeared to be a perfect candidate for some assistance: she was poor, was physically disabled from a central nervous system disorder, and had lost all her furnishings and belongings. Yet, Liz received no aid: "I don't have money to replace anything. I have the bare essentials. I have some resentment. There is all this money coming in, millions of dollars being donated. Yet there are no funds available for someone like me." Actually, Liz did receive $2,000 from the Angel Fund, which helped her considerably, but she had to stretch it out for months because she did not receive any other money. When that money ran out, she survived on her $120 a month in food stamps.

There was widespread dissatisfaction with the way the city handled the Angel Funds from an anonymous donor. The city gave $2,000 from the million-dollar donation to various—but not all—residents. Jean Marie, who lived on the south end of town, felt that her neighborhood was excluded from receiving that money because it was assumed that her area of town was too affluent: "This neighborhood was never called to get the money. They felt, 'Oh, those are wealthy people, they don't need anything.'" On a walk through her neighborhood one day, she showed me a house several houses from hers that was "the most expensive house in the whole town" and whose owner was a prominent figure in town. She also pointed out neighbors who lost their homes, who were not "exactly wealthy," but "because of their address, they never got anything, and they needed it desperately." In this case, both points of view can be seen: the neighborhood had destruction and needed funds to recover, and yet it was the most affluent area of town.

Other women had other reasons for conflicts with the city. Carol, a forty-three-year-old homemaker, was agitated with the city:

> I was proud of the city government during the disaster, but now I'm not. They better get their butts in gear and get something going. We're going to lose a lot of small businesses and the families that go with small businesses.

Many residents were unhappy with the amounts they were offered by the city for their homes. Dana, for example, hired an independent appraiser because she felt that the city was $20,000 short in its buyout offer. Other women felt that the city cost them their homes in the first place. By making evacuation mandatory, residents could not stay and continue to operate sump pumps, which might have kept water out of their homes. Lorna pointed out that the city "did not need to kick us out that quickly. It was slowly rising water."

Lorna, like several other women, said they would stay at their homes if they had to do it all over again.

Many of the women were outspoken and opinionated about the financial situation. Some even spoke out in a way they never had before. Peggy, a forty-five-year-old mother of two teenagers, was infuriated with the city for putting recovery funds into a new corporate center. At a city council meeting, she was so angry that she rose from the audience and walked to the podium to speak. She recalled the meeting:

> The way they were treating people over buyouts, I couldn't believe it. I went to all the meetings, and finally I had to say something. I told them they had the audacity to sit there and tell us that they are going to pay for a building for a corporate center. Why don't you offer the home buyout people the same deal? We have nothing. Everyone [in the buyout program] gave in to lower prices, and I am not going to. *I am not going to give in.*

Peggy and her friend, who was sitting next to her at the meeting, were both shocked that Peggy spoke in front of so many people. Peggy explained her actions:

> I was sitting in the audience, and I said, "I can't believe this." The chairman says, "Do you have something to say?" I had sat through all these meetings, and I said, "You bet I do, you bet I do." My friend couldn't believe this!
>
> [AF: Would you have ever done this before?]
>
> Never, ever, in a million years! My hair was standing on end. If they weren't treating us the way they were, I wouldn't have. My face was red. I thought I was going to faint on the way up there. I couldn't catch my breath. I told them that I didn't think the buyout was "voluntary." It isn't voluntary for me. Give me a building permit and I'll stay; I like my house. Then he says [she mimics his low, stern, patronizing voice], "I think you know the answer to that." Then, one of the other council members said, "Well, if you can pass inspection, then you can get a building permit." I looked right at him and said, "Well, *I think you know the answer to that,* don't you?"

Peggy had never done anything like that before in her life, but feeling so angry and "pushed around" made her feel as if she had no choice but to voice her opinion. The disaster, therefore, acted as a catapult, sending some women into roles of social activism and civic involvement in the public sphere.

Some women felt that it was unfair to distribute money only in town, when many families had evacuated out of driving distance or had returned to work and could not stand in line for hours. Martha Jo, an upper-middle-class retiree, felt it was unfair for her son, who had evacuated to a resort in Minnesota with his family. Because he was out of town, he could not receive the city's recovery money. Interestingly, Martha Jo did not see that having enough money to stay at a resort during evacuation was possibly an indicator of the level of resources that her son's family had for recovery. From her social location, she felt that she and her son were entitled to recovery money. Some residents were upset with the city for using thousands of dollars in city funds to create a winter ice skating rink arena and decorative holiday lights as a measure to lift morale the Christmas after the flood. Karen disagreed with the critics: "The arena was charming, it was wonderful. I thought it was the one thing they did right! I thought it was lovely. I took my kids to skate at night. It was so pretty. We've never had lights quite so lovely."

A few residents also had financial conflicts with contractors and construction companies. The North Dakota Office of the Attorney General printed and distributed a pamphlet entitled "Consumers Beware of Flood Scams" that warned residents of price gouging, problems with landlords, flood-damaged used cars, and advance-fee loan scams during recovery. The conflicts were gendered in that the contractors were almost all male, and the residents at home when the contractors came to do the repairs were mainly women. Most of the women in the study did not report being taken advantage of by contractors, and the few who felt they were victims of scams, interestingly, did not believe it was because they were women. A few women were "scammed," and others were simply overcharged by various workers, such as construction companies, carpenters, and plumbers. Jane and her husband were the victims of a con artist who posed as a construction worker. They needed repairs on their house, and in their desperation to find someone to do them, they hired a man who told them his license was in the mail. They believed him, and they gave him $2,000 up front for materials, even though they knew that they "were doing everything we aren't supposed to do." When he never showed up to do the work, they contacted police, and the scam artist was charged with fraud. When I spoke with her last, Jane still had not recovered her lost money.

While most of those who came in to do work in Grand Forks were reputable, a few understood how desperate the homeowners would be in the recovery period and took advantage of that situation. Other research has also found that disaster victims need to be cautious of being misled, overcharged, or even scammed completely by construction workers after a disaster.[17] Genie blamed herself for being grossly overcharged by the man who put in a new bathroom in their house, saying with a sense of humor, that "When you're dumb, you're dumb." She never confronted him on the overcharging. For Genie and her family, who were experiencing some upward mobility, paying too much for the repairs was not going to affect them too drastically.

While residents often spoke about the wonderful way the community came together during the flood, there was evidence that these feelings of solidarity may have existed in the preparation and response period but not in the longer-term recovery and reconstruction periods. When the stress of financial problems settled in, residents began to speak out, and conflicts surfaced between the city and residents and among residents of different neighborhoods or with different amounts of damage. Julie was furious to hear from some of her friends and neighbors that they had figured out ways to make money on the flood. "Some people I know are turning in claims for a foundation, but they have no intention of fixing it because it was really like that before the flood, and they're getting $10,000 for it." Roseanne felt that after the flood waters receded, the conflicts between neighborhoods surfaced, with many residents perceiving that wealthier individuals and neighborhoods were doing better:

> There were different programs for those who lost their houses and for those who only lost their basements. There are divisions between neighborhoods. Riverside [Roseanne's neighborhood] is middle/working class, and Reeves Drive is upper middle class, and [on] South Belmont Road area the houses are three-hundred [thousand] to half a million dollars. Lots of lawyers and doctors. They have much more political leverage. Lincoln and Riverside and Central neighborhoods, in particular, were much older neighborhoods, lots of retired, less powerful. The north end [which included Riverside] has always been the poor part of town as opposed to the south end. People pushed for their own interests, for their own neighborhood.

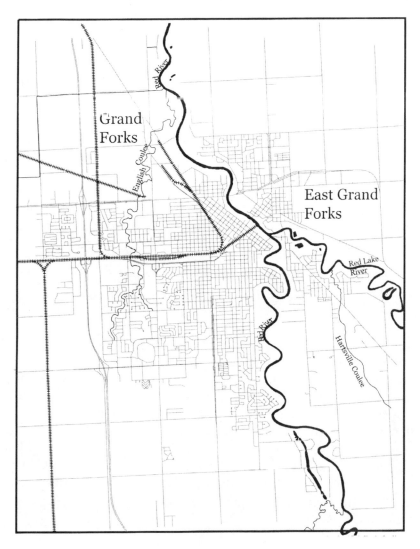

Map of Grand Forks, North Dakota and East Grand Forks, Minnesota. *Map courtesy of the Grand Forks-East Grand Forks Metropolitan Planning Organization.*

The areas that she described as more working class (Riverside, Lincoln, and Central) were the neighborhoods most directly hit by the flood, as they were older areas built right next to the river. Many of these areas have been demolished completely and are slated to become parks and greenways. Roseanne's passionate discussion of what was happening to different economic classes in Grand Forks illustrates the level to which many women became educated on and involved in political, economic, and social issues during recovery. This greater political awareness and civic involvement could be interpreted as an expansion of their community role.

The city, trying to alleviate the enormous housing problems, built houses in the flood aftermath and then sold them to residents. Peggy's friend, Violet, felt that the city had no business in real estate, and when they began to sell lots around the golf course, she said that was a good example of "the disparity between the classes," as only the wealthier residents could afford those lots. Sandy, who lost her home through a divorce prior to the flood and her job because of the flood, felt that other people received help and she should have too. She felt she had fallen through the cracks: "I didn't lose my home to water, but I lost it. Some of those who lost their homes in the flood have moved into brand new homes because they got all the help that they needed. I felt like I was one of those people who was in between the cracks. I didn't lose anything, but I lost everything." From her point of view, it was advantageous to lose your home to the flood as opposed to through divorce. Violet and Sandy, as well as other women in the study, engaged in more economic and political analysis of their social world during the disaster recovery than they did prior to the flood. This engagement in political affairs, even if their activism went no further than the walls of their own homes, marks an expansion of gender roles and some shifts in ideology around women's voice on public-sphere issues.

Resources Matter

Many believe that natural disasters are the true status leveler, in that the disasters hit indiscriminately, affecting all walks of life, both rich and poor alike. By contrast, most research has shown that disasters are discriminating and that the most vulnerable and marginalized members of society are hit the hardest and have the hard-

est time recovering.[18] Popular culture, however, still perpetuates the
status leveling viewpoint.

Some women felt that the disaster did indeed put all the citizens of Grand Forks, wealthy and poor, old and young, powerful
and powerless, in the same position during the crisis. Lydia articulated this idea well in her statement: "We were all in the same boat,
no other way to say it. No pun intended." Amy Sue, a thirty-nine-
year old delivery driver, felt that the sandbag lines were status lev-
elers. She described who participated in sandbagging: "Small
women, older women, older men, farmers, you could see academics
and blue collar and white collar, and kids, and everybody." Carol,
who evacuated to the Air Force base's hangar, felt that the disaster
wiped away status differences during the evacuation: "[The flood]
was a leveler for our community. *Everyone* was evacuated and homeless. The person with her mink coat on was sleeping next to the residents from the mission." For the first few nights the shelters did
have all walks of life, but after several days most individuals with
some financial means left the shelters for other lodging. Furthermore, many residents with more resources never went to the shelter
at all. They went to motels or to stay with family members who had
enough space to host them. Jane and her husband drove to the Air
Force base hangar but decided not to stay when they looked inside
and saw that it was dingy and dank inside. Because they had the
resources, they had the option to stay elsewhere.

After the flood, many charities and programs were set up to
help everybody, regardless of income and status. For a short time,
this produced the feeling of "everybody in the same boat," as everyone was in the same lines for paper towels or vouchers for free gaso-
line. One program that caught everyone's attention was the Free
Prom Dress store in the town's indoor shopping mall. Many of the
high school girls who had planned to attend their junior and senior
Proms lost their dresses in the flood, or their families no longer had
the money to buy them dresses. A program was developed so that
girls from across the United States donated their prom dresses to
the girls of Grand Forks. They were assembled in a store, and the
girls could come and pick one out for free.[19] The prom itself cost
students only one-dollar each for admission.

Often individuals were in the same predicament during the
acute crisis stage and the immediate aftermath, but status differences began to reemerge as the community headed into the

recovery period. Ultimately, the women came to realize that all resources at their disposal—status, power, class, and money— helped them in the disaster aftermath. The flip side, of course, was that the lack of those resources was an extreme liability for recovery. Prior to the flood, many of the women had believed that resources would not matter but rather that assistance after a natural disaster would always be given out more equitably, in other words, distributed according to need.

Many, like Carrie, felt that the flood was indeed a status leveler, but only for a very short period. She described the evacuation situation:

> Down at the church, it was really interesting, all kinds of people were really nice to each other. And then as people started to move back into Grand Forks, it was just kind of, like, a few people left [at the church], and they were very concerned about money. It got to be like the regular poor people and then the middle class. And limited sympathy for the poor, those perpetually out of luck. There were people who couldn't afford to get further in debt or who didn't have transportation.

Clearly, options were fewer for those with more limited funds and no cars. Higher status families did not need to use public shelters for as long, if at all. Families with vehicles left public shelters after only one or two nights.[20]

Louise also observed that before the flood the crisis was a status leveler and people were all working together, but after the flood status divisions and self interest reemerged:

> Before the flooding, everyone was working together. It was great. Everyone was volunteering. "Let's save our city," and everything. People were working together. After the flood, it was more like, "I've got to call this insurance person and this FEMA person," and on the radio everyone was bickering about money, especially the Angel Fund money. You know—"Why did they give money to homeless people who don't even have any belongings to replace?" Things like that. All kinds of anger. "How come that neighborhood got it and our neighborhood didn't?" The Angel Fund was like a magnet for drawing everyone who was upset.

Genie agreed that in the end, not everybody's needs were taken care of, and status and resources played a part in recovery: "It all depends on where you were and what your insurance was and what your situation was. Some people got over like fat rats, and other people are still drowning."

The study participants believed that resources were tied to power and status in the community. Peggy mentioned the fate of one female-owned bakery in town:

> There was this one woman at a city hall meeting; she owns a bakery but won't get any help because she is not downtown. She practically had to beg for help. I feel so bad for her. That poor lady has worked so hard. They are not consistent. They picked and chose. It didn't matter how many tears you shed at these meetings, it wasn't going to change anything. It seems like this handful of people have all the power, and if you don't know them, then you are just shit out of luck.

Cecilia, who lost her home and belongings in the flood, spoke of people wanting to take advantage of the flood situation to make money off of families like her own:

> Our housing situation was really frustrating. The houses were $10,000 more than before the flood, and no finished basements. They justified the expense because of new furnaces and water heaters. I think, unfortunately, that some people wanted to get rich at somebody else's expense. I think a lot of those homes are still on the market. They are just wanting to get rich.

There was a belief also that the city was all-powerful, and that residents were powerless. Dana felt that there was corruption with the relief money given to the city: "You have people who work for the city, you can see where city money is going, and money is going to private individuals. I see now how people can join the militia." While most reactions were not as strong as Dana's, many women felt that one's status did make a difference in how one fared in the crisis.[21]

Personal finances were important during the flood. Carrie explained, "My friend Sallie said if you have a car and credit cards, get out; it is only going to get worse." Because Carrie was middle class and had some money, she took her friend's advice. "I decided to ship my kids off to stay with my sister who lives in Atlanta. Flights were still going out." Carrie was able to avoid the stress and possible danger of having her children in Grand Forks when the flood waters were rising quickly. Clearly, without money she would not have been able to fly her children out.

Lisa's husband's employer paid for a work crew to come to her house to clean out the basement, and each member of the work crew earned $8 an hour. Interestingly, when the work crew was all male, the status and class differences did not really stand out to Lisa. But one day, there was a female member of the work crew, about the same age as Lisa, forcing Lisa to see the class differences between herself and the worker. She offered to let the worker use her bathroom, which she had not offered to the male members of the work crew, and the woman had replied that she would take her up on her offer because she only had one kidney. Lisa thought about this situation: "Here I am just sitting here. And this woman with only one kidney, for $8 an hour, is pulling out all of my belongings. It was very strange. It became very disconcerting to just sit there." Before the female crew member arrived, Lisa could justify the division of labor as gendered, ignoring the class divisions, and thus not question why she could just sit there while others worked.

Knowing that the situation was temporary lessened the anxiety for women in difficult housing situations. While it was still stressful to experience downward mobility for six months to a year, many families in trailers knew that they would eventually find a suitable middle-class suburban home and move in. For seven months, Roseanne and her husband lived in a small apartment, where she felt she had no privacy: "You could always hear somebody else's music. I always thought, 'Oh, I hope they can't hear us,' like a heated discussion or some of the things you say, and I hope nobody hears it." She found that she didn't care for apartment living and wanted to have a yard. However, she knew that they were financially stable and that the apartment was just a temporary situation. As a result, Roseanne saw life in the apartment as "a lark, an adventure" where students nearby would have "keg parties," they could walk to Burger King, and their back yard faced the back of a bar. After seven months they broke their lease and bought a ranch home on a quiet street where everybody owned their homes. While she could smell an unpleasant odor from the potato processing plant from their new home, Roseanne felt happy with her new life.

Others, however, with few or no resources, did not have the reassurance that their downward mobility was temporary. Liz, for example, was worried that she would lose her Section 8 housing when her destroyed apartment was rebuilt. She was already living in poverty and felt that this could force her to live in a shelter. Amy Sue, a thirty-nine-year-old unemployed teacher, did not realize that her economic situation would improve: "If someone came around now and said, 'I am with the Angel Fund; do you need $2,000?' I would say no. But before I didn't have a job, I didn't have a home, I had no way to make bills." When she realized that she was going to end up on her feet financially, she donated part of her Angel Fund to the family who had hosted her through evacuation. Often, having more resources helped in securing recovery financing. SBA loans, for example, were not granted to families with limited income. Both Julie, a social worker who was going back to school, and Joanne, a low-income secretary, were denied needed SBA loans because their total family incomes were too low.

In addition to personal finances, the resources of a social network, especially extended family members, were important to the women's experiences. Many women felt that they were fortunate to have family members who had large enough homes that they could take in an additional family for evacuation. Pat and her family evacuated to her sister-in-law's house: "We were lucky that our relatives had resources, and so it wasn't a huge imposition for the three of us to go there." Other women, such as Liz, were not so fortunate and had to fend for themselves during evacuation. In addition to the importance of personal and familial financial resources, the financial capabilities of the state and the country were also seen as instrumental in recovery. As Fran surmised, "I'm not sure we would have had the outpouring from across the nation or the governmental support that we have been able to get in a different country." The women were cognizant of the importance of wealth on every level.

Having more financial resources and a higher class standing also translated into being comfortable with the bureaucracy after the disaster and sometimes a feeling of entitlement for assistance in recovery.[22] Genie, who had only lived in Grand Forks for a few months when the flood hit, did everything she could to get the money on their destroyed house:

> To get our check I really worked on it. I made calls, I pounded the pavement, I did everything I knew to facilitate our getting our money. I was like the second person to get our voucher money.

> We were in the buyout, and we had purchased a [new] home.
> Then I went to HUD [Housing and Urban Development] to get
> money that is for relocating within Grand Forks.

Thus, middle-class status may have contributed to some of the
women's ease with bureaucracy, and lower-class flood victims may
have found it more difficult to "make the calls and pound the pavement," as Genie did, to get the money and grants and reimburse-
ment to which they were entitled. Fran, a middle-class school
teacher, described how she called FEMA before they even evacuated,
sensing that it would be good to sign up early and be first in line,
and drove down to Fargo shortly thereafter to meet with a FEMA
representative. Because of these actions, Fran received her first housing assistance check long before other residents did. In these situations, social class appeared to have been more important than gender
in how the women negotiated the disaster recovery bureaucracies.

     In sum, the women in the study experienced diverse economic
consequences during the crisis. As much research has found, resources matter a great deal in disasters. Among other things, higher
status and resources enable disaster survivors to feel comfortable
navigating the bureaucracies after the disaster, arm them with a
sense of entitlement, and assure them a near-total financial recovery.
The data showed that social and economic class were significant
factors—perhaps even more significant than gender—in the process
of receiving disaster assistance and resources. The women's experiences, however, were still gendered. For example, when a daycare
was destroyed it was the mother, not the father, who quit her job
and stayed home, but their social location as white, middle-class residents became more important to their ultimate economic recovery.

Chapter 5

The Stigma of Charity

Shame, embarrassment, and humiliation are associated with receiving public assistance, such as welfare. Much research specifically looks at women's experience with welfare, as many women are single parents and accept the assistance to provide for their children but still experience the stigma and demoralization. Indeed, the term "welfare recipient" often refers specifically to women who receive assistance from the Temporary Assistance to Needy Families program. Many politicians and social pundits maintain the achievement ideology by claiming that women on welfare are lazy and promiscuous, and refuse to work.[1]

The cultural stereotypes of people on welfare also have a racial overtone. In the United States, cultural images of black women are associated with welfare assistance. More recently, these images, which include Latinas as well, include the erroneous assumption that the black urban underclass is poor because of a value system characterized by low aspirations or the structure of the black family.[2] Social workers and social scientists believe the stigma prevents many individuals who need help the most from receiving it and ultimately serves to punish poor people for being poor.

The stigma of public dependency is so often attached to the notion that those who receive it are undeserving of the assistance because they are seen as lazy compared to other individuals in society who work hard for a living. Social scientists posit that the majority of individuals receiving some form of public assistance do so not because of a flaw in their character or behavior but due to the persistence of poverty in a capitalist system. The majority of welfare recipients accept benefits only temporarily, and it is often a crisis, such as the sudden loss of a job, a divorce, or a health emergency, that pushes them over the financial edge. For example, divorce often immediately places middle-class women below the poverty line, forcing them to abandon their middle-class lifestyle.[3] However, despite Americans' proximity to needing financial help themselves, the stigma of public assistance remains, and the stereotypes persist. Americans hold on to the achievement ideology that it is an individual's own fault if he or she cannot make it financially without assistance.

The women in Grand Forks felt stigmatized when they received assistance after the flood. The assistance they received included a wide range of public and private items and services, such as staying in shelters or in the homes of strangers, receiving free supplies and donated clothes, and eating food from the Salvation Army. The stigma of charity was a significant part of how the disaster affected them and their overall sense of themselves. The women found the experience of accepting charity to be humiliating and unsettling. According to Goffman (1963), when an individual possesses an attribute, or stigma, that makes him or her different or less desirable, the individual becomes seen as tainted, as less than a whole person, and as possessing a "failing, a shortcoming, a handicap" (pp. 2–3). Goffman (1963) suggests that there are three types of stigma: abominations of the body, blemishes of individual character, and tribal stigma of race, nation, or religion. The women of the Grand Forks flood experienced the second type of stigma, as they felt their personal character was marred by the experience, despite the fact that the blame for the disaster fell on outside forces and not on them individually. In this chapter, I examine the factors relevant to the women's experience with the stigma of charity: the North Dakota culture, the norms of caregiving roles, the loss of class status, the women's management of the stigma using impression management techniques, and the ways in which their perspectives or standpoints changed or shifted as a result of receiving charity in the disaster.

Self-Sufficient Culture

One of the factors that contributed to why and how women felt stigmatized was the self-sufficient culture of this region of North Dakota. In this somewhat remote and sparsely populated state, many residents are proud of their hardy characters and strong wills. They perceive themselves as independent people, able to withstand harsh weather conditions and the isolation of the prairie. Historians have found that North Dakotans have always valued independence. Agriculture has been, and continues to be, the main component of the economy, and with the difficult weather, a frontier ethos remains in the culture. A local radio station, in its video of the flood, described Grand Forks residents as "the hardy people of the North." Overall, the women explained, North Dakota culture produces individuals who are self-sufficient, stoic, hard working, private, self-reliant, and independent. This regional culture, however, reflects the values of individualism (and the achievement ideology) that are pervasive throughout the United States.

After the disaster, however, residents found themselves poor, dependent, and in need of assistance such as food, clothing, and shelter. Participants said that the North Dakota culture taught them how to give, but not how to receive. Many of the women used the expression "swallowed my pride" and the words "embarrassing" and "humbling" to explain how they felt about accepting charity from organizations such as the Salvation Army or the Red Cross. Carol, a forty-three-year-old homemaker articulated the problem:

> In this community, where we are very self-sufficient people, we're very proud, and we're very "I can do it myself." It's been very interesting to find out that we *can't* do it ourselves. Our nature is *not* to go to the Salvation Army and *not* to go to the church and ask for help.

The women felt that receiving assistance was a sign of weakness. Thus, if you were poor and needed help, that said something about you, not just about your situation. Tina, a nurse and mother of two small children, recalled the humiliation of fighting the crowds to receive free towels, which she needed for her family: "I am not going to *compete* for bath towels. You have to have some dignity."

Many explained that the North Dakota culture was based on a Swedish and Norwegian heritage that was especially proud and stoic. Jane, a fifty-four-year-old North Dakota native, explained how accepting charity felt:

> We learned how to do it. We ended up accepting things here and there. But it seemed very, very strange. And very, very hard. I think it was harder for me than for my husband, but then I'm Norwegian-Swedish, and he's not.

Several women explained that because of their Scandinavian up-bringing they could not accept help of any kind, especially not mental health assistance.

The Swedish-Norwegian culture is also private. North Dakotans are friendly and hospitable but private and reserved at the same time. Thus, receiving charity was difficult as there was public exposure at all stages—staying at a shelter or at someone's house and standing in line for food or other donations. Some women in the study explained that staying with family members was acceptable but staying with nonrelatives was more problematic, as it felt like more of an imposition and a greater degree of charity.

Within this culture, the women felt guilty about receiving help and expressed the feeling that an individual or family should accept help only if they deserved it. This issue surfaced acutely during the distribution of the Angel Fund money. Many in the community began to complain about people who did not need help but accepted this charity. Louise, a forty-two-year-old homemaker, explained that this situation prompted her and her husband, Rodney, to decide whether they were truly worthy of charity:

> We talked about that Angel Fund money, and we were like, "Well, we're more well off; we shouldn't get in line for that. But then after the insurance guy came, and he told us all the things that weren't gonna be covered: "Your refrigerator's not covered. None of your possessions are covered." And then Rodney was like, "Well, maybe you should go stand in line." So I stood in line for two and a half hours. We got $1,000.

Others felt they were deserving because of their age or their long-time contributions to taxes and "the system." Maria, a nurse with four small children who lost her home and belongings, discussed this perspective:

> Someone said to me, "You know what? You guys, you both work, you pay taxes, you're supporters of the system. Now it's your turn. Don't be afraid to ask for things. Take it. You need it now. Take it." And I thought, you're right, we do need it. So I thought, okay, all right, I can accept this. But every time I'd swallow my pride and go ask for something.

The women worried about how the flood and the newfound life of charity might change the self-sufficient North Dakota culture. For one, the women disliked being seen as victims, and they did not want sympathy from others. Diana, a forty-six-year-old teacher, explained this notion:

> And the last thing in the world that we wanted was sympathy, to be the object of sympathy. And I think as much as everybody has appreciated the truckloads of apples from Washington and the truckloads of orange juice from Florida, everybody I know at some level is so damn sick of being approached as if they were a victim. It becomes tiresome, tedious, and mawkish to have to deal with.

This sentiment highlights the similarities between the disaster victim role and Parsons's "sick role" (1951). There are certain social expectations regarding how society should view sick people and disaster victims and how they should behave. The duties of the sick role, for example, are to get well and to seek medical help, whereas the disaster victim feels obligated to accept donations, look needy, show gratitude, and become self-sufficient again.

Other women expressed fear that this disaster might change the culture—and themselves—so much that people would find it too easy to accept free things and not work hard for life's amenities. Jennifer, a twenty-six-year-old single professional, remarked:

> I was fortunate. I did get the Angel Fund, and I had insurance, and FEMA gave me money for being relocated. But my fear is that you start getting things for free, and then you don't want to buy them anymore. I can go to the Salvation Army right now, and I can pick up enough food for the next month. . . . Like, one time they were giving away Tupperware, and we were standing in line with these people and that is *all* they're doing. They aren't doing anything else with their time except going from place to place, just getting stuff. So I tell myself, like, I can't go to the Salvation Army anymore because I'm employed, and I have a job.

Others also worried that the culture would change children's attitudes about handouts. Rachel, a single parent of three teenagers commented, "We will have a whole generation that doesn't remember running for the ice cream truck but remembers running for the Salvation Army truck."

The experience of standing in line to accept charity was antithetical to their perception of their culture; one woman compared it to what life must be like in Russia, where she believed one must always stand in line for food and clothing. It is interesting that the first image this woman had of women standing in lines for food was of Russian women and not of the poor women, many of color, who stand in line for welfare checks and food stamps in the United States. North Dakota women may compare themselves with the Russian women, who are also white, with European features, and are seen as victims of a larger social problem (not individual shortcomings), because these women are closer to the Grand Forks women's self-identity.

Emotions were especially strong toward those who were seen as completely undeserving, those who had not been in the flood at all. Some of this sentiment was racially based and directed at migrant workers. Sandy, a fifty-two-year-old unemployed divorcee, found herself upset by this:

> I mean, I'm not prejudiced, because for one thing my daughter was on welfare, and she was a teen mom. But my sister is a farmer, or married to a farmer, and they hire migrants from Texas every fall when they need help with the wheat harvest. And she found people coming from Texas and moving in, more or less, and trying to sign up for, let's say, the Angel Funds or going to the Salvation Army and loading up on groceries. It was like another intrusion. I mean, we're too proud to ask for help. And they were just *loading up*.

Even a year later, in her follow-up interview, Sandy was still angry at the undeserving collecting charity:

> There were probably people who needed [the Angel Fund money] more than John Gonzales that came in from Texas and lived here six months or whatever. I'm not being prejudiced. Even college students that could go home and stay with their parents, they collected the money.

Not everyone was upset about the migrant workers, but many expressed a disappointment in general about people who came in and claimed to have been victims of the flood so that they could receive public assistance and town residents who were becoming just too greedy.

Most of the working-class and middle-class women in the study had very similar feelings about accepting charity and how it ran against their cultural values. By comparison, two of the poorest women in the study, both of whom had lived in chronic poverty most of their lives, did not express guilt or dismay at having to accept free items. Both women lost their homes and all their belongings in the flood, and both felt deserving and unashamed at accepting help from private and public sources. Joanne, a divorced mother in her fifties, described her experience with accepting free things:

> I was delighted with my finds. A used blow dryer, toothpaste, a razor, and some mouthwash. In the food bank I filled a plastic grocery sack with Cheerios, sauces, juice, crackers, plus laundry soap, a sponge, paper towels, a comb, Kleenex, deodorant. Then on to the clothing depot where I found a better everyday wardrobe than the one I left behind. I went to a lot of these clothing places, partly because it was fun. . . . I thought, this is great fun, and you get all this great stuff you like, and you don't have to pay! We didn't take that much, and there was millions of stuff more left. So, no, [accepting charity] was okay. I would be the first person to give somebody that, too. I feel like that is how the world should work. I didn't have like a pride thing there or anything like that.

Joanne's comments point to the enormous class differences in responses to the receipt of charity, as the middle-class women were humiliated when they received public assistance, but Joanne did not have "a pride thing" about getting the help she needed. Because the middle-class women's identities were formed in opposition to poor women, accepting help more closely affected their views of themselves. In addition, Lisa, an upper-middle class woman who did not have to rely heavily on assistance, did not understand why her domestic worker, Catherine, had a hard time with charity:

> In terms of getting charity, it doesn't matter that *I* haven't gotten a free blanket from Kmart, but *we* [the community] have. We all feel like the recipients of this charity, even if some of us need it more. I mean, Catherine, who helps me clean, she laughs

and is a little embarrassed, but she got the new purse and the
new clothes.

From her class position and access to resources, Lisa was not able to
understand the humiliation that others felt.

Caregiving Role

In addition to conflicting with their stoic and self-sufficient
culture, accepting charity clashed with the caregiving role that the
women had been taught. This role included giving of yourself,
helping others, and being self-sacrificial. Thus, not only did the culture teach both men and women to value self-reliance, but it also
taught women to be self-sacrificing and giving. Most of them described a life where they had done housework and childcare most of
their lives, volunteered in the community, such as at their children's
schools, and felt that they were, in their words, caregivers. Accepting help but not being able to help others threatened the caregiving
role that these women had identified with their entire lives.

The women spoke of trying to reconcile the incongruity of
being helpers all their lives and now needing help themselves.
Genie, a homemaker in her thirties, stated that after a lifetime of
helping, the flood forced you "to learn to let people help you." Pat,
a fifty-one-year-old nurse and mother of three, found the switch
from caregiver to care recipient unsettling. She shared this journal
entry with me:

> I have always been a "care giver"—the oldest daughter, a wife and
> mother, a nurse, an educator. Taking care of others—be it elderly
> parents, children and spouse, patients, and even nursing students
> I now teach—has been a significant role my entire adult life. But
> the flood turned me into a "care recipient" in ways I had never
> anticipated. It is one thing to accept a favor from a friend or rela-
> tive (a hot dish after a baby is born; a yard mowed when you are
> sick) but days, and then weeks, of being cared for by others—in
> ways that could never be reciprocal—was an overwhelming and
> humbling experience.

Many of the women shared similar stories with me about the
change. Carrie, a director of a nonprofit organization, explained
that she was a "crazed volunteer," helping numerous individuals

and groups in the community, and was shocked when she became a victim in need herself. Vicky, who had been unemployed and divorced just prior to the flood, needed to leave her children with her ex-husband so that she could take on an emergency job with the city. She had to concede that she could not be the sole caretaker as she always had been before. Many of the women were caregivers at home but also were caregivers in their professions as teachers, social workers, nurses, and counselors. Julie, a social worker, said that accepting charity "was really hard for me because that's what I do here is *give* people stuff like that. I don't *take* stuff like that. . . . I'm used to being the support person." The women felt guilty that they were not able to help others more. Pat, a nurse, had been sandbagging her house for days without sleep but still felt she should be doing more for other people, such as volunteering as a nurse and giving inoculations to residents. The women's sense of self was tied to the caregiving role. Thus, when the disaster made it difficult to fulfill this role in the manner they were used to, they felt that their identities—rooted in the white, middle-class ideal of women as caretakers—were threatened.

The values of the caregiving role had also been passed on to the women's daughters, and thus accepting help had to be explained to this younger generation. Lorna, a hospital manager, expressed this dilemma with her own daughter:

> With my daughter we have talked about [charity]. The church would have a drive for, like, kids in Africa for school supplies, and they were supposed to give a box of colors, and I've always tried to teach her that we have so much that we need to be thankful for. And that because we have so much, we should give to people that don't. . . . So since she was really young, I've been able to instill in her a sense of giving to others. So one day these people came by, and somebody in Texas had donated all these teddy bears. So, Payton said, "So now am I one of those kids that people are giving things to?"

By teaching their children that as middle-class, white females they are expected to give to those in need, the women are reinforcing both class and gender norms.

Many of the women explained that they accepted charity only so that they could pass it on to others. In this way, they could satisfy their need to give. Many accepted free food for their children or got free items for their hosts during evacuation. Julie accepted a $100 food voucher from the Salvation Army because she rationalized that it was for her sister, who was hosting them—and feeding them— during evacuation. Lisa, a teacher with three grown children, also went to the Salvation Army only so that her evacuation host could go, because the host "liked to shop."

Women felt extremely uncomfortable imposing in others' homes during evacuation. Being a guest for extended periods of time was especially damaging for the maintenance of the traditional giving role. Lisa described what an imposition they were on the family that hosted them:

> They don't have a dog, and I don't think they realized that we were bringing our dog. And our dog is a *big* dog. And the husband was allergic. And I'm in this woman's house, who's *sort* of a friend, and very, very nice, and they gave us a bedroom and a bathroom. And then the dog throws up. He drank from the toilet and it had 101 Flushes, so he throws up this blue stuff and ruins the rug. So I try to clean that up and I can't. She keeps saying, "It's okay."

As Goffman (1963) posited, stigmatized individuals do not know what others really think of them, and even when people are nice to them, they still feel that in their hearts others are still defining them in terms of their stigma (p. 4).

Sometimes the women tried hard to find ways that they had helped others even as they accepted help themselves. Tina took her family to her mother's unheated cabin at a lake for evacuation. While she was accepting the help from her mother, she spoke of how good it made her mother feel to help them out, which in turn made Tina feel as if she did something good for her mother. By constructing the situation in this light, she maintained her giving role. Other women also spoke of how they could tell that accepting help from others made the givers feel good. Roseanne, a fifty-year-old with two college-age children, recalled that her elderly mother-in-law felt good helping her children and their spouses by giving them a place to stay during the flood. Marilyn, a secretary and mother of one daughter, also maintained her female role by accepting the charity of others: "They had those free concerts. And there was a free barbecue. I feel like if people are nice enough to do these things for you, then you should show your appreciation and go." Some of the women also spoke of their plans to become Red Cross volunteers later in their life and travel to disaster sites to help victims.

Loss of Class Status

As discussed in the previous chapter, the flood caused many women to experience downward mobility and a loss of middle-class status. Hundreds of residents in Grand Forks lost their family homes, a clear signifier of middle-class status in the United States. In an instant, the women were stripped of a place of comfort, the fully furnished and decorated homes that they owned, a garage with cars, full wardrobes, and lawns and gardens that they cultivated. They quickly learned how fragile that existence was. In addition to the loss of their homes, one of the main indicators of their loss of status was receiving assistance. For many of the women, the act of accepting charity meant they were no longer members of the middle class. Thus, the flood threatened the women's female identity, but specifically, it threatened their middle-class female identity.

Becoming poor instantly, having no way to pay for anything, was a "sad, hopeless, helpless feeling," according to Genie, who had only recently moved to Grand Forks and lost her home and belongings. Losing one's home and accepting help was humiliating. Tina recalled:

> We had $125,000 in this small community. We had a very profitable business. I was an RN. Our children went to parochial school. We owned our home. We owned our cars. We paid no one. We had no credit card debt. We had no debt at all. And all of a sudden, you need to ask someone if they have a shirt you could have. Or you need to go to them for food. You have nothing. . . . My friend said, "What are you going to do?" And I said, "We're going to be a trailer park family." I don't mean anything bad for people that live in trailer homes, that's fine, that's what they choose to do. . . . It hurts really bad inside to have lost everything you own. All of a sudden you have nothing, and you think, maybe we should just move away so no one knows what we ever had.

For Tina and others, falling from the comfort and respect of middle class life to needing the help of others, such as a FEMA trailer, was unbearable.

Approximately 11,000 homes in Grand Forks were flooded, and all but 27 of the approximately 2,500 homes in East Grand Forks were flooded. Total estimates range from $1 to $2 billion in damage. Homes a mile or two from the river, considered a safe distance and untouchable, were also flooded. The river crested at 54.11, about 5 feet more than predicted by the National Weather Service. Dikes were built to protect both cities to 52 feet. *Photo courtesy of FEMA (website)*.

The public nature of the charity contributed greatly to the feelings of a loss of class status. Some of the women stated that their new lower status was easy to detect during the evacuation, as they looked poor and disheveled when they relocated to other towns. Diana, a non-North Dakota native and mother of two girls, explained how Grand Forks residents never needed to ask for help due to their appearance:

> You could instantly pick out the people from Grand Forks because we all looked like zombies, and we were all wearing crumpled clothes. We looked all unkempt and dazed. I went to Dayton's [a department store], and they instantly applied a 40 percent discount.

In other towns, and in Grand Forks, the women struggled with having everyone know that they no longer owned a home, lived in a trailer, and survived on food stamps. Peggy, a forty-five-year-old mother of two teenagers who lost her home in an old, tree-lined, working-class neighborhood, described her embarrassment at this publicity:

> There was an ad in the paper for disaster food stamps. I thought, I don't even want to do this; I'm just going to leave. But then I thought, well, I have been working since I was sixteen, and I do feel I'm entitled to this, but it was just nauseating to me. . . . They gave me food stamps, and I found myself looking around in the store, and when I saw people, I spent more time looking around so they didn't get in front or behind me. Thinking oh God, you know people are looking at people with food stamps. And then the times when I have used the stamps [the store clerk] has not had food stamp dollars to give back to me and she *hollers*, "I need food stamp dollars!" And, *oh my God*, I'm just about dying. Because this is a whole new experience, and I'm trying to get through this gracefully without feeling, like, you know, like I'm using the system or something.

Peggy hints here at her own middle-class bias toward people who use food stamps. While the store clerk may have been trying to publicly humiliate her, there is no indication that anyone in the store actually said or did anything that would confirm her suspicions. Thus, much of Peggy's discomfort came from how she perceived others judged her, based on her own feelings of the poor who use food stamps. Goffman (1963) stated that everyone takes on stigmatized and normal roles in some ways and in some phases in our lives, so that we can all play out either role in the "normal-deviant drama" (p.133). In other words, because individuals used to harshly judge others with their stigma, they develop a "disapproval of self" since they know how others are viewing them now (p. 34). Thus, Peggy and others felt particularly stigmatized and humiliated because when they had played the role of "normal" perhaps they had judged those who accepted assistance negatively.

After leaving their homes, many Grand Forks residents first evacuated to temporary shelters in the Grand Forks Air Force Base hangar or in public schools before they moved on to other evacuation sites, such as the homes of relatives. Staying at the large shelters was difficult for many of the women and their families. As Jane explained, the hangar was "dingy, dark, and it smelled." It was also a very public sign of loss of status to be crammed in a public shelter with hundreds of other people. Jane and her husband decided not to stay there at all and opted to drive hundreds of miles to their son's house. Jean Marie, a divorcee in her fifties about to embark on a second marriage, also found the air base hangar a drop in status and explained that it was difficult because "there were no cleaning facilities, there were potties and handiwipes. She continued, "There was no privacy, it was like living in a really crowded city. And then the people next to us stole our clothes."

Cecilia, who took her four children to a school shelter, commented that it was tough to share space with strangers, especially one woman who became hysterical and scared Cecilia's children. A social worker in her early forties, Rachel also stayed at the shelter and commented, "It was kind of strange for me because I used to work with the mentally ill in town, and a lot of my clients were sleeping around me. They were nice people, but I wouldn't want to sleep in the same room." Others also described their discomfort sleeping next to the mentally ill, some of whom talked to themselves all night in the shelters. Many of the women, by working in helping professions, knew some of the individuals from the Mission, the Grand Forks homeless shelter, and felt comfortable with them. However, having to sleep in a crowded shelter next to them meant that their middle-class status no longer provided a barrier between them and the former Mission residents.

Women who accepted shelter from friends, coworkers, and relatives also felt they were dropping in class status. Genie had trouble accepting temporary shelter conditions below her normal standard of living when she was forced to stay several nights with her husband's coworker:

> It is a huge house, and the man has six kids. Three of them are sick and throwing up. They have a house full of cats, and it smells like cat pee, and it was *so gross*. I was so grossed out. I have sleep fetishes. I have to stay in a nice place; it has to be clean. So this was a *nightmare*. I had died and gone to hell. I am in *hell*. This is *hell*: cats, pee, throwup, sheets with pills. I'm not in my home. This is the end. I am not going to make it through this. . . . Now please don't get me wrong; I'm grateful that someone extended their hospitality.

Genie, whose middle-class background had provided her with a certain standard of living, was unable to tolerate even a short-term decline in lifestyle. Genie found that her children quickly caught on to their new lower-class status. She remembered how her two boys came to expect things for less since they had no money:

> They are turning into moochers. "Can we get that for free?" We are at Sam's [a department store], and Zach says, "Ma'am, can you knock a few dollars off this TV 'cause my momma hasn't gotten her buyout letter yet?" I was so embarrassed. We are not totally destitute. We have food on the table. Their daddy is no longer eating off the Salvation Army truck.

As discussed in Chapter 4, others found that the sudden downward mobility reminded them of times in their lives before they had reached middle class status. For those who had been on welfare before, they had hoped they would never have to go through that experience again. Rachel, the single mother of three teens, was not happy to be accepting public assistance again:

> When the kids were little, and I first got separated from their dad, we lived on welfare. We did anything we could to survive. There wasn't enough of anything, and you just had to make do. That was real stigmatizing. . . . We had a lot of trouble [accepting assistance after the flood] because we had old baggage. We had been through that and didn't need help anymore.

Rachel elaborated on this issue in her follow-up interview one year later:

> [By accepting charity] I felt like I was going backwards. For other people it was a new experience, but for us it wasn't. I remember when I was raising the kids on my own, I used to do laundry in the bathtub. The kids thought that was cool, but I did it to save money. Then they saw Oprah Winfrey's life story, and her mom was doing laundry in the bathtub because they couldn't afford it, and then it wasn't funny anymore. So you go from there, and you work up, and I think we had gone a long way, and all of a sudden you're back accepting help, and it makes you feel like you not only lost the house and everything, but you moved all the way back there. And I had felt a lot of pride in coming so far.

For Rachel, accepting help again was the greatest signifier that they had gone backwards and could no longer feel proud of their rise out of poverty.

Impression Management Techniques

To deal with the difficult experience of accepting charity after the flood, many of the women used impression management techniques to cope with, and distance themselves from, the situation.[4] It was important to them to find ways to demonstrate to others—and themselves—that they were not the "real poor." One technique the women used was to minimize the damage they had, to declare how lucky they were, and to show that "others had it worse" and needed more help than they did. Like many others, Fran, an elementary school teacher, explained that their SBA loan was more than she and her husband needed. Lydia, a sixty-seven-year-old mental health counselor, noted that minimizing damage was common: "Right from the beginning people were saying, 'I didn't have first floor damage,' or 'I didn't have to leave my house for more than a few weeks,' or 'others had to live in a FEMA trailer.'" Jean Marie, the one about to remarry, felt fortunate because her house was filled with silt, but not sewage. Interestingly, older women felt a great deal of sympathy for the younger generations who were in the flood, and the younger people expressed the same sentiments about the older people. Martha Jo, a retiree who wintered in Arizona, was angry with the Red Cross because they did not have separate lines for the truly needy, such as the disabled or very elderly. Jean Marie noticed that the "real poor," the "Mission people," were being helped at the shelters. Cecilia, who lost her home, realized she was minimizing her family's damage and explained why:

> I still have this "Well, I didn't have water up to my rooftop, so I'm not really in need" mentality. It's hard to think that I've lost pretty much everything, you know. It's hard to think that maybe I'm just as bad off as those people who had it up to their roof.

Some women did not accept donated clothes because they believed others in Grand Forks were in greater need; others turned down donations because they felt that there were people in other places in the world who were less fortunate and that Grand Forks residents had received more than their share.

The women's second technique involved finding ways to show that their poverty and subsequent needs for assistance were temporary. Tina explained that their trailer was not really a home:

> The trailer never felt like home. We had somewhere to live. To the boys, they never said "home." Never "I am going home." It was, "I have to go to the FEMA trailer." The word "home" was never used. When I said "We are going home," they thought we were going to the flooded house. "No, we're going to the FEMA trailer." And they would say, "That is *not* home."

Because they framed it as a temporary situation and not a real home, Tina and her family never got to know their neighbors during the full year they lived in a FEMA trailer park: "You wave or say 'hello' but there is no camaraderie. There was only one trailer that put out lawn furniture." Thus, Tina created social boundaries to maintain her privilege, status, and sense of entitlement within the trailer park. Similarly, Roseanne was never really home at their temporary apartment, and, indeed, even after almost a year in the apartment, she never took a single photograph of it. It was so temporary that it did not even need to be recorded. In addition, she was able to see their neighbors, a bar on one side and partying college students on the other, as "entertaining," as it was just a temporary adventure. Lorna, who taught her daughter the traditional female role of giving, made sure her daughter saw their need for charity as transient:

> One day this lady dropped off teddy bears for our kids from the church. I said, "Honey, you can take this teddy bear, and you can love it a lot right now." And I said, "And maybe someday you'll want to give it back to another little kid who doesn't have anything." And so she has really gotten into realizing that now when things happen, now that we are back in our home, that we need to watch out for those other people again.

While the women tried to frame their predicament as temporary, it is important to consider that they did not know if it was a permanent situation, and even if they no longer received assistance, they did not know if their stigmatization would be permanent.

Writing thank-you notes to show that accepting charity was not a way of life for these women was the third impression management technique that they used. Writing thank-you notes has been found to be a distinctly female job in most households (di Leonardo 1987), and in almost every interview women mentioned performing that task. Julie explained:

> I've written thank-you cards to everybody who's done anything for us. You know, the people that hired my kids. The woman who highlighted my hair for half price. The store that gave my husband 25 percent off some boots.

Joanne, who felt fortunate despite her substantial losses, declared that after receiving assistance from friends, "My response now that I'm through this is to make sure that I am in turn very loyal and steadfast and sit down and write letters to all these people every Sunday." To accept charity without a thank-you note would have been to acknowledge the normality of needing assistance, which was how they perceived being on welfare.

A fourth technique was that the women tried to pay, or otherwise compensate, for things that were given to them so that the donated items or services could not be considered charity. Myrna attempted to pay for copies of photographs that family, friends, and neighbors gave her when she lost all of her family photos. Martha Jo wanted to pay the young men from the Salvation Army who helped her haul the destroyed contents out of her home. The women particularly wanted to do things for their evacuation host families to earn their keep. Many, like Lisa, also brought enormous amounts of food to their evacuation hosts:

> I cleaned out the fridge not because I thought that it would spoil, but because I felt I should take something to the family. I took toilet paper. I took the chicken and the vegetables out of the fridge. I took the meat in the freezer. Not thinking that the electricity would be off but just thinking it would be polite.

Leslie, pregnant and the mother of a two-year-old, also took food, because, as she said, she did not want to show up and say, "Here we are. Feed us." The women also cleaned and cooked at their evacuation homes, trying to earn their keep and be good guests.

The fifth impression management technique was educating others—including me—about their previous status, making sure it was understood that they had not always lived in a trailer or a small apartment and had not always received handouts. Sandy, a fifty-two-year-old unemployed woman was grateful for, but embarrassed by, my offer to pay for her lunch. She wanted me to know that she was "used to giving people money and taking them places and buying them lunch and dinner," not the other way around. Many of the women showed me photographs of their old homes and belongings and told me about their class standing. They seemed aware that the usual markers of one's status, such as home, car, and clothes, were not available for me to see. Julie felt the need to explain herself to the townspeople when she evacuated:

> Not that we are poor financially, because I would tell these people, like when I went to ask for grocery money, where I worked, and that I had a good job and where my husband worked in Grand Forks, and we both had good jobs. . . . When we went to the bank, they weren't even sure that they wanted to cash a two-party check. It was like, "We *have* money, but we don't *have* it."

This quote highlights what Levitin (1975) calls the process of "avowal revelations," which are used by people with temporary stigmas so that the people they interact with know that their condition is temporary. They do this, Levitin claims, because they know that a label of a permanent stigma is "far more serious than those of a temporary stigma" (p. 552). In addition, as Goffman (1963) pointed out, the move from "normal status" to "stigmatized status" (p. 132) is extremely painful psychologically, so the women desperately do not want others to see the new deviant part of the self as the entire self.

The sixth and final technique employed to deal with the stigma of charity and their newfound status was for the women, in the midst of accepting assistance, to do things for others. Amy Sue, a single, recently laid off woman in her forties, and her dogs stayed with strangers in their Air Force base apartment for over a month. In turn, she put some of the $2,000 Angel Fund money she received in a savings bond for the family's little girl. Addie, a homemaker who lost her house, stayed with her son and daughter-in-law for seven months; to help she did laundry every day. Carol insisted that her neighbor take a thirty-pack of beer and a quarter of beef from their basement in exchange for moving Carol's dryer to the first floor of their house, and she took ten boxes of cereal from her home to the evacuation shelters for the children staying there. After the flood, she and ten female friends volunteered to plant flowers at a nursing home. Right after the evacuation period, Fran, the elementary school teacher, sent five boxes of her non-flood-damaged clothes to a poor family in the coal mining area of Kentucky. These impression management techniques allowed the women to be spared the embarrassment of accepting charity. In many ways, these stories highlight how reciprocity is a normal feature in lives that depend on others. The women are re-creating the structures of exchange and support—and thus they are attempting to subvert charity with reciprocity.

Shifts in Standpoint

Through their experiences of poverty, loss, and the receipt of charity, the women in Grand Forks learned a great deal about how it felt to be poor and needy all the time, not just in a natural disaster. The women had an opportunity to develop a new sense of empathy for the poor, a new understanding of being on the receiving end of charity, and in some cases, a completely new view of women on welfare. In short, they now knew what it felt like to be needy, hungry, desperate, and stigmatized.

Many of the women, due to their flood experience, realized how difficult it was to depend on others, specifically government agencies or charity groups like the Salvation Army, for food, clothing, or shelter. They had to wait in lines for excessive amounts of time, fill out copious bureaucratic forms, wait weeks for checks, and endure the humiliation of being needy. The women described how much time it took to receive assistance: for example, four hours in line for paper towels, half a day to wait for food, five hours in line for gas vouchers. Carol explained:

> That's one thing we learned through all of this: a new appreciation for anybody who has to jump through all the hoops to get any help and to fight red tape. After a while, you just go, screw it, I don't need any help this bad that I'm going to jump through all these hoops. . . . I think all of us found out that, wait a minute, this is the way some people have to deal with this to get everything they need, everything they need, *all the time*. All of a sudden you realize, I was dealing from the outside; now I'm dealing from the inside. And we've only been dealing with this for a summer, and you think, no wonder people get fed up with the programs.

Cecilia was also surprised by how much work it took to receive assistance:

> Well, I learned that it's much easier to work than to be on welfare. I don't have the patience for standing in line, and filling out all this paperwork, and playing those silly games you have to play to meet government regulations. It's crazy. It's absolutely crazy.

Others also had the same sense that a paying job was actually easier—less work and less hassle—than receiving free assistance from public or private sources. The perception that poor people are lazy and accept free handouts to avoid work was challenged by their new knowledge.

Many of the women, forced to accept assistance, learned that some people donate or give to charity for the wrong reasons. For instance, they believed that wealthier people donated clothes to the poor because they wanted to clean out their closets and get rid of stuff. As a result, many donated items were old, outdated, and in poor condition. Receiving these castoffs made the women feel belittled. The women also objected to people giving just for the recognition. Tina commented:

> You should just give to give. You don't give to get the recognition. You can tell if somebody just gave because "everybody else is giving so I better give something," or if they gave because they wanted to get rid of something, or if they gave truly from their heart.

Many of the women, most of whom had donated to charity throughout their lives, began to realize the flaws in the notion that one person's trash is another person's treasure.

The women learned what it felt like to be poor and to have people look at them and make judgments about them. Genie recalled going shopping with her sons:

> So we went to Target [a department store], and they had on their mismatched shirts, shorts, Sorel boots, tromping through Target. They looked like poor white trash from the South. They had not had their hair cut in I don't know when. And I'm just, like, I know what welfare mothers, I think I know what a welfare mother must feel like when she goes in a store, and her children look less than the rest of the children. I mean, I may not know her total struggles, but what do these people feel when their children look like dirty little urchins and their clothes don't match, and there's nothing you can do. The futility of that situation.

Some of the women believed the flood was a lesson in empathy. They speculated that maybe the true purpose of the flood was that individuals like themselves would learn what it is like to accept assistance, especially federal assistance such as food stamps. Sandy, who lost her job due to the flood, began working temporarily at a job service office several months after the flood. She felt that she did a better job in this position because "people would come in looking for work and I would understand how they felt being unemployed." Genie felt that God made people go through certain experiences, such as the flood, to teach them compassion for others. She felt she needed to accept charity for that very reason: "It was very painful at first to need help. And then you had the realization that God allows people to need help in order to understand, to have compassion, for those that need it." Indeed, Genie, Tina, Sandy, and others came to the conclusion that the flood occurred so that people would develop more sympathy for the poor and needy in society.

Many of the women asserted that they knew beforehand that being on welfare was difficult, and that welfare recipients weren't lazy, but the flood gave them an even greater appreciation for their circumstances. Cindy, who lost her daycare business in the flood, remarked that she did not believe in the stereotypes of the poor but that she, too, had thought more about what handouts mean:

I've always been very liberal minded when it comes to assistance for people in need. I have never begrudged people that needed that. Always felt very blessed that I didn't. But I heard that conversation in lines many, many times. People would comment about how "this sure makes me look at welfare differently." I think things like [accepting charity in the flood], not that you want to wish that situation on anybody, but I think things like that are good teachers. You can make something positive out of it, if you let it teach you.

Pat, a nurse and mother of three children, also felt that while she was sympathetic to welfare recipients prior to the flood, she developed a new understanding of what daily life on welfare was like:

I learned what it's like to be on the recipient end of [charity]. It feels strange. I've worked a lot with people on welfare and all, so I've heard from other people that it is not a fun experience. So I didn't think I came with a lot of biases about welfare, that those are just lazy people. But to realize how time consuming it is to have to wait for that kind of help. You can spend a whole day to get one shopping cart full of cleaning supplies. Whereas, when you have money, you say, "I'll just run to the grocery store and buy it."

Others admitted that they had not been as tolerant of those on welfare before the flood. Cecilia learned during the flood how women on welfare are often treated and what it feels like to endure the stigma of welfare:

Those of us who are taxpayers and see the abuses of the welfare system get frustrated by that and maybe have a prejudice against the recipients of welfare. And I think I experienced that with an SBA lady that I was talking to. She was talking to me, and I was explaining to her how I didn't think this was fair. And she got really snotty to me and said, "Well, I would like to be able to trade in my mortgage for a four percent mortgage!" I said, "I am not a person that is trying to take advantage of a system; I am trying to put my life back together." She was just really not very nice to me. I think she had that perception—and it hit me—that this is how a lot of welfare recipients must feel.

However, despite Cecilia's experience with the SBA official and her belief that she had greater sympathy for and understanding of those on welfare, she described her views this way in her follow-up interview a year later:

> The flood experience said to me, "Why would anyone *want* to be on welfare?" It has made me see that there is a lot of inefficiency in our government and a lot of coldness in our government, and there shouldn't be. I seriously don't know why anyone wants to be on welfare.

Even six years later, when thinking back on what she learned from the flood, Cecilia commented that "I am more understanding of people accepting assistance in times of need. However, I still believe people need to make efforts to get on their feet, and not rely on handouts forever."

The disaster made the women feel their vulnerability. They discovered they were only one crisis away from needing public and private assistance to survive. Prior to the flood they had felt much more secure, stable, and far from poverty, homelessness, and the acceptance of charity. Marilyn, the secretary who, to be polite, attended the free concerts for flood victims, articulated this emotion:

> For the first time in my life I realized this could happen to anybody. You could suddenly find yourself homeless, through no fault of your own, there is nothing you could do, and be totally dependent on the kindness of strangers. I was in the house working, it was cold, there was no way to heat food, there was no water. I thought a hot meal would be really good, and I saw the Red Cross truck, but it was too fast, and I couldn't catch it. I thought, I really want a hot meal, and I can't have it. I thought, this is what it feels like to be needy, to be hungry. I'll always remember that.

Due to her experience losing everything and depending on others for her survival, Tina came to the conclusion that it could happen to anyone. She felt her standpoint shift was so large that she now speaks out in defense of the poor who must accept assistance, such as food stamps:

> And everybody has made comments like "Oh, they're using food stamps," and it's like, for goodness sakes, have you ever had to go somewhere for your food? It's not easy to do that and main-

tain your self esteem. So I think I've become more verbal when I hear those kinds of comments. Now I have less of a tolerance for it. [I correct them] in a respectful way because perhaps they've never had the opportunity to learn. I try to help them advance a little on that.

Not all perspectives or standpoints changed with the flood. Most of the women in the study, however, did speak of a greater sympathy. The poorest women in the study had less of a shift in standpoint, as they had already endured the stigma of poverty and charity prior to the flood.

Because disasters are often perceived to be acts of God and not due to individual incompetence, it is surprising the degree to which women experienced charity as stigmatized. As Goffman (1963) suggested, when individuals are stigmatized, they feel as if their character is tainted. The disaster survivors felt tainted because the stigma of charity was experienced in a larger culture that constructs race and class as connected to charity and welfare. The majority of Grand Forks women, both in the study and in the total population of Grand Forks, were white, and whites are raced, just as men are gendered. According to Frankenberg whiteness is a location of structural advantage, a "standpoint," and a set of cultural practices; therefore, a white, middle-class consciousness is socially constructed. Frankenberg (1993) posits that the construction of masculinity and femininity are racialized; women's lives, therefore, are shaped by race, class, and gender. The Grand Forks women's problematic relationship with needing and receiving assistance illustrates how such experiences only have meaning in a larger framework.

In the United States, most citizens have very negative images of the poor, and of poor people of color in particular. In Bullock's (1995) work on classism, she found that classist attitudes, beliefs, and behaviors are commonplace in the United States, despite an ideology of classlessness. She reported that in studies on class, even young children believed that the poor do not work hard enough and that the rich and poor are actually different kinds of people (1995, p. 123). Classism makes the middle class distance themselves from the poor and see the poor, working poor, and welfare recipients as "other." People on welfare are seen in the most negative light. They are seen as dishonest, uninterested in education, and dependent, while the welfare system overall is seen as wasteful and unproductive (Bullock 1995). Those persons who are most demonized are women on welfare (Bullock 1995), particularly women of color (Collins 1990). In addition to the other stereotypes, women on welfare are seen as promiscuous and as having more children in order to receive more benefits.

The women in Grand Forks were not only classified as poor, which was in and of itself problematic, but they believed they were now seen to have the same status, behavior, and character flaws as the poorest of the poor—welfare recipients, who are often perceived to be women of color. Thus, the Grand Forks women saw themselves in relation to two other groups, the lower class and a racialized group, prompting some of them to resist the role of the other, and other women to take the role of the other (Mead 1934). They wanted to avoid the stigma of the lower class, and the stigma of the racialized other, so it had been important for them to define themselves in opposition to the other. For example, they were more likely to identify with women in Russia than poor women in America, and they were more likely to want to volunteer for the Red Cross in a disaster than want to volunteer in an inner city neighborhood. Yet, some of the women truly took the role of the other and became more sympathetic to the poor and people receiving welfare assistance.

Chapter 6

Threats to Mind and Body

The disaster affected the women of Grand Forks on a personal and intimate level. The flood affected their physical, emotional, and psychological health and well-being. Research has shown that physical and mental health are connected. Good physical health makes people feel good about themselves and have a positive outlook on the world; conversely, a positive outlook, emotional strength, and happiness affect their physical being. Speaking about the women's "well-being" is referring to their feeling good, strong, resilient, and in control over their physical bodies, as well as feeling happy, positive about the future, and capable of using coping strategies to combat any threats to their well-being and health. This chapter explores the ways in which the flood affected the health and well-being of the women, what these issues meant to them, and how they negotiated the challenges to their emotional and physical health in their everyday lives. In the following sections I examine the physical and emotional issues that the women faced in their daily lives during and after the flood.[1]

Physical Issues

In many ways, the women felt that they had little or no control over their physical bodies throughout the crisis. During the days of preparation, sandbagging, and evacuation, women wore themselves out physically by lifting sandbags, moving furniture, and loading trucks. They complained of sore muscles, aching limbs, and in several cases, injuries to their backs. Women spoke of nights during sandbagging as "four-Advil nights" because they could not sleep without pain medication for their bodies. In addition, the women spoke of how they lost all of their daily health regimens: they did not eat well; they did not get regular exercise; they were sleep deprived; and they were unable to maintain daily hygiene (bathing, grooming, haircuts) to the level they were used to or felt was necessary. This is similar to what has been found in other traumatic life events, such as in times of war.[2] For many of the Grand Forks women, the threats to their physical well-being were due to the disruption in their health routines, such as diet, exercise, sleep, and hygiene. In all manners, the women experienced the flood in very physical ways; indeed, one pregnant woman referred to her unborn child as a "flood baby."

Food, weight, and body image were important issues for women in the flood, just as they are in nondisaster times. Many women spoke to me about how they were not able to eat healthy foods or maintain their previous eating habits, and as a result did not feel well and, in many cases, gained weight. Much of the food served during sandbagging and evacuation was high fat and low nutrition. Carrie recalled the food she prepared for sandbaggers, and ate herself, during the crisis:

> I became the specialist of bad sandwiches, ham on white bread with big blobs of butter. Every bag had twenty-four sandwiches. Then, I thought, this is really cheap, you know you're out there working your butt off on the sandbags, so I'm going to give them extra meat and butter. But they were really disgusting, and I can't look at a crock of butter in the face again.

Rachel found it impossible to keep up with her healthy vegetarian diet, because the Red Cross food wagons that distributed food to residents did not have vegetarian options. As a result, Rachel and her daughters fell out of their healthy food routine, and all, to their dismay, put on an "incredible amount" of weight. Rachel said that self-image issues had become a problem in her family. Jean Marie also ate all her meals from the Red Cross trucks for over two months. Although she did not find the food nutritionally adequate, she was grateful for the food and would run to get some when she heard the little Red Cross bell: "We were good Pavlov dogs!"

Genie, in her first interview four months after the flood, reported that she gained a lot of weight during the flood crisis, mainly due to time pressures:

> I gained a lot of weight probably because I've had so many details to take care of, so much correspondence, so many telephone calls to make, and it was just easier to grab something on the run. And food makes you feel good and that helps you with your recovery, and it helps you while you're going down the tubes. I was thinking today, I don't look good. I look really frumpy. We went to Walmart last night, and I saw myself in one of those video cameras, and I'm like, "Ewww." I just looked so bad.

Genie, who had just joined a health club, was optimistic that she would begin working out when her children went back to school after a few weeks. Dana was concerned about her own and her daughter's weight gain:

> Jenna has gotten quite big since the flood. She has gained a lot of weight. Big, but not in a good way; she's gotten really chunky. The doctor did say to try and watch her. I was a heavy kid. I don't want her to be fat. After evacuation, we didn't cook a lot. It was convenience stuff, and it wasn't good food. It was junk. So I'm trying to change our eating habits, more fruits and vegetables. During the flood, chips and stuff were just too handy. [During the flood] I wasn't that hungry, but now I'm hungry all the time. Now my pants are too tight.

Louise was also concerned about her daughter's diet and well-being. During her family's stay at the university's dorm, her daughter would "load up on pop and cookies" at the cafeteria and happily tell her mother, "This is the food that I love!" After they left the dorms, Louise fought with her daughter, who wanted pop and cookies at every meal. Louise was worried, too, about her own eating habits during the crisis:

> I was just eating and eating and eating. I don't know if I was trying to find some comfort or something. I don't know exactly how many pounds I gained, but it was something like five or ten pounds. In the dorms, it was eat, eat, eat, like I had never seen food before. So I just loaded up, and I just ate this amazing amount, and I was gaining weight.

Lisa remarked that she had limited food options and would get fried chicken, potatoes, and bread at the one store open for business, but she felt that "you can only eat that stuff so much." She said that every woman she knew in Grand Forks gained weight, and all of their husbands lost weight. Even the mayor of Grand Forks commented publicly that she gained twenty pounds during the flood.[3]

A few women found that they lost weight with their new diets of Red Cross meals, possibly due to the stress and anxiety of the flood, and they also felt unhealthy. Lydia found that she did not eat much during the flood crisis:

> It was difficult to eat anything because we couldn't use the refrigerator, because we had no power. I found that I pretty much lost my appetite because I got tired of eating cold food, and the only place open in town was the Village Inn. So there was a while there where we didn't eat.

However, overall, weight gain was much more common than weight loss. Body weight and body image are a profound problem for most women in the United States, because the culture equates women's slimness not only with their beauty but with their overall value in society.[4] This ideology—that women's thinness is equated with their worth and value—is so widespread and pervasive that gaining weight affects women's self-worth and self-esteem, even in the midst of a natural disaster.

Directly related to the issue of food and body weight was the women's relative lack of exercise during the disaster. Although many of them engaged in strenuous physical labor sandbagging and gutting their homes, their loss of regular daily exercise compromised their overall well-being. The strenuous sandbagging work was extreme and episodic, whereas their regular exercise routines were low level and regular. The extreme exercise taxed and sometimes injured their bodies. Their regular exercise, in contrast, was gentler and healthier and often rejuvenated their bodies. Lisa spoke of the difference between these two forms of exercise:

> You'd think we would lose weight because we're all doing all this exercise. But it does go to show you that this is the problem in rural areas, the notion of planned exercise that is healthy for you, walking, Stairmaster, aerobics, all of that is laughed at by the rural woman who lives a rural lifestyle and does all sorts of exercise. They're outside a lot, but you don't burn a lot of calories because

it is not good exercise. It's exercise that makes you hurt. Not like walking or swimming or stretching.

Lisa, for example, worked hard on her house, pulling out nails for days, and all she got was "crowbar elbow." In addition, much of the strenuous physical labor was just before the flood, and for some people, it continued for only a few months as they gutted their homes, whereas the low level types of exercise continued throughout the year.

Many women spoke of both the physical and emotional benefits of exercise, the most common form of which was walking. Peggy articulated her concerns about this lack of exercise:

> We can't even get out and take a walk. I'd go in the evening. We used to have a dog, and he used to pull me and he'd keep me at a pace, and that was great for me. Since the flood, it's my own fault, I haven't walked. I haven't done anything. It is something I should be doing. I always feel better. I always did it. Now I feel more flabby. It is easy to find excuses not to do it.

Peggy blamed herself for not exercising, but it was clear that many factors worked against her. Her daily routine had been disrupted, and her new landlord would not let her keep the family dog, her walking companion, at the new apartment. Rachel, who hurt her back sandbagging, also felt that the lack of exercise was difficult for her well-being and outlook. She and her children joined a health club and started to exercise again, and she felt that was "really good for all of us." Genie, a homemaker in her thirties, found that her lack of exercise contributed to her weight gain during the disaster and its aftermath:

> I am still struggling with that. I need to lose weight. For some reason there is so much going on, and I have tried to walk the dogs in the evening, but there have been too many mosquitoes. I guess you can find a million excuses. I have tried to cook healthier. [My weight] is on my mind.

Dana, a working-class mother who moved from an urban neighborhood to a suburban neighborhood, also found that she did not take her daily walk: "You know that's one thing I did every night after supper. Now I have to drive all the way to town to do it.

There are no sidewalks out here." Joanne, like many others, was determined to get back to her exercise routine, and ten months after the flood she started riding her exercise bike again. Lydia started her daily routine of walking three miles a day two and a half months after the flood. Louise evacuated for several nights to a motel that had a pool. She decided to swim laps because she was "so stressed out." One night she swam for two hours, the other nights one hour, an indication that exercise was a necessity for her stress reduction and overall well-being.

Sound, restful, and plentiful sleep was another area of physical health that women could not achieve during the crisis. Many women got no rest during the acute period of the flood and suffered from exhaustion and sleep deprivation. Carrie, the mother of two children, was exhausted when she was working at the armory, and she remembered just lying down in the middle of everything: "I was working at the armory and there were these long lines of people, and I remember getting some z's lying on the floor, on the industrial carpeting." Eventually, this exhaustion took its toll on Carrie, as she described ten months after the flood: "I was really exhausted. It is kind of amazing. We've been sick all winter, and I am usually really peppy and healthy. I was wondering if it was depression. I was so tired I even got checked for mono." Some women, like Cecilia, felt that they were so exhausted that they could not stop, because then they "couldn't get going again."

Dana, who lost her home and belongings, but saved her bed, felt that sleep was very important and could not wait to be back in her own bed: "The biggest thing we couldn't wait for was to sleep in our own bed. We slept on a hard bed in the trailer. I sleep on my side, and it felt like my shoulders were touching. That was something we were so looking forward to, sleeping in our own bed." Dana also felt that sleep was tied to other issues, in her case exercise, stress, depression, and a family routine:

> I am grumpier, I am a grumpier person, I really am. I know a lot of it is exercise, I'm sure. For me, it relieves a lot of stress. It is a good stress reliever. Before we had a ritual at night; we'd bathe, then we'd go downstairs and watch TV for awhile, then go upstairs and read books. We don't do that anymore. Just haven't gotten into a routine schedule. So I really don't see myself as the

same. I am more tired. I am tired all the time. I would sleep
twenty-four hours a day if everyone would let me. Before I used
to like to get up and go. The sun would get up and I would be
out walking. Get up and go for a walk before anyone else was up.
I liked that feeling. Whereas now, I just don't have that feeling.

Lydia felt that she was totally exhausted for a very long time and was
just starting to catch up on her sleep four months after the flood.
She blamed this total exhaustion for some of her marital conflicts.

Some women commented that sleeping in large evacuation
centers was difficult. Jean Marie and her fiancé slept on the cots at
the Air Force base hangar: "We were on the cots out there, with a
hundred people in the room, and every time you rolled over the
cots burped. It sounded like you farted!" Piper, an eighteen-year-
old high school senior who evacuated to the Air base hangar with
her family, found that the cots were uncomfortable, people were up
all night walking around, and no one got any sleep.

On a cold night in April, a few days before the city flooded,
the residents were out in force sandbagging. It was hard work, and
the air was numbingly cold. There, among the sandbaggers was a
woman named Jean Marie, a secretary in her fifties who suffered
from severe, painful arthritis. In between sandbags she would rub
her joints to ease the pain. "I was determined to help," she explained proudly. After the flood, when her home was damaged, she
took part in the gutting and rebuilding of her home. The arthritis
did not stop her, although she admitted that her body was screaming with pain at times, and she needed massages for her recovery.

For those women with physical and mental disabilities, like
Jean Marie, the flood was particularly challenging. Liz, who suffered from a chronic and debilitating nervous system disease that
made it difficult for her to walk or get up from a chair, was turned
away from several evacuation centers because they did not have or
want to create the accommodations for people with physical disabilities. The evacuation centers suggested that Liz's daughter and
her family stay but that Liz drive on to another center that could
accommodate her. Her daughter was livid and told the evacuation
center officials: "My mother is 100 percent disabled, and I know
how to take care of her! You are not splitting us up!" The evacuation center's suggestion was seen as either insensitivity to or ignorance of the realities of living with physical disabilities, including

how the disabled need family members to help them and give
them support.

During the recovery period, there were long lines all around
town, as people waited to receive items that were being given away
or to register with an agency such as FEMA. Billie, a social worker
at the Community Violence Intervention Center, was sorry to see
that there were no separate lines for the elderly or the disabled, even
though these women had to stay in line for hours. As Billie put it,
"It was ridiculous." Other women spoke of how they witnessed
women with mental disabilities in the flood. Jean Marie was distraught over what happened to one mentally disabled woman at the
Air Force base hangar:

> A little elderly mentally challenged gal had a bird cage in her car,
> and she had it all draped to keep the bird warm, she said. Ike and
> I had just said, "Oh, it's a hot day, and she doesn't have a window
> rolled down, and she's got everything covering it." We came back
> and she's crying and sobbing and sobbing, and she had killed her
> bird. She had suffocated it. She cried all day. That was all she had.
> And they didn't allow animals inside.

Jean Marie did not explain why she and her fiancé, who had noticed the potential danger of the heat, had not done anything or
said anything to help her, yet they were clearly upset by what they
had witnessed.

A few women remarked that living conditions improved after
the flood for people living with physical disabilities. Roseanne explained, "One of my sister-in-laws has arthritis, and she put in special railings and rearranged the closet, and they did the same thing
for their sister who has had a stroke. There have been some improvements for them out of this." Liz, who was turned away at the
evacuation center, ended up in a hotel room that was designed for
people with physical disabilities, with a special recliner and a special
whirlpool tub. These amenities were a welcome sight for Liz, who
found that she could barely walk by the time she got to the hotel.

Another health risk reported by women was a lack of personal
safety during and after the flood.[5] Even before the flood, safety was
a major concern to the women of Grand Forks. Many of the women
spoke of the safety of Grand Forks as one of the main reasons they
liked the city. As Dana described Grand Forks, "The air is clean, the

streets are safe."[6] Genie, who moved to Grand Forks from the South six months before the flood, felt that Grand Forks was different from most of the country:

> What people dream about now, but used to experience in the '50s and early '60s, where your children could ride their bikes and go to the ice cream trucks and have a good time, and you didn't have to worry about them, and they didn't know all that much about drugs. The concern and the fear is not here like it is other places. Before [when they lived in another city], I wouldn't even let them go outside unless I was around. Now they can be gone for hours, going to this little kid's house, and down the alley, and it is so nice, it is so refreshing, to let them have a real childhood.

Unfortunately, for some women, the evacuation centers, the streets, and their own homes, did not feel safe during and after the flood. The flood turned the women's safe haven into what many of them referred to as a "war zone." Tanks moved through the streets, helicopters flew overhead, and sirens penetrated the city throughout the day and night. Cindy and her husband came back into town before most people and found a ghost town that was completely dark. She described the scene:

> It was very much like you picture a war zone. Nobody in town, the place was completely deserted, helicopters were flying overhead, airplanes were flying very low, buildings downtown were burning and chunks of ash were floating into our yard. The air was full. It was like a really eerie snowstorm. Very surreal. Made me think of Beirut.

Rachel, like all other residents, had to drive through National Guard checkpoints to get to her destroyed home. "It was an eerie feeling with the military trucks. It was odd because you think the military is to keep you safe, but it didn't feel like safety." Jean Marie did not feel particularly safe at the Air Force base hangar during evacuation. There were many individuals from the Mission, Grand Forks's homeless shelter, who, Jean Marie felt, "weren't very trustworthy." Indeed, Jean Marie's sleeping bag cover and a bag of her clothes were stolen while she stayed there, although they do not know if one of the Mission residents was the culprit.

When the crisis period was over, and the sirens ceased, and the helicopters and tanks had left, a new kind of unsafe feeling emerged: a fear of break-ins, squatters, and assaults. Karen, ten months after the flood, felt the city was unsafe: "Now there have been these child molestations; someone breaking into trailers and popping in windows." Lydia, who had to live alone in her house during the recovery period, felt spooked in her empty and dark neighborhood:

> I had no heat here, and it was thirty degrees, with a window in the basement wide open. I was worried about mice and rats or vandalism. You felt pretty insecure even though Grand Forks is a pretty safe town. You [usually] feel safe around here, always have. It was eerie to have things so cold and everything wide open in the basement where anybody could come in.

Rachel, a lesbian, felt that she and her partner were safer in their home prior to the flood. The safety issues for Rachel were more complex, as the threats to her well-being were on several levels simultaneously, including the fear for her physical safety if she were "outed" in her new housing:

> Before we had some control over our lives. As far as Alana and I, I think a house provides a little bit more safety. When we moved into family housing, they only defined family, even though the university has a policy not to discriminate because of marital status or sexual preference or whatever. So we get in to the housing department, and they go by North Dakota state law, and you have to have a marriage license to live together. So there is this secrecy about our lives now. That is really hard. It feels kind of sneaky and underhanded and that's a horrible way to live. We have built a life here, and now this. If anyone wanted to, we could lose housing just like that.
>
> [AF: Do you think that could happen?]
>
> It has happened before to people I know. It makes you edgy. It's a lot of stress. And I think that is one of the biggest things we've lost is just that ability to have a bit more control.

Thus, not only did Rachel not feel as safe at her new housing, but she was also the victim of discrimination and had to live in fear that she and her partner would be exposed and be forced to leave their housing.

Roseanne felt that her physical safety was compromised when she visited her destroyed home: "It was always creepy that someone was going to be there when you came over. There was one guy sleeping in our yard. I came around the corner, and there he was! It was creepy." Louise felt that the streets of Grand Forks were unsafe for children, especially young girls, with all the construction workers in town. Because Louise had been sexually abused as a child, she felt especially worried about her daughter's safety.

> [I worried that] there is a real person out there who is going to try to abuse her. And it was a real worry for me, since she would just take off and run around with other kids in the neighborhood. There were a lot of people who came in from out of town, it's just all construction all around, strange people everywhere. It's mainly men around, and not many women. There are probably all these strange little cubby areas in all these houses being built. So it's just not a good situation.

For Cindy, who ran a daycare in her home for seventeen years, the flood reaffirmed how important the safety of Grand Forks was for her:

> [The flood] made you evaluate things you thought were important to you. A way of life, very comfortable, very unthreatened. I think overall it made me grateful for a way of life which is normally pretty peaceful and uneventful and secure. Grand Forks has a low crime rate, and we just don't have the same amount of stress.

A few women did say that they never felt unsafe in Grand Forks during or after the flood. Cindy proclaimed that she "never felt fearful." Lorna also did not feel unsafe: "There were windows broken, and you didn't worry about people going in. We still had thousands and thousands of dollars worth of stuff on our main floor, china and crystal, but if you had windows open, you didn't have to worry." The reasons women felt unsafe did not seem to depend on whether the women were low income or high income, old or young, married or not. However, there seemed to be some connection between closeness to neighbors, whether those neighbors were also home, and a feeling of community and safety. There was also a connection between prior victimization and feeling unsafe.

The women experienced a lack of control over the hygiene and daily maintenance of their physical bodies. They were unable to shower, brush their teeth, put on make-up, get their hair trimmed, and use regular toilets. Before evacuation, they could not flush toilets in their homes, so, as Lisa remembered, they were "peeing in buckets." Later, during evacuation, Lisa stayed at a motel that had a big sign on the toilet: "If you use this toilet, you're out of here," so they had to use the portable toilets outside. Roseanne also remembered the hardships of not having running water or working toilets, and Vicky recalled going over five days without a shower when she had to stay in a hotel with no services. Lydia also went without a shower for many days, even though her friends who had running water offered her the use of their showers. She found that she was just too tired at the end of a long day of working at her job and then working all evening on her home to head out to her friends' homes. Genie was dismayed by having to share one bathroom with all her family members:

> We will soon have our own bathroom that is not out in the hall. Excuse my French, I love my husband, and we still do have sex, and I don't like going out in the hall to the bathroom afterwards. I'm sorry, I don't care what time it is. I'm spoiled, I'm Southern, and I want a bathroom in my room.

Joanne was grateful to have been given toiletries when she evacuated so that she could have some control over her hygiene:

> The church had cots, towels, and toothbrushes and soap, and that was so wonderful. And the towels were completely old and faded, but they looked like the best towels and better than the most expensive towels you'd ever seen in the world, because it was just what you needed right then.

Jean Marie was concerned about hygiene at the Air Force base hangar because there were no cleaning facilities at all, only bathrooms and handiwipes. There was also no privacy to perform any hygiene or personal grooming rituals.

Only a few women spoke of using substances such as alcohol, cigarettes, or drugs during the disaster.[7] The women who smoked cigarettes before the flood continued to do so during and after the flood. Liz was unable to stop smoking cigarettes, even though her mother would not let her evacuate to her house because of her "filthy cigarettes." Dana, who lost her home in Lincoln Park, admitted that she started smoking cigarettes again during the flood, after having quit the habit approximately five years earlier. Vicky, a single mother of two, spoke of consuming massive amounts of alcohol after long days doing emergency work in the city because it was a stress release, and "What else could we do?" She admitted that she understood how someone could become an alcoholic after enduring stressful events. Recalling the evening after a particularly stressful day, Vicky remarked.

> That night I went back to my hotel, and I sat there and said, you know what, I never thought I'd say I could be an alcoholic, but I can see where people become that. And I called up a friend and said, "We have got to do something, we got to do something now." At least I learned how to unload, how to let those emotions out to a certain extent.

Jean Marie felt that the bars were doing so well during the crisis because people had given up hope. She reported that in North Dakota the biggest illness was manic depression, the major crime was domestic violence, and without a doubt "drinking is heavy," although she implied that it was men, and not women, who were engaging in heavy drinking.[8]

Several women spoke of becoming ill during the flood due to flood-related contaminants or hygiene-related issues. There were reports, for example, of a "sick house syndrome" and buildings infected with black mold. Liz, whose central nervous system disease compromised her immune system, had a severe reaction to the contamination and mold in her destroyed apartment: "After I went in there, my body was covered with little blisters, and the next day they were popping and bleeding. It was just ugly." Jean Marie, who suffered from debilitating arthritis, got an inner ear infection from working on her flooded house. Amy Sue, a thirty-nine-year-old unemployed teacher, commented on how the flood affected her health and that of her ex-husband:

> We were getting sick on and off, all the port-o-potties, and not washing hands. Bruce got dysentery so bad. We had just water in our system. We'd go to defecate, and it was only water coming out.

Julie, a social worker with two teenagers, believed that she and her children all suffered from bronchitis during the flood because their home had lost power just prior to the flood in the blizzard, and they had to live in forty-one-degree temperatures for fourteen hours.

Older residents had to be particularly careful of illness during the flood. Martha Jo, a seventy-year-old mother of six, said her children were worried about her because her health wasn't "top-notch" and the "air and water were not clean" in Grand Forks after the flood. Myrna's eighty-year-old husband nearly died due to the flood: "He had been dragging stuff out of that flood and not keeping his mask on, and we'd been trying to get him to stop." Their doctor told them her husband's illness started with pneumonia, which was typical in damp, flooded places. Myrna felt especially bad about her husband's illness because it was her clothes and belongings that he was so determined to drag out and salvage. Surprisingly, Myrna's health was excellent throughout the flood and her husband's life-threatening illness. She described her delight, and her doctor's surprise, at a medical checkup: "My blood pressure was normal!"

Health officials recommended that everyone wear rubber boots, rubber gloves, and masks; throw away contact lenses that may have had water splashed on them; and get tetanus shots. Many women spoke of receiving tetanus shots. Louise could not receive a tetanus shot because there was a slight chance she was pregnant, and she was instructed to go right to the emergency room if she received any deep wound. Women with small children were especially concerned about illnesses from the flood water. Cecilia felt that it was her responsibility to give her children a healthy home and she worried about "all the stuff in the water." Some children reported more stomachaches, which could have been a result of the water, the food, or added stress. Louise's daughter had a bad stomachache the day before evacuation, and Louise believed that the water was already not potable.

Tina, like many others, became compulsive with her children about washing hands. "I was like Howard Hughes! Wash your hands! Wash your hands!" Louise said she was always on her daughter's case to wash her hands because a child in their neighborhood had eaten a small piece of mud off his mother's boot and had become seriously ill. Some women said that because of their compulsive hand washing they did not get sick during the flood. As Lisa pointed out, "Never underestimate the value of washing your hands." Residents were told to wash everything because the water left behind many contaminants, including sewage and oil, which could make them sick. The city even recommended hosing down lawns before allowing children to play on them. In order to avoid illness, many women spent hours outside washing items they were trying to salvage.

After the flood, there were some reports of residents becoming sick from the chemicals used during rebuilding. The glue used to adhere new carpeting in homes and schools made some residents, especially children, sick, and the widespread painting and varnishing throughout town also made some individuals nauseated and ill. One woman's daughter, for example, began to have seizures at night, and the girl's mother believed that her small body was reacting to all the chemicals and toxins in her environment. Pregnant women had to be particularly careful. Leslie, who was seven months pregnant, was instructed not to go near her water-filled basement. Sabrina, who was also pregnant during the flood, was cautious about being in the town at all. There were some reports that pregnant women were miscarrying more than usual. Louise, for example, called me six months after the flood to talk about the miscarriage she had just suffered. She had no doubt it was due to environmental factors, such as the toxic glue, paint, and varnishes used in both her house and office during the months of rebuilding after the flood.

Emotional Issues

"There are times when I think or talk about the flood, and instantly I am in tears," Lorna told me matter-of-factly as she sat on a donated couch in her FEMA trailer four months after the flood. The flood, for many reasons, evoked highly emotional responses such as Lorna's. The issues women raised related to their emotional health and well-being included feelings of sadness, anger, and depression, the strain of family conflicts, contemplating or seeking counseling, experiencing feelings of violation, and negotiating the pain of loss. Many of the women said that the many emotions they had about the flood were often very close to the surface. At other times the women felt that they could not get in touch with their emotions because they were too overwhelmed by the situation to be able to sort it out emotionally.

Women expressed great sadness about the flood and its destruction. They spoke of different things that triggered emotions of sadness and crying, such as talking with a friend, being touched, hearing certain music, or seeing photographs of the flood's destruction. Joanne felt that she and other women she met during evacuation "would just break out crying at the drop of a hat." They would be talking, Joanne explained, and then they felt overwhelmed and cried. Pat remembered not being able to hug a friend, because she knew it would trigger too many emotions: "I said, 'I can't touch you long because I don't have time to cry, and if I start now, I won't quit.' Then she started crying—she's very emotional—and I said, 'I can't look at you, I really don't have time to cry.'" During evacuation, Lisa heard beautiful music on the radio one day and cried for the first time. "There is something about music that makes me emotional." Louise talked about the sadness in her dreams:

> I had these dreams before the flood. . . . Something was going to happen, and the dream told me that . . . I would see it as it happens. Time would show me. I have heard of many people having dreams of the city in flames or in the flood *before* the flood happened. My dream was one of terrible sadness. Then the flood hit and this is what the deep sadness is, the sadness of all the loss. All the symbols I had seen in the dream were around me. And the emotions were the same as in the dream. It left me with an eerie feeling.

Cecilia found herself unable to hold back tears at the University of North Dakota Museum's flood exhibit. She knew she was embarrassing her children by crying in a public place, but she felt she had to cry when she saw the photographs of the flood. Other women who attended the exhibit noted that this was the first time they had ever been to a museum. For example, Sabrina recalled:

> My mom kept saying that I should go, and I was like, oh, it's a museum, *ugh*. But I went there, and I had a wave of emotions come over me. The exhibit was great. Photos of dolls all covered in mud, makes me think of the little girl [who owned the dolls]. I think about it, and I get weepy.

Fran felt particularly sad when she saw her own belongings on the berm, waiting to be taken to the dump. She felt a connection to them, was really bothered seeing her bed carted off, and then became very sad thinking about her "poor bed out there in the junkyard." Tina felt extreme sadness when her son remembered that he had left his beloved teddy bear at their house, which was submerged in water. Tina had asked each of her children to bring one toy, and both grabbed new items. Only later did the young boy realize that he had chosen something new over his lifelong bear, prompting him and all fourteen residents of their temporary trailer "to bawl for hours."

Some women, despite feelings of sadness, did not cry at all throughout the flood crisis. Carrie, who dealt not only with a basement full of raw sewage and the loss of many personal belongings but also with medical emergencies (unrelated to the flood) with two family members, was worried because she did not cry during the flood. She commented ten months after the disaster, "What distresses me is that I still have not cried since before the flood, and I think there is still a real denial going on in me that I really haven't come to terms with all this." Lydia was sad about the flood's destruction, but she was not bothered that she did not cry. She attributed this to her older age: "I think a person learns to roll with the punches the older they get, and I've had no tears. I knew that nothing could be accomplished by crying, there's no remorse. It's a reality; it happened; we have to face it."

Some of the women expressed anger at the city, the state, FEMA, the Corps of Engineers, the National Weather Service, their families, or their church. While these groups or individuals did not cause the flood, they may in some ways have made the circumstances more negative. Cindy, who lost her daycare business, believed that there was so much anger after the flood because people needed somebody or something to blame, but that person or thing did not exist. Research in gender studies has long shown how women are socialized to be "nice" and accommodating and discouraged from being outspoken or showing their anger. Thus the expressions of anger, which broke gender norms, were at times difficult for the women to show. Most women did not express anger toward the river directly because they did not actually blame the river for the flood and its destruction. Most were cognizant of the fact that the river water had to go somewhere and that human settlement and human decisions caused the crisis. Indeed, as discussed in previous chapters, many women were angry at the decisions made by city leaders. Dana, who lost her home and was not allowed to rebuild it, for example, was so angry at the city that she wanted to leave Grand Forks and move to Bismarck. Her friend had been told by a city official not to expect any answers (about new dikes, home buyouts, or other relief) for three years, prompting Dana to ask, "How can a person live like that?" She felt that she did not trust the city government anymore, and she felt angrier overall: "I'm just more angry, and I don't like that, I really don't."

Most of the women refused to say anything bad about Pat Owens, the female mayor of Grand Forks. Even if they were angry at the city, they felt that the mayor had done a great job, and they were proud that a woman was the leader through the flood. Julie, for example, was angry at the city and the National Weather Service because she "felt lied to." But she reiterated that the mayor had done a great job, and she was not blaming her for any of the problems during the flood. Piper reported that some of her male high school friends blamed problems in the flood on the mayor:

> So he said that Pat Owens was responsible for losing the town, and that if we had someone more commanding, more appropriate in charge, then we wouldn't have lost the town. I don't feel that way, and I got really mad. I happen to think that she did a wonderful job.

Rachel agreed: "It was interesting having a woman in charge. She was really thinking about things. She wasn't going to do some macho thing and get people killed." Past research has found that even in settings where gender is irrelevant to the task at hand, men are presumed to be smarter and better leaders than women (Ridgeway 1997). In this case, women residents appeared to contradict this finding by perceiving their female mayor as smart and a good leader; however, men's views of the mayor might support this finding.[9]

Some women were angry when they felt that they were being taken advantage of. Martha Jo, for example, was furious at her son and grandsons, who used her house during evacuation but showed no respect for her home. She said that they tracked mud throughout the house and left dirty clothes draped on furniture, and that one grandson left little hairs everywhere from trimming his "goatee or whatever you call these things that teenagers are sporting now." In addition to the mess, she was furious about their "victim" attitude, which heightened what she saw as a "bitter turn of events." She interpreted her son's and grandson's disrespect for her house as disrespect for her personally. Many women spoke of being angry with family members, a situation I discuss in detail in chapter 7, which examines family relationships in the flood.

There was much evidence that stress and anxiety increased as a result of the flood. In her first interview, Fran, an elementary school teacher, explained that she felt lost and felt there was "this anxiety about the unknown." Other women also commented that not knowing what the future would hold was stress inducing. In her follow-up interview fifteen months after the flood, Fran discussed how she was surprised by a recent reaction to the sound of flood sirens:

> Subconsciously, there might be more happening than I realize. Our sixth graders put on a play every year, and this year, of course, it dealt with the flood. In the production they used the sirens, but when the sirens went off, I almost had to leave. *I couldn't take it.* That was interesting to me because [the flood] is not in my thoughts. It's not something that I ever think about much, only every once in awhile. From day to day, the flood is not in my thoughts a whole lot. But my reaction to the siren, maybe there was a little more stress, a little more than I really think about.

As we continued talking, Fran began to remember the tension and stress that she felt at work all year and concluded, "It was definitely a more stressful year." Like Fran, Joanne felt it was stressful to hear the sirens, which she did in a flashback:

> I want to tell you something. For the first time in my life, I had a flashback. It was on New Year's Eve. I went to bed early but woke up to the sound of the fireworks. I looked at them and some of them were red. I went back to bed and then later woke up with a start. The picture turned from fireworks to sirens going off, back to that terrible night, my scariest night of the flood. It wasn't moving. It was like a still snapshot.

Louise had been stressed by the sound, not of sirens but of helicopters. For many mornings after evacuation, Louise would wake with a start in a "total panic" thinking that she had heard helicopters but knowing that there were none in the area where she evacuated. Julie and her husband also suffered from similar ailments. Julie said that she continually heard helicopters "in my head," and her husband heard sirens, even when they had evacuated to a peaceful, quiet place. She felt these were post-traumatic reactions.

Dana felt that all the stress made things more tense, and "you blow up a lot easier." Cecilia agreed: "I let the tension and stress get to me, and I was lot crabbier this summer than normal." Julie noted that many residents seemed to be taking more sick days off from work, and she believed they were "emotionally sick days." Lisa found that due to her stress level, she was grinding her teeth at night. One possible reason for increased stress the year after the flood was that most of the women had to forgo any summer vacation the summer after the flood. They often acknowledged how that "down time" was important to their general well-being, as it was a much needed break from work. Lorna felt the absence of their vacation. "We went to the lake on the weekends, but we usually take a weeklong summer vacation but we couldn't this year. And I can tell that my stress level is a little higher."

Some women felt that the stress of the situation brought on "flood brain" or "flood head," meaning that they had trouble focusing, concentrating, or remembering things. Joanne felt that in addition to crying and feeling overwhelmed, she started to worry about her mental capacities:

> The stage of forgetfulness, that was troubling. What is happening to my mind? You'd be in the middle of a sentence, and you absolutely did not know where you were going with it. And you knew it wasn't coming back. You knew it was just gone. It wasn't just me. It was the department chair, it was the professors, it was everyone.

Lydia, a sixty-seven-year-old realtor, suffered a "flood moment" while speaking publicly:

> My mother turned ninety-five, and we had a party up there at the senior citizens' center, so I had to speak, and here my mind is just, like, Where is it? It's somewhere in my basement! It was totally gone, I didn't even know what day it was, or what anything was.

Lydia felt that flood brain was probably some kind of defensive mechanism to deal with the stress of the flood. Some of the women laughed when describing their "flood moments." For example, Fran joked that "flood brain" was just a new word for "space cadet." However, this "flood head" may have been also a sign of the level of stress that the women were experiencing, in that they could not function in everyday scenarios, such as having conversations with co-workers or friends. Past research has shown that women may be slightly more likely than men to suffer from Post-Traumatic Stress Disorder PTSD after a disaster (Green 1996). In addition, it is more common than ever before for PTSD to be diagnosed in natural disaster survivors.

Some women reported that they suffered from depression as a result of the flood.[10] Rachel was worried about her teenaged daughter, who began taking antidepressants after the flood: "She's just been really depressed. She's been moody." In fact, all three of Rachel's teenage children needed medication for depression after the flood. Rachel felt that it was tough for her family to cope since "after the flood, there were so many losses in a row, like it wasn't going to stop." The death of their three pets during the course of the disaster made Rachel depressed: "It was just like everything was dying." She joked that there was a light at the end of the tunnel now, and she will be getting out of it soon, but then again, that light "might be a train coming my way."

Jane, in her first interview during the summer of the flood, felt strongly that the toll on the psyche was just starting and that people would be more depressed later as the losses sank in. Jane, like many others, felt that if there were another flood, there would be serious levels of emotional and mental problems: "If we have another flood, we will have a big problem, and everyone will be on Prozac!" Genie, who felt emotionally well and even "the happiest I have been in the longest time" the summer after the flood, struggled with depression during the following winter:

> At the first part of this year I was really doing badly. I was very depressed, very down, and I wasn't suicidal or anything, but nothing gave me joy. My husband could have said, "Hey, let's go down to Fargo and see a movie and go to the Olive Garden," and I would have said, "Nah, no, that's all right." I found myself watching "The Waltons" twice a day. That was the only thing I looked forward to. It came on at 8:00 in the morning, and 6:00 in the evening. There is something not healthy about looking forward to *The Waltons* twice a day.

Jean Marie observed that the whole town was depressed: "For awhile it was so glum, any faces you saw on the street had glum expressions, and there was no laughter."

Dana felt that she had been "mean" lately, and "really grumpy," and her doctor told her that she was "really susceptible to depression." In addition to the flood destroying her home, Dana was also faced with the death of her mother during the flood aftermath. She described how she was coping: "Some days are bad; other days are just fine. My doctor told me the symptoms, and if you have it more than two weeks, then it's depression. I remember feeling that way, but I had some of the symptoms, but not all the time." Jane hoped that her feelings of depression would not last long: "I assume this will be temporary. I just feel less happy, less optimistic. I tended to be quite an optimist, and I'm not so sure I am so optimistic anymore. And that may go away." Louise said that she felt so many emotions during the flood: "At times there was just numbness, then at times depression and crying, and then other times, feelings of we can do this, we can make it."

Many women expressed the need for counseling, but most did not seek out any type of treatment. A local human services center sent social workers and counselors door to door to help people, a service some used and others did not. Many women with whom I spoke said that the North Dakota culture, with its stoic Norwegian roots, taught people to deal with problems on their own. Jane did not seek counseling but acknowledged that this was the second time in her life when she even contemplated seeing a therapist:

> Well, I have never seen a counselor. I'm as Norwegian as everyone else. This is the second time in my life when I thought, well, maybe. When my mother died, and then these arguments with my husband, they have made me think. These are the two times that I probably could have benefited from some counseling. We are just fine now, so okay, we made it through.

While Jane felt that counseling might have helped but did not get any, there were other women who never even let themselves contemplate seeing a counselor.

Some women did seek out some form of counseling. Tina was worried about the effects on her young child and called the Flood Crisis Line for counseling because she felt that "we needed someone with more background than us, to make sure he recovers." She finally took her son to the "crisis place," and she felt reassured by the counselor that she "was doing everything right." The counselor told her that they could not expect their son to recover as other children were because her son's losses (loss of home and belongings and a grandparent dying) were much greater and more ongoing (they were still homeless). Cecilia also felt that her children were having trouble accepting what had happened and enrolled all of them in a mental health services program for four weeks. Genie, who was watching *The Waltons* twice a day and could not get excited about going to the Olive Garden, decided to seek help.

> So I went to the counselor and she said, "Well, you're depressed." She recommended that I get a job and go to the doctor and get antidepressants. I took Zoloft, and it really made a difference. I was really happier, and the house started getting cleaner, and the laundry started getting done.

Interestingly, a sign of recovery from depression for Genie was that she was able to resume her household labor of laundry and cleaning, which she had ignored when she was depressed. She eventually stopped taking the medication and said she felt "fine." Genie also got a job, as the doctor recommended, and that seemed as important, if not more important, to her recovery as the medication had been. As research has found, women who are home full-time suffer from more depression than women who also work in the public sphere.[11]

Some women tried other avenues to help themselves sort through the emotional damage of the flood. Many women spoke of writing in journals or diaries throughout the crisis so that they could make some sense of how they felt about what was happening. Sandy, divorced just before the flood and jobless as a result of the flood, was religious about writing in her journal every day because writing was a healing process. Others wanted to write in their journals, but even that felt overwhelming, as Louise, a writer, explained:

> People have been upset with me. "What is wrong with you? You're a writer, you should be writing a bunch now!" And, "Why aren't you keeping a journal every day? What is wrong with you?" I say, "I'm too busy. I'm sorry, my life is overwhelmed with all these other things; I can't do it." I tried to write a diary, but it only covered April, and I never got back to it. I was too busy. I have this calendar, and have jotted down when I have to do things or what is happening. I have been sort of upset with myself. Why

didn't I keep a journal of the flood? I just felt too overwhelmed.
I just couldn't seem to get to it.

Jane, who kept a journal throughout the crisis, felt that it was
therapeutic even though her main intention was just to keep track
of the chronology of the event, because it was difficult to maintain
a handle on everything that was happening. Pat also felt that she
handled things "by writing a lot," so keeping a journal was "part
of my catharsis." Fran did not write in a diary but instead read
novels as her coping strategy: "I was just trying to lose myself.
That was my way to cope." Other women got counseling help
from friends and family inside and outside of Grand Forks. Carol
decided to skip a family outing to Fargo, where they planned to
treat themselves to a dinner at the Olive Garden, and instead
stayed home and had a beer and a long conversation with a friend
about her emotions about the flood. Lydia found emotional support from her "coffee group" at work. "We meet at eleven each
day, and we were just clinging to one another." Lydia also found
emotional support from her neighbors. "The flood brought us all
together again. We were banding together for support, and we
were helping each other out." Lydia felt that talking to her coffee
group, her neighbors, and me about her feelings about the flood
served as a catharsis for her.

Many women said that they felt personally violated by two in-
vasive forces: the flood waters, first, and, later, by looters who stole
from their destroyed houses. As Roseanne described it, "Our home
had been so beaten up: what the river did and the vandals." Cecilia
agreed, noting it that was both forces that made her feel violated.
Women experienced the violation of the flood as a violation of the
body because women are more vulnerable to assault in their lives
than men. In fact, in the United States women are so at risk to
misogynist crimes that these crimes have been termed "femicide"
(Caputi and Russell 1997). As a result of this pervasive violence
against women, the Grand Forks women's frame of reference for
fear is one of assault, so that these violations from the flood became
violations against their own bodies.

The women experienced the river entering their homes as a
very personal and intimate violation. For many, it was the sight of
sewage residue and silt in intimate belongings, such as their under-
wear drawers and the sheets of their beds, which brought on feel-

ings of being violated. Cecilia spoke of feeling violated when the river water saturated her daughter's clothes table and her clothes:

> One thing that struck me was that we had a changing table for the baby. It was an old one, and it had little levels that I had her clothing in, and it had filled with the river water. I remember feeling really sad about that, like you're violated. It's a really difficult feeling to explain. I had that feeling seeing her little pink socks scattered around, all black.

Louise said there were "terrible feelings of powerlessness" about what the flood had done. Tina felt "earthworms in your clothes was too much to handle" and described the feelings of violation she felt:

> The flood water violated you. I felt violated when it invaded my bed, the sheets, and the couch. The bed especially. I know what it would feel like to have someone come in and rob you. Because that is what the flood water did, and that's what the people who came in [to loot] did. It's the same thing.

The women had a special connection to their homes and felt that they were meaningful, consecrated spaces, a belief that will be discussed in chapter 9. Pat, a nurse and mother of three children, felt that her home had been "assaulted" by the flood and equated it to rape:

> There was a loss of control. There are things you take for granted, that you could keep your home secure. You know you're going to lose control, that people will die in your life, that people can get sick. It has never occurred to me that my home could be assaulted. I felt like the house had been violated. Like people who have been raped. I felt like our home had been raped. I felt like pieces of me had been ripped out because of what had happened to our family and what had happened to our home. You just never think it will happen to your home. Home is the place you should go to when everything else is going wrong.

In addition to feeling violated initially by the dirty and destructive river water, many women expressed feelings of violation as a result of looters invading their homes and taking items. Stealing fixtures from condemned houses and plants and flowers from yards was apparently a fairly common activity. Tina was horrified by people stealing from her home and her mother's home:

> There was looting, if you can call it looting. You felt so *violated*.
> My mother's house, it flooded, the city bought it, but it's still my
> mother's house, and my mom has since died, so it's, like, do *not*
> go in her house unless you have the right to go in. I was driving
> home, and there was this pick up truck [at my mother's house].
> So I called the police. They have no right to take a light switch
> even if we choose not to take it. Looters tried to take our big bay
> window, but it broke while they were trying. I thought, "good."
> [People looting] was definitely a violation. It hurt a lot.

Roseanne, who lost her home of thirty years, commented on the
vandals, "People came in and were destructive. I was glad when
[the house] was taken down because then it wouldn't be trashed
anymore." Cecilia, like many others, felt violated when someone
came in her yard and stole all the plants.

For some women, the violation of the flood brought old violations to the surface. Louise, who had been sexually abused as a child
by a relative, began having disturbing dreams, what she called "invasion nightmares," about her young daughter being sexually abused
by the same relative. "[In the dream], I was trying to figure out,
what do I do? What do I do? I felt really helpless." Later in the
dreams her daughter was sexually abused by a man who looked like
the construction worker from next door: "[In the dream], he was
trying to tell me how it would be so good for her to be sexually
abused, and I'm saying, 'No, you can't do this.'" While Louise did
not believe that the construction worker had harmed her daughter,
she realized that she did worry about her daughter playing in the
neighborhood with construction workers at every house: "It is
something that I worry about, trying to protect her, and how can I
protect her. There are some situations that I am unsure of, where she
would be out there and she'd just be running around." Louise felt
that all of these dreams were connected to the violation of the flood:

> I really felt [the dreams] were flood related because the flood, I
> felt the same way about the flood as I do about the sexual abuse
> experiences, like nothing you can do about it. It is an invasion,
> and so for me, it brought up all those issues. You know, feeling in
> vaded and you can't do anything, and then, just trying to clean

your life up and trying to put it back together. So it felt the same to me. So I think the flood brought on those dreams.

Ten months after the flood, Louise was no longer having any "invasion nightmares" about violation or abuse, which she attributes to that fact that her life feels settled. Liz went through a similar experience. The flood brought up many repressed memories of extreme physical and emotional abuse that she suffered at the hands of her first and second husbands. She felt that being so vulnerable in the flood made her remember how vulnerable she had been when she was battered. The memories were so vivid and so horrific that Liz needed counseling to deal with them.

What both Louise and Liz have described could be classified as post-traumatic stress disorder.[12] According to Herman (1992, p. \37), for many traumatized individuals "the traumatic moment becomes encoded in an abnormal form of memory, which breaks spontaneously into consciousness, both as flashbacks during waking states and as traumatic nightmares during sleep." Traumatic dreams, like Louise's invasion nightmares, are often experienced with terrifying immediacy, as if occurring in the present. Because both women were assaulted by family members, they suffered "repeated trauma," which happens in "circumstances of captivity," including prisons, slave labor camps, religious cults, and families (Herman 1992).

Women spoke of the emotional issue of loss. Cecilia was overwhelmed by feelings of loss: "You could never imagine this feeling, this feeling of loss, that I hope I never have to go through again." Tina equated the losses from the flood to the loss of a family member, and when the one-year anniversary of the flood happened, she was happy to have someone remember her losses:

It was nice to have people remember. Like if you lose someone very special in your life. Like an unborn child, where somebody miscarries, where not everyone can understand how you are feeling, how the person who miscarries is feeling. So it was nice at the anniversary.

It is interesting to note that in Tina's discussion of loss, she uses gendered imagery, as she equates the loss to a miscarriage, an experience inherently and profoundly female. Roseanne felt that watching her home torn down and coming to terms with that loss was "a long grieving process." In the immediate aftermath of the flood, Dana also felt the loss could be equated to someone dying and she began to cry as she said, "I told my sister that you can almost compare this to a death. It is the only way I could explain it to her. I'm really devastated." Liz agreed: "I'm in a grieving process. This has been a death." In a video of the flood produced by a local radio station, a female resident said that losing her home of ten years in the flood felt the same to her as if a friend, relative, or family member had passed away.

Some women felt that the disaster affected them emotionally by making them feel powerless in their lives and not having any control over what happened to them. Karen, a teacher and mother of two young children, explained the powerlessness she felt just before evacuation:

> I know [the flood] changed me profoundly. I can't say exactly how. It's not like I haven't had adversity. I live in this place, and that is an adverse kind of thing. Living here, it is hard to live here. My dad got cancer and died when I was ten. I've had to take care of myself in a lot of ways. I've had two miscarriages. So I've had bad things happen to me. But I've never not known what to do. I didn't know what to do. I just cried.

Cecilia felt that she was more vulnerable in many respects as a result of the flood, and she did not believe that she was stronger "because I just used the strength I had." She felt that sometimes she feels panicked that they need a two-story house in case there is another flood. "In that respect I am more vulnerable and more insecure." Olesen (1992) found in her research on survivors of the 1989 San Francisco earthquake that by going through such a traumatic event, the survivors' vulnerable selves overwhelmed their other conceptions of self. In Grand Forks, the reactions were complex, and the women felt both vulnerable in some respects and more emotionally empowered in others. Genie, who believed that she and her children were going to die when they lost heat during Blizzard Hannah before the flood and cried to God when the flood sirens went off, felt empowered and no longer felt like complaining:

> This has been a life-changing experience for me. It's just incredible. Being a survivor. You survived these big things, and you

think, "Why should I sweat the little things? If I can do this, certainly I can do that." You see what's important to you, and that you can make your home where you are, if you want to, or you can be miserable. I think I was trying to make myself miserable before. "Poor little me, I didn't get my vacation, it's so cold, I have to shovel all this snow, and waa, I don't have any friends, it's cold." All whining.

Liz felt emotionally and psychologically empowered by surviving the flood on her own, and as a result she changed what she expected from relationships. "The flood has taught me that it's okay to have high standards. Not just in relationships with men, but all relationships in my life. I can't just keep giving, giving, giving." Liz felt that she could now demand healthier relationships because the flood had given her "incredible inner strength" and she now can "count on myself and trust myself."

Diana also felt emotionally stronger because of the flood, as she discussed in her follow-up interview a year after I first talked to her:

> I don't feel anywhere near as fragile as I did. I feel like I sort of quavered my way through the interview last year. I think you do develop a certain amount of strength having gotten through so many months of that much pressure and fearsome worry. One has the emotional resources you didn't know you had before. So that is something that's valuable.

Lydia, who coped with the help of her "coffee group," agreed with those sentiments:

> I think any type of tragedy is a building experience, and a person is stronger from having survived it. It was just a horrible thing to go through, and at the time I remember thinking, "This is just awful." But I had no doubt in my mind that I would face it. It was a challenge, but I knew I could handle it. Life goes on, even though it seemed like it wasn't going to.

Rachel reported that her friend, who was proud of all that she survived during the crisis, wanted to make a T-shirt that said, "I survived the flood, the fire, the storm, and menopause all at the same time!"

Others spoke of feeling like stronger women because of work-related issues that emerged in the crisis. Louise took on a new work project that originally she believed was over her head:

> It was a very empowering thing, sort of like, "I did that!" And I am sort of amazed that I did that, and I didn't know anything about it. I don't even know if I could do it again, because it was sort of like the flood helped me to be able to do that. It gave me a lot of power to do that.

Amy Sue, who was fired from her job during the flood, was distraught and felt that her self-esteem had been shattered. Ultimately, however, she landed in a job a flood-related agency and felt like she was "quality" again and could hold her head up high.

Other women who felt empowered and emotionally stronger due to the flood found themselves more likely to stand up for themselves or to speak their minds. Rachel's children were amazed when she drove through a National Guard barricade that was preventing her from getting to her house: "What are they going to do, shoot me? After awhile you get to the point where you said, 'Why listen?' I got sick of being told what to do all the time." Peggy asserted herself in the same manner when she needed to get past the National Guard when the dikes broke: "I said, '*Look*, my home is down there and my family is down there, and I am going down there *one way or the other*.'"

The flood greatly affected the women's physical and emotional health and well-being. An expression I heard repeatedly in interviews, and often in conversations on the street in Grand Forks, was that people were committed to "making lemonade out of lemons." The women of Grand Forks made the most of what happened to them, struggling to remain optimistic and hopeful in the face of traumatic losses and personal upheaval. Despite depression, sleep deprivation, and feelings of violation, the women did not complain; they did not present these issues as if they were victims. Rather they explained to me, because I expressed interest, all facets of their flood experience. The women's experiences with their health and well-being were gendered: experiencing weight gain and a lack of exercise as a threat to body image and self-esteem; feeling unsafe in their homes and experiencing the flood as a violation of the body due to the climate of violence against women; being responsible for their children's health (and suffering miscarriages) among contaminants and black mold; defending their female mayor; and searching for social connection in the midst of loss. Surviving and coping with physical and emotional losses contributed to the women's sense of self as vulnerable, but ultimately they felt strong and resilient and able to face their new vulnerability.

Chapter 7

Family and Religion:
Havens in a Flooded World?

———————

A ll aspects of the women's everyday and personal lives were disrupted by the flood, including their relationships with family
members, their relationships to their churches or other places of
worship, and their views about spirituality or religion. Religion and
family were important issues for the women during the flood disaster. Social observers have often suggested that these two social institutions are of utmost importance to Americans, as families
provide support and sanctuary away from the larger community,
and religion provides a necessary link and connection to the larger
community. The family, which has been conceptualized as a "haven
in a heartless world," is considered a place where Americans expect
to be unconditionally accepted and supported (Bellah et al. 1985).
Crises, however, can put strains on this supportive domain. Research has found that crises such as economic depressions, homelessness, or the loss of a job have wide-ranging ramifications for
family relations, both producing more solidarity and creating more
conflict and strife (Arendell 1986; Newman 1989; Liebow 1993).
The family is also the main social institution in which gender is produced and displayed; thereby making an examination of the
women's location in the family worthwhile (Risman 1998).

Religion is one of the most important ways in which Americans are involved in the life of their community and society. Approximately 40 percent of Americans attend religious services at
least once a week, and 60 percent say they belong to a church. Approximately 95 percent of Americans believe in the existence of
God and life after death and state that religion is important in their

lives. Research has also shown that religion is often very important to individuals and families who survive traumatic events such as war, persecution, oppression, or immigration to a new country (Jacobs 1996). Some researchers have found that belief in God and the workings of fate played a role in how people reacted to, prepared for, and perceived a natural disaster threat (Sims and Baumann 1972). Religion and spirituality can also be a coping strategy to deal with trauma and loss.[1] In this chapter, I examine the women's relationship to these two critical social institutions, family and religion.

Family Relations

The flood affected family relations in several ways. Some families experienced many conflicts, while others felt closer to one another and found the flood to be a time of bonding. For many of the women in Grand Forks, their families were the first priority throughout the crisis, and their families' safety was their largest concern. However, the consequences of the disaster, including stress, exhaustion, and economic downward mobility, did contribute to conflicts with spouses, parents, and children. Other research has found that crises such as downward mobility, can affect a family's ability to get along.

One type of family conflict that surfaced was strained marital relationships. Past flood disasters have been found to have been hard on marital relationships, resulting in fighting and blaming each other for losses and sometimes leading to separation and divorce (Erikson 1976; Davis and Ender 1999). In Grand Forks, some of the women felt that they and their husbands had different priorities. Lydia and her husband were "at each other's throats" throughout the crisis. She said they would start fighting over nothing because it was a reaction to the "desperate situation we were in." The fighting was "really hard" on both of them. Carrie stated that she and her husband had several "huge marital fights" during the crisis. The first fight came when she gave animal rescuers permission to break open their house to rescue their pet, which appalled her husband because there were reports of looting. Another large fight was over what she referred to as "the god awful phone bills" every month, a result of her calls to her friends for emotional support. She felt that she and her husband had different priorities.

Julie and her husband felt differently about the safety of their children. Julie was worried about them on the dikes and wanted to have them at home, while her husband felt they were big enough to take care of themselves. Julie said, "Not that he doesn't love the kids, but he was never worried about them like I was." While they did not fight about this situation, Julie did feel a strain due to their different viewpoints. Diana was angry with her husband because he failed to take her warnings, and the city's warnings, seriously. When the city was evacuating the east side of their street, Diana's husband still did not worry because they were on the west side.

Others spoke of emotional needs not being met by their spouses. Jane described a "real bad fight" with her husband about two months into the flood recovery. In general, she felt that she had "gotten angrier at him this summer more easily than I usually do" and that led to their fight, which she believed stemmed from her anger that "no one was paying attention to my needs." Jane felt that she "was the strong one in the family, so people assume that I'm doing fine." Her anger grew when her husband paid no attention to her work situation and the state of her office after the flood, although they had paid considerable attention to his place of work. "I was just furious. It was as if my work was worthless." When I spoke with her again, months after their "major fight," Jane and her husband were doing better, she reported, because they had learned to be more attentive to "what emotionally might be going on" with both of them. Jane had noticed that many of their friends also had difficulties, but she felt that much of that was "the ups and downs of relationships that happen normally, but just more exaggerated and more visible" in a crisis. Some women felt that they were more emotional than their husbands during the flood, while the men took on a strong, more rational protector role, and the two did not necessarily complement each other.

Some couples faced conflicts because of the changing work demands of both women and men. As a hospital manager, Lorna needed to be at her office throughout the crisis, leaving her husband, Andy, alone at the house because their children were out of town with grandparents. Lorna reported that this situation was difficult for Andy:

> He was worrying about the kids, worrying about me, then learn-
> ing his office was on fire, he wanted my support, he wanted me

there. But I had a staff that I had to deal with. It was very hard for him. I think the most difficult thing is that he has always been the emotionally strong one. I am the more emotional one. He's always been very supportive of my role at the hospital, and he's understood that there are going to be times when I have to drop what I'm doing and leave. When I had to return to the hospital, it was hard, and he got real teary eyed that day and said, "I need you just as much." . . . [In the end] did we learn some things about each other? Yeah. Like I have a need with my job, and he has real sensitive emotional needs sometimes, too.

Other conflicts surfaced around the women's partners' work demands. Several women's spouses had their offices destroyed in the fires downtown, often forcing them to set up home offices during the summer after the flood. As a result, many women, like Carol, had to make sure that the phone line was always free and that the work they were doing on the house was not bothersome. Martha Jo found that her husband had new expectations of her now that he was working at home: "It has been a very difficult summer. I am *not* his maid, and I am *not* his secretary." She was grateful, however, that he played bridge and golf occasionally: "I'd go out of my mind if he was around here twenty-four hours a day." Lisa and her husband found their troubles stemming from the public/ private spheres of work. Her husband went to work every day in the public sphere and gained information about recovery operations (for example, what the city's plans were and where to get supplies), while Lisa was at home and felt isolated from that information network: "I would get angry because he never told me anything."

Other martial conflicts were less severe but difficult nonetheless. These often stemmed from having less living space. Louise and her husband, Rodney, had an experience that was fairly typical. Louise wanted to prepare the house for the flood, and Rodney believed that it was not necessary and felt that Louise was overreacting. At a later point, Rodney decided to help, and he moved some items to a higher shelf in the basement. Louise, fearing the entire basement would flood, as it eventually did, decided to move the items upstairs, even though she knew such a move would anger her husband. Thus, she pretended that she did not know he had moved it to the shelf. Many items that she left in the basement were lost in the flood because she felt she could "not undo what he had done."

Diana had similar feelings, saying that by carrying things up from the basement it appeared that she was doubting or challenging his judgment as her husband had made it clear that he did not think the flood would affect them.

Sometimes the flood brought up issues that needed to be addressed in a marriage. After the crisis, Louise felt that Rodney had no sympathy for her; while she was upset over the flood, he would only complain that he had not been able to play golf. Louise, who had decided to stay home from work and be a full-time parent several years before the flood, found her husband upset with her for cleaning so much after the flood:

> Before the flooding, Rodney was always on my case. Why don't I clean more? I mean, his view was, once I quit working, the house should be immaculate. And for me, I never wanted to be a house-wife ever. So, okay, I'll do a little cleaning. I'll do a little housewife stuff, and I'll do stuff with cooking. So before the flood he was like "Can't we get this place a little cleaner?" And ever since the flood, I'm downstairs cleaning, cleaning, cleaning, and he's been on my case: "Can't you stop cleaning?"

Louise felt their troubles stemmed from having to live in chaos, and the stress of having to make so many decisions: "Are we gonna stay in this house? Are we gonna fix it up, or is it gonna flood again next year? Should we be moving out? Where would we move?" However, it was clear that strain over their gender roles existed prior to the flood, with Louise's husband expecting her to fulfill a more traditional role.

Fran, an elementary school teacher in her forties, and her husband Phil used to watch separate televisions on separate floors of the house. After the flood destroyed their basement, they were forced to watch television on one level, he in the living room and she in the kitchen. They could now hear each other's shows, prompting Phil to shout at Fran to turn it down. Fran was not worried about their relationship because she knew that as soon as the basement was rebuilt, and they moved one television downstairs, they would be fine. Fran's story raises some interesting points about the dynamics of marriage in general, as it seemed to her that spending every evening on separate floors was a typical arrangement. Some women spoke of situations in which their partners were angry or intolerant, and they felt they needed to support them and be more tolerant. Addie, a

Homes such as this one had to be gutted, scrubbed, and disinfected after the flood, and the insides of their homes sat on the berm for weeks. The debris from the flood cleanup was immense, with over 100,000 tons of debris going to the landfills. Some homes were repaired, others torn down. Homes with more than 50% damage were not allowed to be repaired and reinhabited. With money from FEMA and HUD, the city of Grand Forks established a buy-out program, buying approximately 1300 homes. The program was met with criticism and resistance by some residents. Similar buy-out programs have been used for several decades throughout the U.S. *Photo courtesy of FEMA (website).*

retiree, found that her husband seemed "less tolerant and very frustrated about everything," and she felt the only thing she could do
was to try and be more patient. Alway et al. (1998) argued that men
feel that they have "lost" when a natural disaster destroys their
home, and they experience anger, powerlessness, and feelings that
they have not fulfilled their role as "protector."

Some marital conflicts were much more serious and ended in
divorce. Peggy, a forty-five-year-old homemaker, found that the
flood was the "straw that broke the camel's back" with her marriage, and she and her husband sought a divorce during the flood
aftermath. In her first interview after the flood, she admitted that
she and her husband "weren't there for each other" during the crisis. A year later, in her follow-up interview, she said that the timing
was right for their divorce, as there were no house and no belongings to divide: "It was the time for me to do this. Because we have
nothing to fight over, nothing to bicker about. So let's do it. The
flood was not a direct cause, but it determined the timing. The divorce should be final in the next month. I am looking forward to
being on my own." While no statistics were available, the common
sentiment was that many marriages were dissolving during the crisis.[2] A few months after the flood, Louise commented that although
she did not personally know the couples that were divorcing, she
kept hearing about divorces. She admitted that she could understand how it could happen, acknowledging that if were not for their
daughter, the stress of the flood could have led her to divorce as
well. Indeed, two years later Louise e-mailed me to tell me that she
and her husband had filed for divorce. It was hard for her to know
how large a role the flood had played, but she felt it was at least part
of the downfall of the marriage.[3]

In addition to conflicts with spouses, the women spoke of
increased conflicts with their children. Peggy found that many conflicts with her teenage children were due to a lack of personal
space: "If there is a squabble about something, then you have ten
feet this way and ten feet that way. You've got no place to go. That
was really hard on me. Sometimes I would just get in my car and
drive on the highway to Thompson and back." Louise also felt that
family members were more irritable with one another after they
moved back into their crowded house: each room had only narrow
aisles through which to walk because all their furniture and belongings from the basement were stacked in the first floor. Diana

was displeased with her teenage daughter, who, she said, was detached and self-centered during the flood and did not want to participate in sandbagging efforts or other projects. Carrie also was mortified by her teenage son's behavior during the crisis, as he complained of being bored and did not want to contribute to volunteer efforts. It appeared that the women felt that their children's selfish attitudes reflected badly on them as mothers, who are seen as the teachers of values and morals in the family (Hansen and Garey 1998).

Some women reported that the flood improved their marital and familial relations. Pat, a nurse with three children, felt that she and her husband were closer as a result of the flood. She and her husband had endured a major trauma years earlier when they discovered that he had multiple sclerosis, and having been through that crisis together helped them support one another in the flood. Pat also found that she felt closer to her children and also to her sister and her husband's sister, who had helped them during the flood. Other families also spoke of feeling immense gratitude and closeness to family members who hosted them for evacuation, sometimes for weeks or months, and selflessly gave material and emotional support. Sabrina felt that she and her husband and her mother were much closer because they had a common enemy in the flood.

Some couples worked hard to stay close throughout the crisis. When Cecilia and her husband had a miscommunication, they made a point to say to each other, "Let's remember that we're in this together." They felt that this attitude was important not only to them but also to their four children, who needed them to get along. Julie, like many other women I spoke with, was upset that she and her husband had to be separated during evacuation: "I didn't want to be separated from him. I could have gone with him, but then I would have had to leave the kids. He called me every day, though." Lisa remembered that just before she and her husband abandoned their house, he turned to her and said, "Stop a minute." He gave her a hug and kiss, and then they drove off.

Jean Marie, a secretary in her fifties who suffered from arthritis, found that the flood was "a real bonding time" for her and her fiancé and that their relationship flourished. During evacuation, when they had to spend hours at the Air Force base hangar, they read the book *Women Are from Venus, Men Are from Mars* together and would stop and discuss each chapter. They felt that what they both learned about gender and communication improved their relationship. Later, when they were working on their house, they both realized the flaws of their previous marriages: "In his previous marriage, he did everything, and in my previous marriage, I did everything, so we saw a whole new side of give and take and working together." They treasured their relationship during the flood because they "talked and found great comfort in the support from each other."

Relations with children were also sometimes improved. Louise's friend from church, Chloe, confided in Louise that the flood helped Chloe's two foster children feel that they were definitely part of the family, as the crisis brought them all together. Prior to the flood the children had not felt that they completely belonged in the family. Many women reported that they were impressed and proud of their high-school-age, college-age, and adult children, who showed great maturity and sensibility in how they dealt with the flood. Many, like Jane, felt that their adult children, instead of focusing on their losses of childhood belongings and rooms, put their energies into helping their parents recover and providing them with support. Lisa, an upper-middle-class teacher, felt that she and her adult children, who lived out of state, became very close during the disaster because she would send them daily e-mails sharing how she was feeling. Teresa, a Latina store clerk who spent the evacuation period with her daughter and son-in-law, felt that she now considered her son-in-law to be her own son.

Many women felt that they were seeing their children in a whole new light. Some believed this event served as a rite of passage from childhood to adulthood for their teenagers. Pat, the mother of three, said:

> My youngest son and some of his high school friends, they really grew up years through this experience. Some of his friends lost everything they owned, but they came back and helped us, and then months later came and had their graduation. Their maturity level was high. Some of the things that are usually a big deal for seniors became minor. They had moved beyond those things.

Piper, an eighteen-year-old high school senior, explained that sibling relationships also improved, as she felt much closer to her brother and sister as a result of what they went through together in the flood.

Religion and Spirituality

Women's well-being in the disaster was often affected by their relationship to their church or place of worship and by their feelings about spirituality and God. Religious issues in disasters have been notoriously underresearched by social science disaster scholars.[4] Research has often reported that church is more important to American women than men. The Grand Forks women were from diverse religious backgrounds and affiliations: They were Lutheran, Methodist, Baptist, Catholic, Jewish, Evangelical, and agnostic. For many, their faith or the support they received from their religious community helped their overall well-being during the disaster. For several women, however, religion and spirituality played little or no role in their coping and recovery. The flood did not seem to affect these women's views about their religion. For example, most did not question why God brought the flood to their town.

Women had diverse feelings about how their spirituality was affected by the flood and also how their spirituality affected their coping with the flood. Many women in Grand Forks felt that their spirituality, belief system, or faith was not affected by the disaster, and their faith did not play a large role in their coping strategies. Rachel, a mother of two teenagers, expressed these views about religion and spirituality:

> I don't belong to a formal religion, but I am spiritual. I don't think our spirituality changed at all. I don't think [the flood] affected it at all. When the kids were little, I used to joke about "direct action karma," and I think that confused the kids when the flood came around. It has always been a joke, but I think they thought they had done something.

Fran, an elementary school teacher in her forties, who was not a member of any church or organized religion, felt that spirituality during the crisis was personal and not affected by the flood:

> Phil and I believe, but we are not part of any organized religion, in the sense of belonging to a church, that sort of thing. So I think

for both of us it was a pretty much a personal thing, it remained with each of us, how we were feeling. For myself, I didn't feel any different than I did before the flood. It didn't change my beliefs, and it wasn't something that I used a great deal for comfort.

Kimberlee, who happily became a stay-at-home mother because of the flood's destruction of her child's daycare, held similar sentiments:

> I don't think [the flood] strengthened our [faith]. We're very spiritual. There are spiritual people, and there are religious people. There are people who need their church. But you are supposed to have a connection to God, not through other people. I don't believe one religion is better than another. I realize bad things happen, and that brings people closer. So the flood had nothing to with [our faith] for us. If the church is gone, that doesn't mean that God is not there for you. Should [your faith] be an hour in church every week, or should it be every minute of your life?

Louise, the homemaker who did not clean the house to her husband's satisfaction, was not thinking about her spiritual beliefs at all in the days before evacuation. She told the story of how Jehovah's Witnesses came to her door, talking about how the flood was the end of the world, and asking if Louise wanted to be "one of the saved." She told them she could not talk because she was rushing to take her daughter to gymnastics, and she said they looked dumbfounded that she was not considering her spiritual faith at a time like that. Pat, a nurse and mother of three, felt that in terms of religion, she still "felt in touch," but that, as a result of the flood, she was no longer concerned about "the trivial things going on within the religious dogma." Tina's beliefs did not change, but she did question why God would make them go through the trauma of the flood:

> I am a strong believer in God, and God oversaw that I could see how to do this. I think of religion as a private thing. We have always had strong belief. Through the flood, there were different emotions, there was a strong disappointment that we didn't get support. Also, there was the classic self pity thing like asking God, "Why would you do this if you are there?" . . . Then you just realize that things are better than you think they are, and no matter how hard it is, maybe we had to go through this to learn something.

Tina, and others who also asked this question, concluded that they learned something from the experience and that God must have had his reasons. As Lydia, a sixty-seven-year-old realtor, remarked, "I'm sure the Lord had something in mind for all of us by having this happen." Research has found that traumatic events can often have one of the following effects on individuals: they can destroy people's faith in God (how could God let this happen?), or they can reinforce that God is all powerful (Lipstadt 1993).

Other women felt more connected to their faith as a result of the flood and used their religion as a coping strategy. Myrna, an eighty-year-old woman whose husband almost died during the flood, found her faith to be a very important factor in her survival: "Without my religion, I wouldn't have made it last summer. I prayed every chance I had. I think religion helped us through." She felt that "the Lord was helping us, there is no doubt about that." Cecilia, who lived with her four children in a trailer for a year, felt that her family's strong faith got them through the crisis, and she worried about those who did not have strong faith to help them. Genie, who was alone at home when the emergency evacuation sirens went off, felt that she needed God to help her with such a frightening moment. She cried while telling this story:

> Those sirens started going off, and I was by myself, and I wasn't ready for it. I was so scared. I remember standing there thinking, or saying out loud to myself, "Oh God, God, God, what am I going to do? Oh My God!" And I just cried. I didn't even have the presence of mind to say a good prayer, like "Oh God, please protect me; keep the children safe." All I'm doing is calling out His name, "Oh God, what am I going to do?" The sirens are going off, my children are at school, I have nothing packed, and my husband is somewhere, I have no idea.

Evidence that many residents felt that faith was important in the flood can be seen in the most popular name for boys born in Grand Forks during and after the flood: Noah, a Biblical name. Sabrina, a Latina homemaker, named her son "Noah" for its religious meanings:

> I would say that I have become more dependent on my religious values. I named my son "Noah"! It used to be that we only went to church as a family. If one doesn't want to go, then we don't go.

We used to be that we could take it or leave it. But now I find myself going by myself. I find that my faith has been strengthened. I have learned that there are some things in God's hands, and you just got to deal with it. I wouldn't say that I'm a fanatic; I'm not a Bible thumper.

Liz, who escaped an abusive husband during the flood, also felt more spiritual after the disaster:

I have discovered this last year a deep spiritual belief about everything. Everything happens for a reason. I got totally wiped out during the flood. I'm disabled, [and] I didn't think I could get back on my feet. But I did. I'm like a little kid that's been given every single little toy. Maybe the flood, the abuse, all of it, maybe I had to go through that to be the person I really am. Not because God was punishing me, not for any reason other than so I can be all that I deserve to be.

Liz continued:

The flood taught me that there's a lot of power in prayer, if you use it. Instead of praying for stuff, pray for His will. The Lord's prayer doesn't say *My* will be done, it says *Thy* will be done. You put your trust there, and it will take you through anything.

Sandy also felt more spiritual as a result of the flood disaster: "I have to take one day at a time. I am on a spiritual journey. For me it has to do with faith. It can get you through it, and you don't have to be afraid. I now have tons of peace. I have always prayed for that."

Genie felt that God had helped her family by steering them toward buying a home in the flood plain, prompting them to buy insurance, which they would not have done in any other area of the city. This saved them financially. Genie said, "So we were blessed in that way. I really believe the Lord led us to that very house. And that instills faith in me. A stronger faith. Even in the midst of adversity, the Lord does take care of you." While Genie felt that God led her to that house, Joanne, a single secretary, felt that God led her to evacuate to places where she met very helpful people. She started to cry as she said:

I felt these people were angels, and God had put them there for me, there was no doubt in my mind. The good Lord is looking out for me every second of the way. God gave me everything I needed to deal with it. I have never felt the grace of God and the love of God and just the presence of God so much. This Bible verse was repeated to me many times: "When I am afraid, I put my trust in Thee."

Tina, who lost her old Victorian house in the flood, felt that the positive things that happened to her family during evacuation were the "work of God."

Cecilia also felt that her faith was stronger as a result of the flood: "My religious convictions are very important and are my first priority. They have been reaffirmed and strengthened." Cindy, who experienced downward mobility but remained positive and upbeat about the situation, felt that her faith was important to how she coped: "I have a very deep faith in God, and I think that made a big difference." Four months after the flood, while many were still homeless and recovering, there was a Billy Graham crusade event in Grand Forks for flood victims. Lydia felt that the Billy Graham appearance was a positive experience because he talked to them about how "there is a higher power, and this tragedy brought us to our knees."

Some research has found that in the southern United States, residents had such faith in God and fate that they did not evacuate when storms were approaching (Sims and Baumann 1972). While many of the women of Grand Forks were very religious, none of them expressed any similar fatalist sentiment along the lines of not taking protective actions, such as evacuating, because God would protect them. However, at times the women spoke of events happening during the course of the flood that they attributed to fate. For example, Cecilia's children were scared on the way to an evacuation center, so they all prayed. Cecilia told them not to worry, "that God would take care of us, and that's why we are going to the center." Thus, unlike the research findings from the South, Cecilia felt that God was safeguarding them by providing them with protective actions to take.

The women expressed diverse perspectives on their places of worship and their religious institutions. Many women attended their place of worship less frequently after the flood. Pat, who found that her church was a place and community of support during the crisis period, remarked that it was "bizarre" that she and her husband, who are "consistent church goers," did not go to church at all after the crisis. She felt that they had just been too busy to get there and were trying to get themselves "remotivated" to return. Eighty-year-old Myrna said that this was the first time in her life that she neglected church. Roseanne described her feelings about churches in Grand Forks:

> I was grateful for churches as an organization. I liked how churches handed out stuff to their own. But as far as attendance at church, I would say we go less now. We really lost contact there. There was a squabble within the diocese over money, and that turned me off. There aren't too many things that we want to battle over. Not with the city over the price of the house, not with the church over money. We go less to church now, but spirituality hasn't changed.

Many other women expressed similar sentiments. They attended their church less in the year after the flood, but their belief system or their spirituality had not changed. Martha Jo explained that she did not go to church because she was very independent: "I can do my thanks to God walking around the house. Having a flood doesn't change how I act or deal with my faith." Genie gave this admission over a year after the flood, explaining why she did not attend her church:

> To be honest with you, I'm just going to be honest with you, we have not gone to church very much this year. Several reasons, nothing to do with the church or the pastor. Darryl has to be at work a significant number of hours, so he's not too motivated to go on Sundays. The kids are hard [they have attention deficient disorder], even on medication. I'd hook them up to an IV if I could. And the guy who was helping us for free on the house came on Sundays. I saw that the last check we wrote to the church was months ago, and I thought "Oh my God." I'm a Christian and I believe in God and Jesus, and I know that he wants you to assemble. But our beliefs haven't changed.

Tina, who lost her home and belongings, was very upset with her Catholic church for not supporting her during the disaster. No one from the church ever visited her at her FEMA trailer or expressed any concern about her situation. She explained her relationship with her church: "There is still strain, but we stayed. The structure, church, is irrelevant and always has been to us, but with children you need a specific area to go to and a doctrine for them to comprehend." Dana also did not attend church much after the flood because she lacked the "ambition" to get up early and drive a long distance:

> Religion has never been real important to me. When I was younger we had a pastor who would just yell, and he would scare the crap out of us! I think that is why I really never got into it. But Gary takes the kids to church every Sunday. I wouldn't say that I don't believe. It's just not an important thing in my life. It has probably gotten worse since the flood. It's that ambition thing again. Getting up on a Sunday morning when you don't want to. And it's not five minutes away anymore. It's a little ways away now.

Karen, whose husband became abusive toward her after the flood, also felt that going to church was not that important to her, but she decided not to attend services for her safety and the safety of her children:

> My belief is more important to me that my religion. Culturally, in this area, church affiliation is somewhat important for social reasons. I think it's particularly important for the kids because their friends are there, which is not the only reason I do it, but it's a factor. They learn things that are value based about being nice to people and kindness, and a bunch of things that are good. I'm not a big churchgoer. I don't take the kids now because Greg goes to all the services now in hopes of seeing us, so I'd have to switch churches.

Liz had been very active in her church but stopped going to church a few years before the flood because she found out that her brother had been molested by the minister at her church. She said, "Organized religion, it's too much of a betrayal. But my spiritual beliefs are strong and brought me through this." Some of the women who attended church less frequently after the flood by their own choice found that decision to be somewhat liberating. They sheepishly admitted that they had not attended church but did not seem particularly sorry to miss the services. And they even seemed pleasantly surprised by their bold move of not attending church on Sunday, especially if their families did attend.

A few women found that they were more attached to their church and attended services more often after the flood. One church in town, the Catholic church on the University of North Dakota campus, was partially destroyed in a fire several months before the flood, and then it was completely flooded and destroyed in the flood. It took months to rebuild it. Services were held in another church or in a lecture hall on campus. Sabrina, a mother of two and a resident of Grand Forks for three years, felt very attached to this place of worship:

> Last Sunday the priest took us on a walk by the old church, and they were starting new construction, and he wanted us to pray over the construction. So we walk over there, and we see the evidence of the flood and the fire. And to walk around it, I got emotional. I said, "I must be premenstrual or something because I am feeling very moved by this whole thing, and I'm like, it must be close to my period, because I am very sensitive." It was like, "Oh my God," I had never realized the intensity. They had totally taken the roof off. You could really see the charredness on the inside. The structure was intact; it just looked like an old boarded up church before, but now you can see the black. It looks like ruins. It was like, *Oh My God*.

To make the situation more traumatic, the church transferred Sabrina's priest out of state, leaving them, as Sabrina said, "without a leader." Carol also felt emotional about her church being rebuilt:

> When we went to the church, there were all these volunteers from all over the country, three pews full. They had cleaned out the church, and we all stood and clapped and cried. I don't think there was a dry eye in the house, men or women.

Some women were sorry that they could not participate in the rebuilding of their church. Lorna, for example, said, "I felt really torn. You want to give to your home, you feel you need to give to your church, you feel like you need to give to your work, and yet you couldn't give to all those things."

Sandy, who had a traumatic flood experience, felt her church was critical to her recovery: "I've gone to mass every morning, and pray that God will put me where he wants me. The Church has been a source of spiritual strength." Diana, who is Jewish, at first remarked that her feelings about her faith and her synagogue did not change as a result of the flood. Then, as she thought about it, she admitted that since the flood she had taken her first leadership position in her synagogue. She wondered if maybe that did mean something, that she felt more connection to her place of worship and her religious community. Louise also felt more connected to her religious community, a Unitarian Universalist church, and evacuated, along with several other families from her church, to the home of a fellow church member. When the church members were all back in town, they reunited by holding a potluck dinner.

Cindy and her family created their own place of worship when they could not get to their church. They had evacuated with two other families to a friend's house thirty miles outside of town. With more than twenty people there, they decided to hold their own Sunday services:

> We actually had church ourselves. With all the other families, we are all very musical and have always been in the choir together for years, and they have a piano and an organ. So on Sundays we would set aside a time, and it was encouraging and supporting. In fact, we have a flood survivor reunion with those families. We're planning a little potluck. We were able to be there for each other, cry, support each other, hear each other's stories.

Months later when she was able to return to her church, Cindy felt that it was a "place to vent and share and be heard again, and it was a lot calmer than town hall meetings." Cecilia and her family could not attend services for a month but then attended regularly. She enjoyed hearing church member's stories of how they had "seen the Lord work in their lives" during the flood.

Many churches geared their services for many months on dealing with the flood, the recovery, and the emotional losses. In the religious services I attended during my visits, the sermons focused on issues from the flood, such as healing, grief, and forgiveness. Several women who had no flood damage felt that they overdid this. Kimberlee commented, "There is a point where people need to move on. Sermons *every Sunday*. I know people need to talk about it, but it seems like venting and obsessing. *Move on.*" Genie, who suffered from depression after the flood, found it helpful to have the sermons focus on the flood. One Sunday, her minister at their evangelical church spoke about depression. "[He] said that depression was very normal in a big disaster, and that you don't get depressed right away, you get it later, after the work had been done." These words were comforting to Genie as it reassured her that she was not alone in her struggle with depression and that it was a normal reaction to such a crisis. Lydia found it helpful when her minister spoke about marital conflicts during the flood:

> [He] kept saying that there has been so much fighting because you're so tense and so worn out and everything is major, even minor things become major episodes. We were both aware of what was going on, but then to hear our minister say that there's more of this bickering between spouses because of the tension involved, and the exhaustion. That made us feel better to know that it was a reaction, and it was not normal, but it was happening.

Since Lydia and her husband had been fighting, these sermons were especially comforting to know that conflict with your spouse was a common response to the situation.

As sociologists have long reported, the social institutions of family and religion are among the most important for social stability and cohesiveness (Bellah 1970; Bellah et al. 1985; Coltrane 1998). In Grand Forks, the women found their relationships to their families, and especially to their spouses if they were married, were strong determinants of how the flood affected them overall. Whereas some women experienced more conflicts with their family members, others thought the flood was a bonding experience. For some women, the family conflicts were more severe and the conflicts more profound. Religion was also an important coping strategy for some women. Other women received support from their religious community and relied heavily on their own spiritual beliefs during the disaster. Some women, on the other hand, did not get support from their church, and others felt that their beliefs did not play a large role in their coping. The findings show that the women's feelings about their own spirituality and their relationships with their place of worship are complicated and varied, and would benefit from further study.

Chapter 8

Domestic Violence

Two facts are generally undisputed regarding the abuse women receive from their intimate male partners. First, the home is not always a safe place.[1] Second, because woman battering frequently occurs in the context of the home and is stigmatized, it is a largely invisible offense (Belknap 1996). However, the phenomenon of woman battering is so widespread that it is considered by some scholars the most frequent form of family violence. Indeed, it has long been recognized that calls related to woman battering are among the most common police calls. Yet research on woman battering was almost nonexistent until the second wave of the feminist movement in the 1970s.

Unlike the other chapters of the book, this chapter presents case studies of two women, Karen and Liz. While these two women were the only women who spoke to me about their experiences with domestic violence, there may have been other women in my study who also experienced this violence. Due to the stigma and invisibility and what is known about woman battering rates, it is likely that other women in my study were also battered but did not report it to me or anybody else. Indeed, Karen did not reveal her situation to me until our third face-to-face interview, after we had known each other for over a year and exchanged phone calls and letters, a time period that illustrates the need for us to establish a relationship of trust before she could confide in me.

In this chapter, I begin by presenting the two case studies of woman battering in my study in Grand Forks, allowing you to hear Liz's and Karen's stories directly, thereby letting their voices contribute to the conversation on domestic violence in disasters.[2] As social scientists know, police records, official statistics, and even survey research results do not often match the stories told by women who have been victims of physical violence, and thus it is critical that we let women speak for themselves (Erez and Belknap 1998). It was through such traditional grassroots efforts, from listening to women, that wife abuse was first uncovered in the early 1970s (Gelles 1997). It makes sense, therefore, that listening to women now will help us to discover how intimate violence plays out in a disaster. Second, I discuss the information gathered from the Grand Forks domestic violence organization, the Community Violence Intervention Center, to give a larger context to the woman battering situation in Grand Forks.

Karen's Story

On a hot day in July, 1998, I went to see Karen in her new home, the dorms at the University of North Dakota. I walked upstairs and knocked gently at her door. Karen, a bubbly, petite woman with a big smile, led me into her small family housing apartment. She had filled it with handmade crafts and quilts and embroidered pillows. The room was full, even stuffed, with belongings, but it was neat and decorative. Despite the gray cinder block walls of the dormitory apartment, Karen had managed to make it feel cozy and homelike. She moved hurriedly around the room, turning off the television, moving her son's backpack from the chair, pouring lemonade for both of us. She talked quickly as she moved about the room. She was not nervous, just an energetic woman. Karen and I have met many times over the last few years, and she was comfortable having me there. While we had talked about various parts of her experience in the flood, we never talked about domestic violence, and I never suspected it based on her previous accounts. Now she has changed her mind: she has decided to tell me about what happened to her after the flood. She has decided to tell me about being battered by her husband.

Karen is a forty-two-year-old white woman who has lived in Grand Forks her entire life. She is a college-educated high school teacher who has been married for twenty years and has two children, ages six and thirteen. She and her family lived in a modest, well-kept, two-story wood frame house on a quiet tree-lined street of single-family homes. The family members, who were evacuated in the flood, were not physically hurt. When they returned to their home several weeks later, however, they found that their basement level, which had been their family room and the hub of family activity, was lost in the flood waters. In addition, Karen's elderly in-laws lost their home and all of their belongings.

Things were very tense around the house, Karen explained to me. Greg, Karen's husband, became more and more angry—at the flood, at the city, at the Corps of Engineers, at his family, and most of all, at his wife. Karen assumed that his anger would subside as time passed, when the town and their home were rebuilt. Instead, Greg's anger grew with each month following the flood. Indeed, a year after the flood his anger erupted into violence, and he began beating Karen. She explained how the situation began:

> Over the last year, almost every day, it's been sort of a slow onset of sort of a paranoia about, first of all, other men, of which there are none. And then he started getting more aggressive about it, going through my work papers. It got so bad that I couldn't go anywhere. He's never had a very good temper, but it's gotten really bad. Pretty much isolates me from my family. The first year after we were married there was an incident, but nothing until now.

While he had always had a bad temper and was always highly critical of her, Greg had not been physically abusive to Karen in almost twenty years, and she had not contemplated leaving until the physical violence began after the flood. She explained how she decided to leave:

> The crystallizing incident took place on Mother's Day, May 9. That's when Greg was pushing me, and Jonathan walked in and lunged to defend me. He had a clenched fist, ready to hit his dad. He looked like he *wanted* to hit him. . . . My son had had enough of his yelling. He [Greg] yelled at him daily. I think Jonathan felt like, "That's my mom, and I'm going to protect her." I realized I had to go.

Karen's thirteen-year-old son Jonathan wanted to protect his mother, and he also told Karen that he wanted them to get away from his father. Many children in domestic violence situations become very protective of their mothers, and their willingness to leave a violent father helps the woman decide to leave (Dobash and Dobash 1979; Ferraro and Johnson 1983).

In Karen's description of what was happening in her home, we learn that the flood may have been a major contributing factor to the onset of the violence. She described how the flood affected her husband:

> He likes things ordered. And when things are out of order, he doesn't like it. So the flood was a nightmare for him. It's not like his temperament completely changed with the flood, but I definitely do consider us to be a flood casualty. The flood did bring on his anger.

Karen continued her story:

> He was kind of already on that path. He's always had a short fuse. He was getting worse with age instead of better. I can't explain that. His anger was always thinly veiled, and he was always highly critical, picking on me all the time.

After the violent attacks, Karen decided to leave. She moved out and got a restraining order. She explained how it felt to have left the situation:

> I got a protection order that he violated three times. Now he's being charged by the state with stalking. He can't do too many more things before he ends up in jail. I haven't regretted my decision to leave for a minute. It's so much better now. Nobody wants to do this, but in the long run it's better for everybody. I feel like a huge weight has been lifted.

Several months after Karen left Greg, she reflected back on her experience:

> You know, when I used to think about women who were victims of abuse, that if you were privileged to some extent, then your experience would be vastly different. And now I think not. I think not. Because no amount of privilege can stop that person. You know? I am no better off than an uneducated, poor, Native American, ethnic woman. I am no better off really in that respect. Apparently, when a man in our society gets in that mindset, there is so much latitude for them to act out, to do damage that a reasonable person can't imagine would be allowed to continue. You can be smart, articulate, educated, competent, but it doesn't matter, it doesn't help.

Karen came to the difficult realization that being somewhat affluent and educated did not protect her from her husband's violence, no matter her race or economic background. She was acknowledging her own vulnerability, the vulnerability of all women in our society, and the power differences between men and women. Karen noted that she was also vulnerable financially:

> Somewhere in the last year he started putting money somewhere. I think he was hiding it. I've never been somebody that worries that much about money. The truth is that my name is not on any of our assets. I don't know how that happened. It's just not something that I attended to.

Yet despite her financial concerns, Karen did have resources available to her, including middle-class family members who were willing and able to take her in and support her. In addition, with her educational background and occupational status, she knew that her job was secure. These factors may have helped Karen to leave immediately after the beatings, something many battered women are not able to do. Thus, while Karen's status did not protect her from becoming a battered woman, it did help her successfully deal with the situation once she was in it.

Karen felt that the flood brought on the violence, but that in a way that was good, in that she could deal with it sooner rather than later. In a conversation I had with Karen a year and a half after the flood, she expressed regret that she did not leave Greg earlier because he had been mean to her and the children for years. She believed that if the flood had not brought on the violent incident, there would have been a more violent and more dangerous incident down the road. She explained:

> I think when you're living in it you make all kinds of excuses. You try to find a way to frame it that is not quite as damaging. You have to rationalize it or you can't stay. There you are one day, with your kid thinking they have to beat their dad to protect you. I really think someone in my family would've gotten hurt. Maybe me, maybe one of my kids. I would rather have it be me. And considering that, it's better sooner than later. . . . I think I stayed too long. I should have known better. But, now, I'm really excited about what I'm doing now, and my kids are safe.

Karen felt the Community Violence Intervention Center was very useful for her, helping her get a protection order and providing counseling services when she needed them.

Two years after the flood, Karen was living in a small apartment with her two children, working, and going to school at night for an advanced degree. She lived in fear as Greg continued to stalk her, drive by her apartment late at night, and follow her in his car; on one occasion he broke her door and entered her apartment. It is difficult, if not impossible, to know if his violence would have occurred if the flood had not happened. Karen believed it probably would have happened but maybe further in the future. The important thing to consider is that Karen needed assistance—a protection order, counseling, housing—in the midst of the disaster crisis. Without this assistance she might not have been able to leave or keep herself and her children safe. When I left her apartment that hot July day, I felt worried for Karen, for the crisis was not over. But I also felt hopeful, for she felt fortunate that she got out when she did, and she felt optimistic and determined about her future and the future of her children.

Liz's Story

Liz is a likeable woman, a chain smoker with a hearty laugh and a raspy voice. She is friendly and looks you right in the eye when talking to you. You have no doubt that she is telling it to you straight. Liz, like Karen, is a Grand Forks native, white, and in her early forties, but she is less privileged than Karen in many ways. Liz is from a working-class background and is disabled from a central nervous system disorder leaving her unable to walk without assistance and unable to work. She went to high school but never to college. She grew up in an abusive household and has been in abusive relationships since she was a teenager. Fred, her partner of the last nine years, and husband of the last two, has beaten her many times, and she had been to the hospital with serious injuries on several occasions. Liz described a particularly bad beating two weeks before their wedding that left her hospitalized:

> I came home from shopping, and he was intoxicated. I didn't start screaming, I didn't start yelling. I asked him to leave. The police had told me not to confront him. He began throwing

things, screaming at me, threatening to kill me. Then he lunged at me, and he grabbed me by the collar of my shirt and started shaking me. I remember screaming at him, "You're killing me!" Then I lost consciousness. When I came to, I was on the recliner, and he was hitting me on the head with his fist and screaming at me. At this point I was going in and out of consciousness. . . . The police took me to the hospital, and people were staring at me. My neck was so swollen, my face was so swollen, I think I was in shock. He nearly severed my spinal cord. The doctors said had he shaken me one more time, he would have severed my spinal cord, and I would have been dead. They called the counseling center, and the advocate came, the poor girl, and I was her first call ever. I felt so bad for her.

Liz told me this story the first time I met her, sitting at a booth in a Chinese restaurant in Grand Forks in the summer of 1997. The details of the beating and the relationship were upsetting, but she seemed to want to tell the story and explain what happened in her life. After relaying the story of beating just two weeks before the wedding, Liz paused, and, as if anticipating what might be asked next, explained why she decided to go through with her marriage to Fred:

The invitations were out, and he said it would never happen again. This is someone you love, you want to believe it is the last time. But, I mean, I just can't tell you why I went ahead with the wedding. I mean I really can't answer that question, because I don't know why I did. But I did.

After the wedding, Liz continued to suffer extensive physical abuse:

The police have been to our house so many times, it isn't even funny. I mean, he is a man that has nearly killed me I don't know how many times. . . . But I have always been minimizing the physical abuse. I repressed a lot of the memories of the beatings—until the flood; then all the memories came back.

Despite the beatings, Liz was emotionally attached to Fred and did not have the confidence or independence to leave him. She explained that she felt afraid when she was not in a relationship.

Just before the flood, Fred entered a residential drug and alcohol treatment program. Therefore, Liz was on her own during the flood and had to deal with a difficult evacuation period and the loss of her home by herself. Her basement apartment was flooded with ten feet of water and raw sewage. In photos she showed me of the damage, the walls, furniture, and carpet appeared to be painted black but actually were covered with sludge from the flood waters. The apartment, which tested positive for a variety of bacteria, had to be gutted, and all the contents were thrown away. She described her feelings about the loss:

> The night I got into town, the third of May, was when I found out that I had lost everything. I mean, I was about as vulnerable as I could be. It's been terrifying, especially when I've been hungry, and there is no money. And I didn't have the money to replace anything.

Liz had to face the destruction of the flood in addition to the continuing crisis of poverty. She believed that surviving the flood without Fred was how she discovered she was strong and competent enough to leave him. She discussed her newfound strength:

> But I've been really lucky with the flood. I've learned so many good things through this. I have really worked on myself and reevaluated things. I've taken the flood as an opportunity to grow personally. I have found an inner strength that will carry me through anything. How else could I have made it through this? I now know that I can count on myself. I can trust myself. It's been painful, and I've been lonely. . . . I still love him with all my heart, and there are many things about him that are very wonderful, but there's his dark side, and that dark side will cost me my life. I'm just not willing to pay that price anymore.

The experience empowered Liz and gave her a sense that she could make it on her own, something she never believed before. For Liz, the flood required dealing not only with violence and poverty, but also with a physical disability. In my conversations with Liz, she discussed how her disability affected her flood experience, describing here her evacuation with her twenty-one-year-old daughter, her son-in-law, and her two young grandchildren:

> When my daughter and I evacuated, we went to the air base. But they wouldn't take me because they said all of their accommoda-

tions for people with disabilities were full. So they turned us away. They told me to get in my car and keep going. . . . So we drove on to Devil's Lake, and the shelter there said the same thing. No accommodations for me. We couldn't believe it. And I have no proof if they were actually full or not, or if they didn't want to deal with extra needs. We go on to Rugby, same thing, we got turned away. It was about one-thirty in the morning and we pulled into Minot. . . . They told us that they weren't giving any assistance to Grand Forks flood victims, and we should get back in our cars. . . . I said, "Where am I supposed to go?" . . . And I'm standing there in my *pajamas.*

Liz eventually found a place to stay until her apartment was rebuilt, but her disability posed additional problems. She explained how her disability affected her ability to leave the town where her abuser lives:

I've had to get over my stubborn will and realize that I have a chronic illness that is progressive. I live with intense physical pain and intense physical symptoms that I can't control. I don't have a choice there, but I have to learn to listen to my body. And when it says stop, I have to stop. That's one of the reasons I can't leave here, even though [Fred's] here. My doctor's here, and I can't start all over finding doctors. And I need to be near my daughter because she knows how to take care of me.

As Chenoweth (1996) found in her work, women with disabilities need to combat their isolation and exclusion to avoid being victims of male violence. Liz continued her story and acknowledged that the Grand Forks Violence Intervention Center and Amelia, a staff member there, helped her tremendously:

When he got back to town, I'd call Amelia all the time. Boy, did I need them then. If I couldn't make it in, we'd do the counseling over the phone. I used this time for personal growth. It wasn't easy. Had the center not been there, or my daughter, you know, I wouldn't have made it. There were times in the middle of the night when I've needed the center and called. I can't give up my counseling when I'm in the same town as my husband.

In addition to noting the importance of the Violence Intervention Center, Liz also was admitting that the flood, and the struggles involved in recovering from it, may have had positive consequences. Other women in this study expressed positive consequences of the disaster, such as new skills acquired and personal strength and confidence discovered. Liz revealed how her personal growth and inner strength carried her through the disaster and how, with the help of the battered women's organization, she was able to leave a life of violence. She described how she felt to be free from battering, over a year after the disaster:

> For the first time in my life, I feel free. I can go where I want. I can do what I want. I don't have to look over my shoulder anymore. I don't come home, turn the key in the lock, and get beaten. Now I can do whatever I want. No one is going to tell me you can't do that. And no one is telling me I'm ugly, and no one is telling me that the world is falling apart 'cause of something I did.

The flood disaster may actually have been the catalyst Liz needed to leave the abusive relationship and gain a better awareness of herself. Ferraro and Johnson (1983) found that catalyst events are important for helping women leave batterers. Yet while Liz was free of the violence, she still faced extreme poverty after the flood. Liz described her situation:

> I'm applying for disability, and, boy, I hope I get it. I have no income. I can't eat three times a day. I just go hungry. Luckily I do get a housing voucher because of the domestic violence. I lost all my clothes, my furniture, everything. I mean, I have no money, no money. I have $3.96 in my checking account.

A year after the flood, Liz was back in her basement apartment, living on her own, and had just started to receive disability payments. She was still seeking counseling to help her hold on to her new strength and keep Fred from reentering her life. Looking at her experience with the domestic violence and the disaster, Liz contemplated what had happened:

> I'm starting a new life. So I'm going to take that flood, and all that abuse, and when the flood waters left Grand Forks, well, *that was my old life leaving*. All the abuse left with the water. That's how I look at it.

Research has found that battered women often have low self-esteem and a very poor self-image, both of which contribute to their feelings of dependence and powerlessness (Gelles 1997). Therefore, if a disaster provides an opportunity for a shift in one's view of oneself and an increase in self-confidence—in other words, a redefinition of the self—then such a catalyst could encourage women to leave domestic violence. As Liz explained to me, the disaster put things in perspective and forced her to determine what is important in life. Enarson and Morrow (1997) found in their work on Hurricane Andrew that one woman planned to use disaster assistance money to buy a bus ticket out of town and out of an abusive relationship. Thus, disasters can provide, both financially and psychologically, an opportunity to leave an abusive relationship. On the flip side, because of financial and emotional pressures, many women cannot leave batterers during a time of crisis.

Services and Resources

The Community Violence Intervention Center, the organization for battered women in Grand Forks, provided me with information illustrating how the demand for services in the disaster increased even as resources were depleted. The center provides many battered women's services, including crisis counseling, legal referrals, and assistance with obtaining protection orders. The center was completely destroyed in the flood. The staff lost everything in their offices, including their furniture, phones, and computers, and they had to hand dry their clients' records. In 1997, at the time of the flood, the center did not run a shelter for battered women, but shared with a shelter for the homeless, a situation far from ideal. In 2000, the center opened their own shelter, a "beautiful facility," to serve battered women and their children.[3]

The Community Violence Intervention Center found their services in demand after the flood. In July 1997 they had a 21 percent increase in all the services they provided, a 159 percent increase in the Abuse and Rape Crisis Program's services to ongoing clients, and a 29 percent increase in the number of Abuse and Rape Crisis Program clients. They saw a small increase in the number of crisis line calls. Compared to the usual average of forty calls a month, they received forty-two calls in June 1997 and forty-four calls in July 1997. They found significant increases in the services provided to clients they already served, but not a lot of new clients. The center had to relocate approximately five times after the flood, making it extremely difficult for new and existing clients to find them.

The number of protection orders, issued to protect women from their perpetrators, can also be used as evidence of the demand for services. The Community Violence Intervention Center found that prior to the flood, during the period of January to March 1997, twenty protection orders were issued by the local courts. However, after the flood, from January to March 1998, thirty-three protection orders were filed to protect women in domestic violence situations, a substantial increase. One of the social workers at the center also reported that there had been an increase in the number of battered women who needed to be treated in the emergency room, showing that the severity of battering had increased. To measure available resources, we can analyze the number of volunteer hours, the total amount of time given to the center by local residents who volunteer their time. In the first time period, January to March 1997, volunteers gave 3,475 hours to the Center, while in the second time period, January to March 1998, they were only able to give 1,903 hours of their time.

An increase in the number of protection orders may be explained in several ways. The increase may indicate an increase in violence, a greater propensity to report the violence, or a woman's greater inability to handle the violence on her own. No matter what the explanation, the increase in protection orders clearly represents an increase in workload for the center's employees. In addition, volunteer hours were down, even six months after the event, as volunteers were still working on repairing their own homes and lives. With fewer volunteers to help in the office, the staff faced even more work.

The staff had additional work for several other reasons. The homeless shelter, which served battered women, was lost in the flood, so staff had to find housing for battered women at local motels. This was a difficult task, considering that most residents of the city were also in need of housing at that time. In addition, there was the increased need for other services, from existing and new clients. They also told me that some women, not having any other resources, called their batterers for assistance during the disaster and as a result found themselves back in an abusive relationship after the flood. Since housing was such a problem after the flood, the staff found that some women let abusers live with them, while other women moved in with their abusers. The staff also reported that the local jail released some batterers during the evacuation period, an action that frightened and angered the battered women and the center staff. This occurrence is important because it illustrates the community's role in enabling the violence.

Understanding Domestic Violence

Little is known about the issue of domestic violence in a natural disaster context.[4] Many who work in the field and study the issue report that woman battering does increase following a disaster.[5] In nondisaster times, battered women are often overlooked as victims by the public at large, the criminal processing system (for example, the police and court professionals), and service and health agencies and professionals (for example, physicians, social workers),[6] so it is possible that they are overlooked after disasters as well. Wilson, Phillips and Neal (1998) report that the community, domestic violence, and disaster organizations in their study that were aware of the existence and extent of domestic violence prior to the disaster were more sensitive to the presence of postdisaster violence.

Therefore, if a community defines domestic violence as a problem predisaster, it will be more able to identify and respond to it following the event. Wilson et al. (1998) argue, then, that a community's ignorance of a domestic violence problem could increase women's vulnerability and possibly contribute to more injuries and deaths after a disaster. Enarson (1998) found that most grassroots women's organizations are not prepared for a disaster and that few domestic violence programs participate in local or regional disaster planning groups, although many are interested in increasing their disaster readiness. Australian social service workers advocate that disaster workers be trained and become informed on issues of woman battering in order to be prepared for increases in this violence during disasters (Honeycombe 1993; Dobson 1994). Thus, domestic violence organizations are ill prepared for a disaster, and disaster organizations and communities are poorly prepared for domestic violence situations in disasters.

There have been numerous attempts to understand the causes of battering. While there is a strong history of blaming the victims for the battering perpetrated against them (see, for example, Dobash and Dobash 1979; Tong 1984), more recent research has attempted to understand what places men (and women) at risk of becoming batterers or escalating their existing battering practices. Some disaster research has found that men use more alcohol after a disaster (Green 1993), a combination that some believe would increase domestic violence rates (Pleck 1987). Yet Kantor and Straus (1987) examined the role of alcohol as a cause of woman battering and concluded that while excessive drinking is associated with higher woman battering rates, alcohol use is not an immediate antecedent of battering. Dutton (1988) identified the excuses and justifications batterers frequently use to deny wrongness and responsibility for their battering behavior. Dutton found that batterers use situational characteristics, such as being drunk or fired from a job, to excuse their behavior, and characteristics about the victims, such as not having dinner ready or allegedly having an affair, to justify their abuse.

Thus, a disaster crisis could be used in this manner, to excuse the batterers' behavior, essentially blaming the flood for their loss of control. For example, Morrow and Enarson (1996) interviewed one woman whose husband beat her so badly that she had to be hospitalized. The husband supposedly lost control because he could not handle the effects of the flood, which included losing household belongings, not having enough food to eat, and losing his job, because his business was destroyed in the flood (Enarson 1998). Experts in the field maintain that perpetrators are very much in control: crisis conditions do not cause the abuse, nor do they cause men to lose control. Gelles (1997) notes that stressful social factors such as poverty and illness may be related to violence and abuse but that abuse would not occur if there was not widespread social and cultural approval of violence in the home.

Some women may be more at risk for woman battering than others. In addition, social status and resources affect the subsequent vulnerability of those who are battered. For example, women with disabilities may be more vulnerable to battering and are much more likely than women generally to be victims of physical and sexual assault; almost all the perpetrators are men who are known to the women (Sobsey 1994). These women face a high incidence of violence and abuse in their lives because they are seen as being of little worth, invisible, and less than human (Chenoweth 1996). In addition, the violence that disabled women experience is largely unknown and invisible as they often experience societal marginalization, powerlessness, and exclusion (Chenoweth 1996). In disasters, therefore, disabled women may be at increased risk for battering.

Poor women are also more at risk. In disasters in general, research has found that poor women's concerns are not taken seriously, and they lack the resources and support necessary for recovery and reconstruction.[7] Poor women may also be more vulnerable to battering. Schwartz (1988) argues that "universal risk" theories are so popular, as a result of efforts to see women as a unified group under patriarchy and to repudiate past class biases in research, that researchers have overlooked how working- and middle-class women have distinct experiences with battering. In fact, empirical studies have shown that there is more woman battering in families with low income and low socioeconomic status (Okun 1986). Schwartz (1988) argues that if you examine the effects of both patriarchy and capitalism, it is clear that there is not a universal risk to all women but that socioeconomic status is related to chances of victimization and consequent treatment and resources. Thus, some women *are* more vulnerable than others.

Disaster studies have found that disaster events can affect relationships between men and women and their views on social roles. Ketteridge and Fordham (1998) found that women, many of whom had gained a new self-confidence during a flood disaster, separated from unsupportive partners. This finding is relevant because many women in battering relationships lack the confidence to leave their abusers (Gelles 1997). Alway et al. (1998) found that men's role as protector and provider is threatened in a disaster, a pertinent finding considering that domestic violence concerns issues of male dominance and control. Davis and Ender (1999) found that married couples who reported strong relationships prior to a disaster reported their relationships were stronger after the disaster. In contrast, couples that reported weak relationships prior to the disaster generally reported that their relationships were even weaker after the disaster.[8] Interestingly, Davis and Ender found the stronger couples experienced more tension and strain during the disaster, while the weaker couples reported feeling closer during the acute period of the disaster. While their results do not address domestic violence specifically, they do touch on some relevant issues concerning conflict between intimate partners.

Woman battering situations are diverse and complex. Knowing and examining the full social and individual context of a battered woman's life is considered essential to understanding her domestic violence circumstances and choices. In this chapter, I emphasized the context of woman battering in disasters, using two case studies to shed light on the realities of two women's lives, thereby showing not the frequency but the range and variation of the kinds of problems women will face in a disaster. As shown in this chapter, whether the rates of domestic violence increase or not, there is an increase in the demand for services for women who are victims of battering in a disaster.

Chapter 9

The Re-Creation
of Domestic Culture

Historically, the private domain of the home has been women's domain. As discussed in previous chapters, women have long been associated with the private sphere and men with the public sphere. Specifically, women have traditionally been responsible for childcare, food preparation, and household maintenance such as laundry and shopping. In addition, women have traditionally been responsible for preserving, maintaining, and transmitting "domestic culture," a term I use to capture the norms, values, routines, foods, ceremonies, and artifacts of family life. For example, maintaining domestic culture could entail making a family meal every evening and preparing special foods for a Christmas dinner.

Women are especially likely to be the transmitters of culture during times of threatening and adverse social conditions, such as religious persecution, slavery, and other times of oppression and crisis (Jacobs 1996). During times of slavery, for example, African American women maintained African rituals to preserve an African identity. While most of the research on women's roles as transmitters of culture has involved political crises, this work is also applicable to natural disasters. However, no research has been conducted previously on this aspect of women's roles.

The women of Grand Forks were re-creators of domestic culture after the 1997 flood. They took responsibility for preserving and re-creating their preflood domestic culture. In Grand Forks, the need to preserve domestic culture became significant as families lost all the markers of their previous lives: homes, belongings, neighborhoods, churches and synagogues, schools,

parks, community centers, and shops. The women of Grand
Forks talked about their desire to re-create the domestic culture
that existed for their families prior to the flood. They often spoke
of their homes and neighborhoods with nostalgia and needed to
fill the void when their homes and belongings were lost.[1] They
felt that their homes, belongings, and the routines of life that
played out in the home were sacred to them, and they believed
that it was their job to re-create them or negotiate new versions
of them. I found that the women re-created three main areas of
domestic culture: (1) *place,* a family's actual physical space, which
is the sacred home; (2) *time,* the rituals, routines, and the other
ways that a family organizes their time and spends time together;
and (3) *objects,* the things or artifacts that symbolize the family's
culture. In this chapter I will examine these three areas of domestic culture and the meanings associated with them.

The Home as Sacred Space

The place component is perhaps the most important aspect of
domestic culture as the home is constructed as a sacred space to
most Americans. For women, the home is a place set apart as holy,
a place of belonging and reverence, a place they where they feel
connected to others—in the past, present, and future. The home is
an extension of the women's self, so that losing their home threat-
ens their core identity as wife, mother, and woman. In writings on
the homeless, researchers find that a home symbolizes one's sense
of self and one's sense of belonging. Women without a home are
conceptualized as out of place, and they must struggle to maintain
an authentic sense of self (Liebow 1993; Hatty 1996).

In Grand Forks, as in most of the United States, the domestic
domain was women's space and responsibility. Women spoke rever-
entially of their lost homes because their homes were more than
buildings; they were places with meaning and memories. Addie, a
homemaker in her sixties whose house was destroyed, expressed
why a home is so meaningful:

> Because over the years it provides a lot of security and warmth, for
> who knows how many people. You have your family and your rel-
> atives and your friends, and all the things you do there. Gradua-
> tions, barbecues. So then you have to think, "What is it? Is it just

A month after the flood, the city engineers and the Army Corps of Engineers began the difficult work of establishing new dike lines that would determine which homes, schools, and neighborhoods would have to be demolished. At the same time, Grand Forks Mayor Pat Owens banned scavengers from picking through flood debris and destroyed belongings that families placed by the curbs. The home shown here, in the Lincoln Drive neighborhood, was lifted off its foundation and dropped on the resident's car. *Photo by Alice Fothergill.*

the material things? Or is it the people and the things that you have done in your home?"

Others also commented on how they viewed their homes. For example, Karen, a teacher and mother of two children, explained that "home is the place where life is played out day to day." Lydia, a realtor in her sixties, said, "My home is my life. It is where I raised my three children; the home is mine." Liz, whose basement apartment was completely destroyed, commented, pointing to her chest, "Home is what's in here. Home isn't the possessions we surround ourselves with. It's the feeling we have in here, when we're home." Carol, a middle-class homemaker, smiled as she recalled how much she had adored the home they lost, even though it had some problems and they had briefly considered moving before the flood:

> In our home we did not have a second bathroom on our main floor, and part of the basement was only six feet two so our son was always ducking because he is six feet four and a half. But we *loved* our little house. We put in a patio and a deck, and it was *us*. Last summer we were thinking of moving so he wasn't ducking all the time. We found a house, but our sixteen-year-old sat and cried and said, "We can't leave this place!" Every corner of this house and yard says *us*. We'd redone it all contemporary. I spent two months painting all the woodwork in it, very contemporary, very crisp and clean. It was incredible, just a fun-looking house, and the patio, just like a picture out the back window with the gardening and things.

Many made a distinction between a "house" and a "home."[2] Lydia, for example, worked long hours so that, as she stated, "Each day my *house* feels more like a *home* again." Lorna, the hospital manager, also remarked that in their new house they "try to make it look like a home." Amy Sue commented on her apartment that was lost in the flood, "Granted, I rent . . . it's my landlord's house, but it's my home." Myrna, eighty, lost her home of forty years and moved into an apartment: "It doesn't feel like home. It doesn't feel bad. It's a nice enough apartment, but it's not home." Addie agreed, commenting that she felt like she was "living in somebody else's house." Peggy, who also felt as if she was visiting somebody's house in her temporary apartment, kept thinking, "God, is it time for me to go home yet?" Sometimes very small changes made it feel like home again, as Martha Jo found when she put up her curtains: "It is amazing what it is psychologically to have them up. It adds a soft, homey, furnished feeling." Rachel, who had to move into college housing with her partner and children, referred to her home as a "nest" and was finding it difficult to deal with her child leaving for college at the same time she lost her home: "I was going through that empty nest stuff and still am, and I was trying to go through it when I didn't have a nest. The empty nest without the nest."

Carol and her family felt that the most important thing about their house was that their teenage son and his friends had a place to "hang out." So in their new postflood home, creating that space for their son was a critical piece of re-creating their domestic culture:

> We used to have six or seven big kids down in the basement, playing their music and stuff, and the kids lost that. Where else could they go? Movies cost too much. There was a refrigerator down there, and they thought it was like an apartment, and they said, "Your parents don't even come down here, except to bring food once in a while." Teenagers get going late at night, so they were down there, and all we heard was "tromp, tromp, tromp" when they left at midnight. At the new house, what we did was, it has a nice sized master bedroom, and for the next two years, we gave our son the master bedroom, and there's room in there for a couple of bean bags or something so he can have his friends over, so he'll kind of have that space again.

In addition to giving their son the largest room, Carol planned to begin making some improvements to the new house, and it did not seem to bother her that it would be "the same work that we did for the last thirteen years on the old one." This work would help make this new house more like the home they had to leave.

Peggy, who was pursuing a divorce after the flood, had trouble being as optimistic as Carol about leaving the home where she raised her children. Peggy explained that even though their house was condemned, she and her family were often drawn like a magnet to it and went down just to look at it. Some of the women went back during the summer to pick flowers and berries from their old yards even though the houses were condemned. It is clear from these stories that deciding what to do after the destruction of their homes was difficult for many of the women. Some were able to focus more on the work needed to be done to make new houses into homes while others, like Peggy, were still drawn back to their old homes, unable to let go.

Many of the women explained that they could not enter their destroyed houses because it was too emotionally upsetting. Some, like eighty-year-old Myrna, could barely bring herself to see the outside of the home. She explained, "I haven't gone in. I thought, I don't need that. I can remember it real well." Others also chose to concentrate on the memory of how it was prior to the flood. Some, like Addie, who lost her home, were willing to look at videos of their destroyed homes but would not go in them. Cecilia described her family's first look at their destroyed home: "We just walked around the house. We didn't go in. We just walked around. You could see the water line. None of us dared to go look in the house." When she and her husband decided to open the front door, they "held each other for awhile, and then we went in." Lorna, when she had to gut her family's destroyed home, felt that she had to distance herself from the task:

> I did help tear out the sheetrock. You had to distance yourself as you did it, because as you were sitting there with a crow bar, hacking away at the sheetrock, you had to not think about it. Because if you thought, "I am tearing apart my house," that was too depressing.

For Dana, a blue-collar mother of two young children, the loss of her home was so devastating that she could not bear to leave it. After the flood, she and her family lived in a small trailer in their yard next to their destroyed, abandoned home. Dana explained that she did not know how to rebuild their lives without their house.

In fact, many women wanted to rebuild their homes, but the city would not let them. Tina, the nurse who lost her Victorian house and lived in a trailer for a year, declared, "It is not my decision, whether or not it is condemned. Our house was classified as 90 percent damaged, so it is condemned, but it was not my decision." Liz, who is disabled and lost her basement apartment, showed her joy at having a home again:

> When I saw the walls up last week, I was practically dancing. The contractor was worried that I was going to fall down, and I said, "I don't care. I have walls, walls, walls!" I was so happy. He said that

he had done so many homes, and nobody quite had that reaction. He said that he realized that my reaction was what he was waiting for. He said, "You made my day." I hugged him, I really did!

For Liz and others who were able to rebuild their original homes, there was euphoria at each step of rebuilding, as it signified rebuilding their lives.

Many women anthropomorphisized their homes because they were the site of their familial and emotional lives. Diana, whose home suffered basement damage, stated that her home is "personified" because it "has human qualities to me." Sandy, an unemployed fifty-five-year-old, felt that the home was so sacred that it could be compared to a marriage:

> With my marriage, with all broken marriages, it's like a broken mirror. How do you fix a broken mirror? And it's like that with the houses in Grand Forks. Maybe they just can't be fixed. If my husband and I ever got back together, it would never be the same because the trust was broken. With the flood, Grand Forks is not going to be the same.

Karen, who was one of the victims of domestic violence, explained that if the homes in her neighborhood were people, she would "give them a hug," and relayed a comment that her young son, whose grandmother had just passed away, made to her when looking at the destroyed houses in his neighborhood: "They've all died, like Grandma."

In contrast to the emotional feelings women had over losing their homes, many did not feel upset over the loss of their workplaces, as there was no emotional attachment to those places. As Phoebe, a longtime director of a local social service agency to which she was deeply committed, commented:

> When my husband first saw [my destroyed office] on TV, he turned around and said, "Get in here and look at this!" The water was up to the sign, so it was up to the roof. So you knew the whole place was gone. My husband turns to me and says, "You can cry now if you want to." But I said, "It's a building." I said, "There is not one single person that we lost in town. Why am I going to cry over a building?" I never did get upset over the loss of that building.

As committed as she was to her work, the building was not a sacred place to her and thus not an emotional loss.

Many of the women felt a need to make new living spaces into a home before their children returned from having been evacuated to the homes of relatives and friends. Some of the concerns were health related, but many believed that there should be a feeling of warmth and familiarity in the new living quarters when the children arrived. Maria, a nurse and mother of four small children, explained how she felt when a family donated their farmhouse to her family for several months:

> So we walked into this house, and it was, like, I don't know, a gift from God. It was furnished, they had made up all the beds, they had stocked the fridge with milk and eggs and butter, and there were cooking utensils. They were our biggest angel. They said, "As long as you need to stay, you stay."

For most of the women, re-creating the home as a sacred space was primarily for their immediate family. They spoke of the needs of spouses and children for a place that felt familiar, private, and similar to the old home. However, there were situations in which women worked to re-create the home as a consecrated space for others. Jane, for example, was planning a wedding for her son just a few months after the flood. She felt the need to prepare the house for all the guests, mostly extended family, who would be coming to stay with them from out of state.

For many of the women, their sense of self and their identity was tied to their home, and they expressed "not feeling like themselves" when they were not at home. Peggy described this identity issue:

> There was a movie one time, where somebody came home and everything was gone. It was like a "Twilight Zone" or something, and everything was gone, and their whole identity and everything was gone. That is how I feel. Just weird. Weird. It feels like you're you but you're not.

Dana felt similarly when she lost her home: "It was like a standstill. It's hard to explain how it felt. Like a whole 'nother world. Like this isn't my life. That kind of thing." Many of the women tried to verbalize how their sense of themselves and safety was tied to their home. Pat articulated how her sense of security was shattered:

> I realized what a basic security is. Like, you should always be able
> to go home, and suddenly, home is not what is was before. Home
> is the place you should go to when *everything else is going wrong*.

Pat felt that she was lost when she could not go to her home, her
sanctuary. Erikson (1976), writing about the Buffalo Creek disaster,
also found that identity was tied to home, as the home is not simply "an expression of one's taste; it is the outer edge of one's per
sonality, a part of the self itself." And when they watched their
possessions being destroyed in the flood, the flood survivors "were
watching a part of themselves die" (p. 177). He argued that "urban
dwellers" would not understand the residents' attachment to a particular home or a set of rooms because they do not confuse their
own history, their own identity, with that of the structure that
houses them. Grand Forks residents may be more similar to Buffalo
Creek residents than to the idea of "urban dwellers," in that they do
not move frequently and are very attached to family homes.

Women in Grand Forks worked to normalize new family
places such as government trailers or temporary apartments. Some
women decorated temporary places, and some decided to wait until
they were in a more permanent place that could really become
home. Peggy explained the difficulties of making their temporary
apartment feel like home:

> We can't put things on the wall here. The landlords want you to
> use double sticky tape, not nails. I tried putting that thing on the
> wall, but it was up about ten minutes before it came down. It's
> just that everything is so *unfamiliar*.

Cecilia also tried to make her temporary trailer feel like home: "I
got that table cloth, and I put up that little quilt. I found some wall
decorations that I put up in the bedroom."

To make their homes sacred and meaningful again, the women
had to buy many items for their new accommodations or for their
old homes which had been gutted. Interestingly, they did not enjoy
shopping, despite the predominant theme of American con-
sumerism (Schor 1988) and stereotypes of white women's love of
shopping. Many reacted to this stereotype that women always want
to shop. Lisa stated:

I still have to buy all these things. There is this notion that all women want to do is shop. But I bet for most of them buying this stuff is not fun. Even if you have a generous budget. It doesn't matter. I can't tell you how many times I have been to Walmart in the last two weeks. It was not fun.

Tina, who lost her Victorian house in East Grand Forks, her cars, her furniture, and her clothes, reported a similar reaction to shopping:

People say, "Gosh, you *get* to buy all new things!" It's like, it is not *fun* to go shopping when you have to buy things that you never planned on buying again. Or buying vehicles because you *have* to buy vehicles, not because you want to, not because you actually have time to find what you want.

Peggy, a forty-five-year-old who lost her home and clothes, asserted similar feelings about having to go shopping:

We have a wedding to go to in August, and I've got to get something new to wear. All my clothes are gone. So I've got to get something to wear to that, and some shoes. I just don't feel like it. I just don't feel like it. Ordinarily I would be very happy about this, but I just don't want to go shopping. I just don't want to, but I'll have to, since I've got nothing to wear.

Marilyn, a middle-class secretary, took her daughter shopping, and they both felt awkward about all the "opulence" in the stores. To appease her two young children, Genie told them that buying new belongings was fun, although she was not convinced of it herself:

I tell the boys that bad things happen to good people. I say that I'm sorry that the flood happened. I said, but look at all the new stuff you get. You got a new bike and new toys, some new clothes, and Momma's gonna get some new furniture one day, and we got this nice new house. I told them that we were getting lots of new stuff, and they'll make lots of new friends in the neighborhood. I was really trying to accentuate the positive with them.

Liz also spoke to the issue that shopping does not replace meaningful items, as the items are not there: "A lot of people said, 'Oh, it must be so much fun; you get all this new stuff.' And I said, 'No, it's not fun, because all you want is what you had, and you can't find it.' Going shopping, I was looking for what I had, and it just wasn't there." The women were speaking to the idea that the re-creation of family space was not about buying things to replace what was lost. Rather, this process was about finding ways for a place to feel like home, reconstructing the more intangible ways people make a space a home.

An important part of creating a familial place was the desire to reprivatize lives. Many women felt that the disaster made their lives too public, especially when all their destroyed belongings sat on the berm, for all to see. Lisa explained:

> When the contents of everybody's houses was on the road, you could ride down the street and see some butt-ugly couches. I mean, one after the other of orange and black couches. Their whole life was exposed with those couches on the curb. You could drive down, and you realized that there was a lot of awful stuff they got out of there.

As discussed in earlier chapters, many of the residents spoke of how their Scandanavian background made them private people, making this public exposure all the more difficult. In addition to not having any privacy, evacuating to someone else's home meant you could not really make yourself at home. Maria, a nurse and mother of four, explained that she could not relax when she and her family stayed in her coworker's house:

> You don't feel like you do when you are in your own home. With the kids, I kept saying, "Don't put your glass there, it may leave a water mark!" You have to be more careful when it's other people's stuff. . . . They are starting to get those trailers ready. I'm hoping for one of those, so we could have our own space.

Maria's story illustrates the anxiety of not living in your own home, especially for those who had young children.

In addition to the lack of privacy in respect to outsiders, there was also the issue of having enough privacy within the home. For long periods of time, many families had to live in half or a third of their normal living space. They often had to use their dining room or living room as a bedroom. As Marilyn explained, "What is really different for us is having the family room furniture

in the garage and having Jessica's bedroom set in the dining
room." Carol discussed how difficult it was for her family to live in
one room together:

> For awhile it drove us all crazy, and we were snapping at each
> other. We were in that little apartment, and we had two twin
> beds—probably when we needed to snuggle the most, and my
> husband and I have twin beds! For our son, there was just enough
> room to put an inflatable bed on the floor. . . . We were used to
> having our own place to get ready, and here we were all packed in,
> and that kind of thing drove you crazy. We like being together,
> but we still like our private times, you know. There was nothing,
> there was no time when you were by yourself.

Rachel, who was grateful for her friend's apartment, found it very
small for a family of four: "One person on the bed, someone was on
the floor, one on the futon, and one on the couch." Often families
had campers or trailers in their front yards while they were rebuilding their homes. These trailers were small, making privacy next to
impossible. Some families negotiated these arrangements for periods of months, and others for a year or more.

Reestablishing Rituals

In addition to the actual physical place of home, the rituals and
routines that the family engages in are also important to the re-
creation of domestic culture. Durkheim ([1893] 1964) and Collins
(1988) posit that rituals are key ways by which individuals reaffirm
what is important and valued in social life. In a disaster, these activities and schedules provide the "sense of permanence that charac-
terizes everyday life" that is important because a disaster disrupts
not only lives but "realities" (Smith and Belgrave 1995, p. 247).
Smith and Belgrave (1995) note in their study of Hurricane Andrew, "The schedules we keep and the places we go to work and to
shop and the roads we travel structure our lives, making them
predictable and meaningful" (p. 247).[3]
   The Grand Forks women attempted to maintain or reinstate
certain family routines and schedules in order to retain a sense of
continuity from their predisaster culture.[4] Some women, for example, enrolled their children in school during evacuation so that they

would have that routine continue. Marilyn commented about what helped things feel normal for her daughter during the evacuation:

> Getting some structure in her life and doing things with her friends her age. And the public schools got up and running. Now she's in a summer performing arts program with some friends. They were going to do Hello Dolly, but all the costumes were ruined in the flood, so now they decided to do an original musical about the flood.

Lynn, a post office clerk, agreed:

> I put the children in school during evacuation. I figured they needed to do something besides sit around and worry. Now it is summer, and the middle one plays softball, and the oldest one has a babysitting job. They've got a life. And the little one I put back in daycare again. Even though the older girls could watch her, she needs the routine.

Most schools in Grand Forks were closed from the start of the flood, April 18, through the remainder of the school year. As a result, parents had to find alternative arrangements for their children through the spring and summer if they wanted to re-establish their children's routines. During evacuation, women also worked to locate their children's friends who had evacuated to other towns in Minnesota and North Dakota. They felt that playing with friends would also help their children and the family to regain normalcy. Interestingly, the search was often thwarted because children frequently stayed with maternal grandparents, and the women did not know the maiden names of the other mothers.

One significant familial ritual the women reestablished was sitting down together for family meals. DeVault (1991) noted that meals allow members of the household to come together as a group and have significance for the family relations, but they do not occur "naturally or automatically." Instead, "women do this work to produce home and family" (pp. 59–60). Family mealtimes were often a challenge during evacuation when homes were not accessible, or later if the homes were destroyed, particularly because the women had no recipes, no spices or staples, no pots, pans, or other necessary cooking utensils, and often no dining tables. Some women were in FEMA mobile homes, so the kitchens were not stocked, and some were with relatives or friends, so they had limited access to the kitchen because they were guests. Cecilia laughed as she explained how she finally tried to make a family favorite, mashed potatoes, in their temporary trailer, only to find at the last minute that she did not have a potato masher.

Many of the women lamented that there were no longer any regular meal times since the disaster began. Tina unhappily pointed out, "We used to eat at noon and five, and now we eat at two and eight. I mean, I just can't seem to get the meals done anymore. That part is not together yet." Maria, who had moved into the furnished farmhouse, also faced dilemmas with reestablishing meal times while they lived temporarily outside of town and had a longer commute:

> Meals are something that a family kind of centers around, and part of the problem is that I leave the house by six-thirty in the morning to get to work by eight, so I don't see them in the morning at all. And I don't get home until late also. But they wait for me. But it's late. It's not normal yet.

Reestablishing the family meal was a benchmark for the women, as it revealed how much their home lives had recovered. Peggy also spoke of the difficulty of reinstating the family meal:

> We don't have family meals together because, well, we don't have a table. It is so unreal to think about putting a meal together. You don't have anything. No seasonings, nothing. You have to plan, plan, plan. Just to put a meal together, I have to think, what should we have to eat, what do I need, and then, well, I don't have a pan to put that in, so you know. So then, maybe I'll have a bowl of cereal or something.

Carol also spoke of the problem of not having a table for family meals, as well as the emotional strain and exhaustion that surfaced at mealtimes:

> There was no table, so we could never eat a meal together. We'd sit on couches and eat whatever we brought home. . . . We'd sit there and kind of snarl, let's get this over with so we can go to bed. Now it's back to it's a good time to catch up. All our son's friends have the same dinner hour, six o'clock. So all the kids disappeared, and you always knew that you could have dinner together.

For Carol and many other women, their families were able to reestablish the family meal as a time to share about their day and to reconnect with one another. Jean Marie also mentioned that having good friends over for dinner was another important meal ritual. Durkheim ([1893] 1964) stated that eating together is the most important solidarity ritual, and these women worked to create family solidarity in this way.

In addition to sitting down to regular meals, the women mentioned concern over the loss of special foods and treats. Peggy, for example, confided in me that she longed to make her chocolate chip cookies for her children, but she had no ingredients or pans because she lost her home and all its contents. The cookies, Peggy felt, would remind her family of home. Baking was also important to Dana, who had to bake in her old garage while she lived in her backyard:

> I was at my sister's the other day, and she was baking these nice big banana muffins. I was like, "Goll, I have nothing to bake with, I'd have to go out and buy it all again." And I don't know how to work the little stove in our garage. But I really want to bake something.

As Hodder (1994) found, the simple act of smelling and tasting a cookie can awake strong feelings and memories. Research has found that food preparation is seen as an especially important part of the preservation of religious and ethnic culture as it represents a form of ritual adherence, and the food itself becomes the symbol system through which a connection to the religious and cultural heritage is maintained (Jacobs 1996). Indeed, because one's ethnic identity is expressed through food, it is even more important when you are away from home as even everyday food becomes special (Ronn 1998).

This idea translates to secular domestic culture as well. It is important to note a distinction: there was the food item itself, and there was the preparation of that food. The women did not want just to purchase the food items for their families; they wanted to prepare the food for them. Addie was disappointed that she could not cook for her youngest daughter's wedding, as she had for her other two daughters:

> We had the wedding at the Marriott, and it went well. It was frustrating because usually when we have something like this, you are

doing the baking and you're doing the cooking, but I didn't feel
like I could do that at my daughter-in-law's place. So we just went
with what they served at the hotel. They had muffins and bagels
and fruit at the gift opening. I didn't have to fix it or clean it up!

Interestingly, while Addie was sorry not to bake and cook, she
sounded as if she was also a little surprised, and maybe even pleased,
that her daughter could get married and she, Addie, did not have to
do all the work.

In the fall of 1997, Roseanne told me, "I must have a house for
Christmas. I need a place to cook. That is important." Many of the
women shared Roseanne's sentiments. Addie decided she was still
going to host the Christmas meal at her new small condo, after years
of serving Christmas dinner to all her family members at her home:

> We are kind of stubborn, and we decided that we can have
> Christmas here at this place. My mother—she's eighty-four years
> old—was very concerned about what we were going to do for
> Christmas. We were lucky that Christmas day was a nice day, and
> we put tables in the garage with heaters, so the kids ate in the
> garage. Some ate in the dining area. And we had Christmas din-
> ner together.

For the women in Grand Forks, food preparation at Christmastime
was an especially important tradition to preserve for their families.[5]
Many spoke of Christmas foods and meals as important. For all of
them, food held special meaning as it linked them to a life that was
lost, at least temporarily.

In addition to meals and special foods, family leisure activities,
hobbies, and vacations created normalcy, solidarity, and unity in the
family. Family rituals develop around common and repeated events
such as holidays, birthdays, meals, bedtime, vacation, and leisure activities, and they are powerful and meaningful times. Families have
changed dramatically in the last several decades, but the idea that
families value spending time together holds true, as does the idea
that spending time together makes them a family. The women in
Grand Forks spoke of how, especially during the weeks of evacuation, they would take their children to the park, the museum, or the
zoo, fly a kite, visit their friends, or go to a county fair. Genie evacuated to "the Cities" (Minneapolis/St. Paul) with her family, and
she felt that having economic resources helped her family to have

fun together, regain normalcy, and begin healing faster than families of lower socioeconomic status:

> We went to the Cities and went shopping and went to the zoo and had so much fun, and it was so good to have fun. Then we came home and read the paper and watched TV and listened to the radio, and, all of a sudden, we are a flood victim. It's like this burden hits you again. I'm sick of everyone wearing their flood shirts. Let's move forward. I have one, but I don't wear it anymore. [Seeing everyone in their shirts] was so depressing. But I was thinking, "Well, what a spoiled thing I am. I bet everyone would like to go to the Cities and spend a couple hundred dollars eating and shopping." We didn't spend much, but it really costs to go on vacation. So I'm thinking, "You spoiled thing." I felt so judgmental of all these people. They didn't get to go to the Cities and everything. But, still, let's go forward.

Genie recognized the extreme importance of family leisure while acknowledging that family leisure time was an economic luxury many others did not have.

In addition to family vacations and leisure time, the women found that reestablishing hobbies was important. Peggy explained how important it was to resume her hobby, knitting:

> I lost all my knitting and crocheting and all my patterns. All of my patterns and needles and everything were gone. So somebody sent me a box of patterns and things, somebody I don't even know, somebody from Wisconsin. There are some knitting needles and boxes filled with yarn, and there are some patterns in there, and I *just couldn't wait* to dig in.

Carol, a forty-three-year-old homemaker, also felt that leisure activities were important in reestablishing her family life:

> One of the reasons that we have enjoyed my being [a homemaker] is it was a luxury that then, when we did have free time, it was time to enjoy as a family. [Since the flood] there has been no free time. There has been virtually no time to just horse around, and that we've missed. And we also lost all our hobby stuff—woodwork, start plants, you know. Lots of the hobby books were lost, things like that. Fortunately, my favorite gardening books were saved. I am *very* interested in gardening, my husband is

pretty interested, and our son is *somewhat* interested. So right after the flood, anticipating that we might move, we started picking out their favorite plants, and we got those potted up. That was very therapeutic for us, and it gave us an excuse to be doing work outside, in the sunshine and fresh air.

Carol and her family, like many of the other women and their families, worked to reestablish the time and place for leisure activities, even though many hobby-related items were lost. In some cases, there was also no space for hobbies or leisure routines or even holiday rituals. At Christmas, many families in trailers had trouble finding room for a Christmas tree and decorations.

Many families had a basement or first-level family room that was destroyed in the flood. This family room had been the family hub where they would relax together, watch television, read, or play games. Marilyn longed to get back her "old, dull, uneventful life," which consisted mainly of hanging out at home, in the family room. Many women admitted that their formal living rooms on the main floor were not able to serve the function as a family place to gather, as they were stiff and uncomfortable. As Lorna described, "We just don't want to be inside in the formal living room, and we don't want to sit in the bedrooms." Larson and Richards (1997) found in their research that healthier families spend more time in leisure activities together, which could include going to the zoo, visiting relatives, doing recreational activities, or just being together watching TV. After the disaster, when families had to live with relatives, sometimes just watching TV was problematic, as Addie found when living with her adult son and his wife:

> We didn't have a TV of our own, and we wanted different TV programs. But we couldn't ever say that, you know. Like with sports. My son likes sports, and so does my husband, but his wife isn't quite as understanding about sports all the time. She wanted to watch something else. So I had to kind of bite my tongue and not say anything because it made no sense to make any trouble.

Most families in the United States spend a fair amount of leisure time watching TV, and thus, it was a familial ritual and routine that the women wanted to re-create after the flood.

Planting flowers was perhaps the next most important ritual after preparing and serving family meals. Some literature has found a connection between women's gardening and the notion of women's fertility and rebirth. For example, Walker (1983) wrote about how black women who have had their homes taken away cultivate gardens to establish a connection to the earth. In this way, when they feel under siege in their life, the women find other avenues for stability and connection. Gardens were a way to continue domestic culture in a crisis. In Grand Forks, planting flowers was significant to many of the women, as it was both a process and a product that symbolized their family life and culture before the disaster. Planting flowers helped make their damaged homes, or new homes, seem more familiar, more like home. Louise thought she would forgo her annual planting of flowers, with all the work she had in the basement of her flooded home, but decided to do it after all. When she finished, she realized that planting flowers had become a chore in the past few years, but this year it felt good. Lydia explained that she planted flowers right away because it made her feel as if she "had something that was okay." Myrna, eighty, recalled: "I used to plant flowers; there were days of planting ninety-five flowers! This year my sister-in-law brought a beautiful bouquet of peonies from our yard. That was real nice." Addie, who lost her home, dug up and moved her rose bushes and ferns to her lake house so that she could save them. Tina, who lost her home and belongings, felt that planting flowers was a sign of normalcy, and because the disaster had hit her family particularly hard, she could not fathom recovering enough to start a garden:

> If I see flowers, planted flowers, annuals, it is so bizarre to me. I was trying to explain it to people at work. Flowers become a luxury. It's like, who has time for flowers? I'm an avid gardener, I canned all my food, and I had flowers, but this year they seem bizarre to me. It seems strange that people plant them. At the one end of town, where they only had basement flooding, you go by now, and you see them mowing their grass and they have flowers. It creates the illusion that everything is all right.

Like family meals, planting flowers was a measuring stick: it measured how far along you were in the recovery of your home and life. Lynn, a post office clerk and mother of three, agreed with Tina.

Flowers were a symbol of a home becoming sacred again, which had not happened for her yet:

> It was like you were paralyzed with the enormity of the job ahead of you [gutting the damaged house]. Everyone was kind of paralyzed at first. You did the essential things you had to do, but everything else, you just had to leave it. [For example], I haven't planted flowers this year at all. I always do flowers. But I'm still trying to get the house back together basically.

Many, like Roseanne, were frustrated that they could not plant flowers at their new apartments. Peggy put some potted plants on a small balcony instead in an effort to replace the annual planting. Carol, a homemaker in her forties, was discouraged to discover that she had lost all of her gardening tools in the flood, thereby thwarting her efforts to plant flowers in the summer of 1997. Some women who were not able to produce their full garden modified their planting ritual. As Pat remembered, "I normally garden a lot in the summer, but I just threw a few geraniums in a pot, and that was it." Carrie, whose home sustained major, but reparable, damage, was pleased when a female disaster relief worker thought to plant flowers for her, while the male workers were gutting her house: "That is one thing I really appreciated. It is a typical woman's touch. She put in our annuals. That was very nice. That never would have happened."

Preserving Artifacts

Finally, the third aspect of domestic culture that the women of Grand Forks struggled with was the preservation of family objects or artifacts that symbolized their heritage. Both Durkheim ([1893] 1964) and Collins (1988) spoke of the importance of cultural representations, such shared cultural forms as objects or symbols that represent the group experience to its members, such as a flag, a totem, or a song. In this light, the domestic cultural objects lost in the flood were connections to the self, and even seemingly mundane objects, like furniture, held symbolic meaning. Indeed, Erikson (1976) referred to the furniture and belongings lost by the Buffalo Creek survivors as "furniture of the self" (p. 174). For the women of Grand Forks, these artifacts connected them to their families, their home, and their past.

Saving personal belongings, or the family's cultural artifacts, was important to the women in the study, as these objects symbolized the family's life, culture, and heritage. As Sabrina, a twenty-eight-year-old bank teller, told me:

> We've only been married for three years. We have only three years worth of joint marital possessions, but, you know, little stuff, like pictures. Pictures of my father who's been dead for twenty years and that kind of stuff. And Tyler's crib. He's gonna sleep in it for at least two years, and then we're gonna have another baby; and then one day it will be passed down to our kids' grandkids. And all sorts of stuff. I thought, "Oh, jeez, if we lost that crib, I'm just gonna be sick."

Sabrina understood that these belongings tied her to both past and future generations. Others spoke sadly of prized family items—such as a child's teddy bear or a handmade table—that could not be replaced. As Lorna put it, "Going through my mind were my pictures, my kids' christening gowns, our home videos, stuff I knew *no money could replace*." The women had "boundary confusion" as a stuffed animal became a representation of the child. Women often have more "fluid boundaries" between themselves and others (Chodorow 1978). In the flood, women endowed objects with the feeling that they held for the people who owned the object or who the object represented.

Genie, who had tried to accentuate the positive with her children, admitted that the loss of artifacts, especially her Bible, was difficult:

> My husband had given me a Bible a few years ago, and when he was telling me about the things we lost, I cried, "What about my Bible?!" We lost so much. We lost our Christmas tree, but I got my ornaments. But we lost our bikes, tools, toys, a dehumidifier, tables and prints, and just so much.

Jennifer, a twenty-six-year-old graphic designer who had to evacuate quickly, had her parents help her find her videos, photo albums, and a jewelry box given to her by her grandparents. However, after she returned from evacuation, she realized she had forgotten one meaningful artifact. Six years after the disaster, Jennifer stated that everyone has their favorite flood story—and this was hers:

> My grandfather had made me a Christmas stable for my nativity set. Years ago the music box quit working. This happened to be the only item that I had left in the basement that had any meaning to me. As I carried it out to the pile of trash, it was evening and I was probably one of the only people left in the neighborhood. I tossed the stable onto the pile. And wouldn't you know it, the damn music box started. I'm standing on this deserted street and it's playing "Silent Night." The music box that hadn't worked for years said its goodbye. It was like a made-for-TV movie!

Only one woman, Amy Sue, a teacher, mentioned that she first saved many nonemotional, nonfamilial items such as "personal records, credit cards, taxes, an address book, and a disk with all my grades on it" for her students. However, she, too, said the most important things she saved also included emotional items, such as a teddy bear her brother had given her and family photo albums. Hoffman (1998), who wrote about gender patterns after the Oakland fires of 1991, also lost her home and belongings in that disaster. She painfully recalled how "nothing I owned carried the aroma of my family" (p. 61).

Peggy expressed how much meaning a seemingly unsentimental object, a store-bought piece of furniture, had to her:

> I wanted a fainting couch for my bedroom, and I had seen one and had been hinting to my kids, and I knew they would get it for me. So, on Christmas I was sleeping in bed, and they're giggling 'cause they're hitting the walls and everything, and they bring it up and put it in the bedroom for me. And when I saw them carry that out [of the destroyed house] all cut up and everything, I said, "Oh no, you aren't throwing that away." And I started crying. My son said, "Mom, you gotta go, you can't stay here." And then I saw the baby stuff in the pile, stuff we saved from when our kids were small, and I thought it was best for me to not be there. So I went away and thought about all the stuff that was in each room.

For Peggy and many others, the emotional attachment to the artifacts made it extremely painful to witness them being discarded.

Roseanne articulated how she went about saving her most important items:

> I took out all my photo albums. My wedding pictures, significant things that had been my children's. I'm a real pack rat for that sort of thing, like baptismal gowns and stuff like that. I took those things. And my husband has taken trips to Alaska, so things from his trip, those kind of family mementos. I boxed up eighteen boxes, and I got them all in sizes that I could carry, or some of my lady friends could carry. I wanted all the boxes to be a size we could handle, because I'm not going to have my lady friends come here and bust up their backs. Then I had a Saturday moving party, and we ladies moved all this stuff to my sister-in-law's, since her elevation was fifty-two feet. So I moved all of it there, all my scrap books and photo albums and all of it. At the time my husband was saying, "Aren't you kind of overreacting?"

Many other women remarked that their husbands believed that they were overreacting by placing objects on higher ground. Unfortunately, Roseanne's sister-in-law's house also flooded, because the water crested at fifty-four feet, but even though Roseanne lost many items, she was happy that her photo albums were not damaged.

Not all family members agreed with the women that familial artifacts were meaningful, symbolic, or even worth saving. Martha Jo, who was out of the state during the flood, found that her adult son trivialized her loss of family artifacts, a loss that was his fault:

> I had all my treasured family Christmas decorations, our little artificial tree, and a lot of collectibles. I told my son, "I want my things moved up, just put them in the bedroom or bathroom." I was concerned about the coulee.[6] But he thought, it's not going to flood, not to worry. So he tells me that everything is taken care of. And he told his sister it was all taken care of. But he *never did anything*. He was just so convinced that his mother was being too cautious, and he just wouldn't accommodate my wishes because he felt that I was too far off center. So we lost everything: boxes, books, a dozen bottles of wine, antique mirrors, sewing materials, things like that.

> [AF: Did your son acknowledge his mistake?]

> Yes, but it doesn't phase him that much. So it's old stuff that Mom has; who needs it? They didn't sympathize with me. One table was my grandmother's, and the dining room set [belonged

to] my folks. And so much of what I own is family, and it can't be replaced.

Martha Jo felt both angry and powerless to have her request dismissed and to have her loss trivialized by her son. For the women in Grand Forks, their belongings were meaningful and connected to the lives they had lived. For example, Diana described how she felt when she looked down into her basement: "There were boxes floating around. I am a fanatic about keeping things. Every box of my life was just floating around." Maria also felt that her belongings were not just "things"; they meant something:

> Everything we own fits in a storage unit and that's depressing. We've been married for seventeen years, and everything we own fits in a storage unit. You kind of start all over. It is kind of commercialist, or capitalist, or something, but we judge people by your possessions. It is a major judgment, in our country anyway. . . . But you also have memories associated with your things.

Liebow's (1993) study of homeless women found that giving up their belongings was one of the most difficult aspects of being homeless, resulting in many women paying the last of their savings or their small paychecks to keep their belongings in a storage unit while they resided in a homeless shelter. For the women in his study and the women in mine, their belongings represented who they were and where they had come from.

Peggy grew up in Grand Forks, married her high school sweetheart, and spent her whole life in Grand Forks. Tragically, one of their children died when he was an infant. Twenty years later, when the flood hit and their home was destroyed, it was understandable that her first thoughts were of the photos of her son: "That's all we had of him." She worked for days following a complex system that involved freezing the albums to save the photographs. Peggy told me that losing the photographs of her deceased son would be like losing him all over again. Almost every woman I interviewed mentioned that she saved, or attempted to save, family photo albums. This action has been documented by journalists in other disasters, as seen, for example, in newspaper articles on the Los Alamos fires in 2000. In Grand Forks, many, like Peggy, felt that photographs of deceased family members had the utmost sentimental value. Carol was touched that her son saved her albums before his own belongings:

> The first load that my son brought up was my picture albums, and he said, "Ma, I know it would kill you if we lost these." I'm a camera freak, you know. So he brought up boxes of negatives and photos and albums. And then he went and got his snowboard and CD player and his CDs.

Many women also mentioned preserving family videos, especially ones of their children at young ages, yearbooks, and baby keepsake books. In a letter I received from Myrna four years after the flood, she mentioned that she still mourns the loss of her family photographs. And six years after the flood, Cecilia admitted that her family videotapes and old home movies are still in the freezer, waiting until she has time to send them to a facility in Canada to see if they can be restored. All of these items, such as photographs and home videos, can be interpreted as representations of connections to others, which women worked to preserve.

After photo albums, Christmas items were perhaps the most meaningful artifacts to women. Martha Jo, a seventy-year-old retired woman, determined that her Christmas decorations, collected over many generations, were the most difficult belongings to lose. Lynn, a working-class mother from East Grand Forks, agreed:

> The first thing I did was to get the Christmas decorations and the toys. I wanted my Christmas decorations 'cause they've gotten one every year from their grandma, and I got to get those. I don't know how many people I've talked to now who lost their Christmas decorations, and that was their biggest loss to them, their Christmas decorations.

This sentiment was echoed by all of the women who lost their holiday decorations and Christmas tree ornaments, most of which were handmade by themselves or their mothers or grandmothers. The homemade holiday decorations were representations of relationships and emotional attachments, thereby making the loss of such items more unbearable and disconnecting.

In addition to the Christmas items, mementos from other special occasions were also critical to rebuild their lives, reconstruct the domestic culture, and maintain a link to their past. Fran, a married school teacher in her forties, explained how she lost some items:

The Federal Emergancy Management Agency (FEMA) established several large temporary trailer parks to house hundreds of families while their homes were repaired or while they found other housing. While thankful for the lodging, many families found the experience of living in the trailers to be difficult. East Grand Forks, anticipating the need for future housing, asked FEMA to construct the temporary trailer parks in such a way that they would serve as the infrastructure for new subdivisions of permanent homes in the future. *Photo by Alice Fothergill.*

> I did lose my wedding dress and a little dress I wore as a flower
> girl when I was six. The only time the flood really bothered me
> was when I lost those things. I had put them on a high shelf, but
> the flood got them. I tried to think, "Well, you weren't ever going
> to wear them again anyway." I tried to rationalize it.

Despite her attempts to rationalize the loss of these familial artifacts,
Fran was devastated by losing items from her childhood and the be
ginning of her marriage that were symbols of her personal life.
Many of the women, like Fran who rescued her husband's *Star Trek*
collection, recognized the importance of their husbands' mementos
and belongings. Roseanne made a point of explaining how it was
important to recognize that men also lost items:

> My husband lost a lot of his things, too. In the basement he lost
> a lot, his hammers, nuts and bolts, nails. His stuff was important,
> too. The tools were important. He was sad about it. His father's
> chainsaw completely disappeared in the flood. His father died
> young so it was significant. You think of women losing so much in
> the home—linens, kitchen stuff, albums—but men lost their
> things, too. And I didn't really realize that until my husband said,
> looking very sadly at our home, "Well, we had collected a lot
> there over the years."

Lydia, who had proclaimed that the home "is mine," was also sad
that her adult son lost the football, baseball, and hockey cards
that he had collected for over twenty-five years and that were
worth $15,000. Cecilia felt badly for her children: "It wasn't so
hard to lose my things, but it was so hard to see those things that
the children had carried up that they lost. All the effort that they
took, and it was gone." Because the home was so clearly recognized as the female domain, and thus women's losses there were
more obvious, a few of the women felt the need to point out that
men or children might also have lost items that meant something
to them.

Some women mentioned that they worked hard to save some
family artifacts in order to save money, as many of the families were
working class and did not have insurance to replace lost items. Their
efforts to save many artifacts, however, were hindered by warnings
of contamination. Tina felt that the city officials should not have
advised everyone to throw everything away:

People threw way too much stuff away that could be saved. Why? You feel so contaminated yourself, and it is just drilled in your head about contaminants. . . . You become sort of compulsive. "You touched your toy, so wash your hands. Mommy hasn't decontaminated that yet." We almost threw away all the children's toys, but then I went back and reconsidered. Why did I reconsider? Because it was incredibly important that the children have something of their own. People were giving things to them and sent them some toys, but it is important for people to have something of their own, that was theirs.

Many other women agreed with Tina, believing that the radio announcements about contamination were misleading and that many families could have saved more belongings and keepsakes. While it was unclear what the real risks were of contamination, it appeared that the city officials erred on the side of caution, as they did with evacuation, and broadcast warnings through radio announcements, which prompted many to discard more than they now feel was necessary.

In addition, the women revealed that the artifacts also represented the family's hard work, an important value in North Dakotan culture. Many of the women lamented that to lose their belongings meant that the symbols of their sweat and labor for their families over the years were gone. Jennifer said:

While I like to think that I am not that attached to objects, a lot of the stuff, I could say, well, if I lost the couch, the VCR, the TV, you know [it would be okay]. But the bottom line is, I worked really hard for this couch, I worked really hard for this TV, and for this VCR, and they may not be much, but it's all I have. Your lifetime accomplishments are housed in your house.

Hoffman (1998), who lost twenty-five years of her anthropological research in the Oakland Fires of 1991, felt that trying to describe losing her life's labor was like "trying to define eternity or infinity—it defies words" (p. 55). Women losing their homes, the sites of their labor, meant losing a connection to their self. Tina, who lost her home in East Grand Forks, described how she felt about these family artifacts and the labor that went into them:

I came to the realization that we all think we own things. You know, you think you own your car, and you think you own your house. I don't think we own anything. I really don't. It is all on borrow. It can be wiped out at any minute. . . . It was everything that we had worked for. It's everything. We had a grandfather clock that [my husband] Frank's great uncle had made for us before he died, and Frank had hauled the trees for this thing.

Marilyn explained why the loss of these belongings should not be downplayed: "Everyone says, 'Nobody died, we didn't lose any lives, and this is just stuff.' True, but this stuff is important to people. It was stuff that people worked hard for and fixed up and bought."[7]

The line "No lives were lost" was a mantra of pride for city officials, but many believed that while that was something to be extremely grateful for, there were still personal losses that were traumatizing. Peggy took issue with the mayor and other city officials constantly downplaying the losses:

> She has said on TV, "We've lost no lives, only material things." I agree. But these material things we have worked very hard for; the memories that are there, the sweat and tears put into a home of twenty-three years are more than "material" things to me. That's just my personal opinion. People will say, "It's just things." Yeah, you're right, and I don't say anything. But the more I think about it, I know I shouldn't be so upset about losing everything, but those things meant something to me. We worked hard to get where we were, and now we have nothing. So, I know it was just material things, but it meant something to us. They were more than "material" things to me. I know we are all safe, and I am grateful for that, but there is a "but" on the end. If they had told us the truth, and we had prepared for a higher level, we could've gotten out the most important things. We put our things up to the level that they said.

Like Marilyn and Peggy, others expressed reluctance to sound materialistic when they spoke of their grief over lost objects, as they knew the most important issue was that no lives were lost. On the other hand, they wanted to acknowledge, without sounding superficial, that these artifacts held a great deal of meaning for them and their families. Clearly, the women felt that the most important thing was that their families were safe, as Carol summed up:

> My husband and son were sandbagging, and I was moving stuff up from the basement. I heard on the radio that dikes were breaking.

I thought, "Please get off that dike, please get off that dike." [She starts crying]. Finally they came home. I said, "We are getting out. There is nothing in this house that's worth losing our lives for." So we got up and left.

Lorna, the hospital manager and mother of two small children, agreed, although she added a caveat:

> When I needed to take stuff, I didn't care about the things that I could take money and buy. It was the pictures and the movies that I wanted. And even if I didn't have that, I still have my husband and my kids, and that's what's really important. But if I could get that stuff, I really wanted it!

The women in Grand Forks assumed the role of preserving the domestic culture and fulfilled what Jacobs (1996) contended was the "traditional woman's role of culture bearing in the patriarchal family" (p. 106). They felt obligated in many respects to do this work, as it was an aspect of their traditional role of family caretaker, and they also wanted to do this work, as these objects and rituals had meaning to them. The loss of their homes and their families' artifacts was not just about the material loss but also about emotional loss and pain, and a loss of connection. The women worked to reestablish a connection to their families, and to themselves, when their sense of self was also altered by the loss of domestic culture. As Sarup (1994) found, identity is linked to home, so that women who lose their homes, from a natural disaster or any other crisis, must construct identity without the home, without its rituals, routines, and artifacts, as a framework. The reconstruction of home as a sacred place, the reestablishment of rituals such as family meals, and the preservation of family artifacts such as photo albums were all part of the women's work to reconnect to others and to maintain a sense of self.

Chapter 10

Everything in Her Path

M any of the women in this study experienced the Red River flood of 1997 as a "turning point" moment (Strauss 1959). The women found themselves face-to-face with social and familial upheaval, emotional and physical trauma, and feelings of loss, vulnerability, and violation. They were thrust into a situation where they had to examine their vulnerabilities, their capabilities, and their lives. As Denzin (1997) argues, individuals go through major redefining events in life, and these epiphanies are powerful and life altering. Warner and Feltey (1999) also found that experiencing traumatic events leads to identity transformation. Thus, the flood was a window of opportunity for the women to examine and change their own lives and identities.

This study illustrated how women's social roles and identities can change with extreme life events, and also maintain some constancy. In other words, there was both role and identity continuity as well as role and identity shifts in the wake of the flood, a seemingly contradictory phenomenon. My data helps to clarify how these competitive realities—the role and identity shifts and continuity—are constructed and maintained. There was a mixture, simultaneously, of determined behavior and autonomy.

There are three major examples of how women's role changes and solidification led them to develop a positive sense of self and undergo change, especially in regard to beliefs and ideologies. First, the women experienced "role accumulation" which led to the expansion of a positive sense of self. Second, the women took the role of the other, which pushed them toward changes in their ideologies. Finally, the women re-created their domestic family roles and identities by re-creating domestic culture, which contributed to a

positive sense of self and feelings of both autonomy and connection.
Each of these three theoretical areas will be discussed in the sections
that follow.

Women's Role "Accumulation" and Positive Sense of Self

The women of Grand Forks performed three salient roles:
volunteer in the community, caregiver in the family, and employee in the workplace. While the workplace role temporarily di-
minished for most women in Grand Forks during the acute phase
of the disaster, overall they found that all of their roles expanded
and changed qualitatively. Women participated in community
work such as sandbagging and community support work such as
preparing sandwiches for the sandbaggers. They fulfilled their
family roles, including childcare and housework, and they came
through as employees, working in their regular or emergency
jobs. As a result of their expanded obligations and the accompa-
nying time and energy demands, the women had to fulfill three
roles, all with expanded responsibilities, simultaneously. At times,
these expanded roles produced conflict. As a result of both the
new demands and the role conflict, women found that they began
to see themselves differently, as more competent, confident, and
capable, and worthy of multiple roles and responsibilities, especially in the public sphere.

Much discussion of U.S. women and their roles includes the
problems associated with their increased participation in and identification with the public sphere. Research shows it is difficult to fulfill the obligations of several "greedy roles" without experiencing
role engulfment, being overwhelmed by role demands, and distanc-
ing oneself from one or more roles (Coser 1974; Adler and Adler
1991). Historically, women's greediest role has been the family
role, including the roles of wife, mother, and home manager.
Lopata (1994) argued that American culture still defines the most
important social roles for women as wife and mother. As a result, it
justifies the neglect of other roles, such as work roles in the public
sphere, if they interfere with the obligations of wife and mother. In
her extensive work on the changing roles of American women,
Lopata (1994) stated that the division of the world into private and
public is in itself a major cause of role conflict for it allows men to
solve their role conflicts by neglecting private roles and pushes

women to ignore public roles. Indeed, she posited that there has been considerable backlash toward women's efforts to break down barriers between private and public domains.

Breaking down those barriers can have benefits to women. For example, some of the positive aspects of role accumulation for women include greater authority, status security, ego gratification, and feelings of competence (Lopata 1994). In my study, I found these advantages of role accumulation to hold true. Most of the women in my study spoke of how competent and self-sufficient they felt by accomplishing new tasks, or multiple tasks, on their own and in a time of crisis. The tasks may have been operating several sump pumps on their own through the night or safely evacuating their children and the neighbor's children when the streets were filling with water. For women with disabilities, elderly women, and lower-class women enduring extreme financial hardships, their ability to perform these roles competently added even more to their positive sense of self. Jean Marie, for example, found that as a woman with physical disabilities, she was proud of herself for her participation in sandbagging. No matter the specific accomplishment, it was obvious in talking with all the women that they, themselves, were in awe of their deeds. Indeed, many women felt guilty that something as terrible as this flood ended up having very positive effects for them. The women such as Esther and Beth who took on high-intensity emergency jobs spoke of their new level of authority and responsibility with amazement. Both of them retained their higher status after the disaster and found that they felt more self-confident in their work roles and were treated by colleagues with more respect and deference. Their feelings of self-efficacy and self-worth increased. As Sieber (1974) theorized, the benefits of role accumulation can outweigh any stress the roles produce.

As women's roles expanded, so did their sense of self. According to Mead (1934), the self arises in the process of social experience and activity and can only be achieved through interaction with others. In particular, others respond to a person as a performer in a specific role, and the meanings of the self are learned from that response (Burke and Reitzes 1981). In Grand Forks, the women's selves may have chosen certain role behaviors, but their role performances expanded their senses of self. Roles can be stable and learned through socialization, or, as Blumer (1969) and other symbolic interactionists have argued, they can also be negotiated and changed in a given situation or through a historical shift in the definition of a role. Thus, roles are not simply learned but also made. The women in Grand Forks both enacted old established roles, such as family caregiver, and took part in making new roles, a more creative endeavor to adapt to the particular situation. I found that the self was lodged in some respects in all three prominent roles but that emergent roles in particular changed the women's ideas of who they were and what they were capable of achieving. In essence, they changed their sense of self. The disaster provided the opportunity for women to experience extreme role accumulation, taking on both bounded and creative roles, and as result experience some profound changes in their self concepts.

Ideology Shifts and the Role of the Other

While women experienced an expansion of the self due to their role accumulation, they also faced challenges to their sense of self in terms of class and status. Accepting charity challenged their traditional middle-class gender roles as the women had been socialized to give to others. By experiencing downward mobility and accepting assistance in the disaster, women confronted their beliefs in the achievement ideology and were forced to examine how their views of themselves were created in opposition to their views of the poor. These self-definitions were only possible within the larger cultural context, the American culture of individualism. Indeed, their own identity as middle-class women[1] rested on their opposition to the other, that is, poor people of color. The disaster, however, forced them to take on attributes of the other and pushed them to change their views, particularly toward a lesser investment in the ideology of achievement.

In the flood, the women of Grand Forks had the opportunity to change their views of people on welfare. During economic recessions the middle class have often become poor, and as a result, some classist assumptions are challenged (Bullock 1995). The Grand Forks crisis offered the potential to alter the women's attitudes toward the poor. Bullock has proposed that people use three broad explanations of poverty: individualistic, structural, and fatalistic. Individualistic reasons for poverty include the notions that people are poor due to their own shortcomings; for example, they are lazy, uninterested in self-improvement, and have loose morals. Structural explanations stress the role of the economic and social conditions of capitalism in the creation of poverty, such as low wages, unequal educational opportunities, and discrimination. Fatalistic reasons focus on circumstances out of one's control, including illness or bad luck. A natural disaster such as the Grand Forks flood would most accurately fall into the last category because it was an event beyond the women's control.

Most Americans, especially those moderately educated, believe in individualistic reasons for poverty, while the structural reasons are most often cited by those with the least amount of education (Feagin 1975). There is a relationship between the explanations for poverty and the way people feel towards welfare recipients: Broadly, those who believe in individualistic reasons for poverty, as most Americans do, see the poor as undeserving of public assistance. Some groups, such as single mothers and middle-aged women, are considered especially undeserving of public support (Bullock 1995). Most of the women of Grand Forks, in alignment with other working-class and middle-class Americans, believed to a large degree in individualistic explanations for poverty. This belief explains why they were so stigmatized by receiving charity. They believed that accepting assistance spoke more about who they were as people than it did about their economic situations. The upper-middle class women and the lower-class women in the study had less trouble with the stigma of charity than the working-class and middle-class women in the study. The two upper-middle class women, Lisa and Diana, who accepted assistance but whose livelihood did not depend on it, were insulated from the stigma of charity because of their resources and status. The lower-class women, such as Liz and Joanne, felt that the charity did not reflect negatively on them as people, and they were less invested in the achievement ideology, having worked hard and lived in poverty their whole lives. These women, however, were the exception.

While most of the women believed in individualistic reasons for poverty prior to the flood, many of them began to understand fatalistic explanations after the disaster. As a result, many of the women became sympathetic to other natural disaster victims and to those who became poor due to some other type of crisis, such as illness. It was easy for them to see that those who are poor for those reasons are deserving of public assistance. To a lesser extent, some of the women began to see the structural reasons for poverty as a result of the flood, the explanation that must be embraced in order to remove the stigma of assistance. Interestingly, even those women who maintained their individualistic reasoning increased their sympathy for welfare recipients. They now knew that charity was demoralizing and difficult and that the rest of the social world treated recipients poorly. The women of Grand Forks began to comprehend some of the "hidden injuries of class" (Sennett and Cobb 1972), such as being talked down to by SBA loan officials or grocery store clerks. Bullock (1995) claims that such classist behavior maintains the status of wealthier individuals and reinforces individualism as America's ideology.

This study shows that a natural disaster may provide the potential for middle-class Americans to challenge the achievement ideology, or the ideology of individualism, and to resist classist behavior, as the women of Grand Forks joined, albeit briefly, one of the most powerless groups: women on welfare. It also illuminates the construction of race and class in white, middle-class consciousness, as the stigma experience only has meaning in a culture where race and class are linked to welfare and charity. Ultimately, the women of Grand Forks felt stigmatized when they switched from helper to helped, but the experience opened up a window of opportunity for change, as they began to have more empathy for those who must accept assistance in nondisaster times. Thus, taking the role of the other and understanding how their identity rested on being in opposition to the other, ultimately changed some—but not all—of the women's beliefs. They expanded their awareness of others, which in turn led them to be less invested in some of their previous ideologies.

Domestic Roles and Identity

Research has found that crises may threaten one's sense of self, but also may help people construct a "momentus and lasting sense of self" (Lois 2003, p.186). The Grand Forks crisis may have served that function. The women's sense of self was transformed by their role accumulation, and their middle-class identities were challenged by experiencing downward mobility and having to accept charity. In addition, they often lost altogether the social context in which the self exists: their homes. By re-creating domestic culture the women were re-creating their domestic roles, ones based on serving the home and family, and solidifying a gendered self, or feminine identity, based on connection and relationships to others. By examining these roles, we see more evidence of how women experienced simultaneous shifts and solidification of roles and identity. They experienced role accumulation, which was a mixture of traditional and nontraditional roles, and at the same time maintained and reconstructed a traditional role and identity. This role of re-creator of the domestic culture, however, also had positive consequences for the women's self-identity.

The home is a gendered structure, and the normalization and ritualization work at home after a disaster is also gendered. In fact, in their efforts to re-create domestic culture, women are "doing gender" (West and Zimmerman 1987), meaning that "gender is not something we *are* but something we *do*" (Risman 1998). The re-creation of domestic culture is tied to the women's sense of a gendered self. In contrast to the public sphere, where a loss of material status contributed to their stigma of charity, the material losses in the private sphere were not about material status but rather about the emotional meaning that women give to objects. Thus, these losses were not about the loss of comfort or status; they were about the loss of emotional connections.

As discussed earlier, the women's role expansion altered their sense of self. In addition, women's identity and sense of self are tied to their work as re-creators of domestic culture. Through their work normalizing and privatizing their homes, reestablishing rituals and routines, and preserving or replacing family artifacts, the women were able to restore some of their original conceptions of self, a self tied to family and home. Risman (1998) argues that gender relations in American families are hierarchical and that women, especially married women, are expected to fulfill certain roles within the family. Indeed, Risman claims that marriage is the only institution in which the social roles and responsibilities are based on ascribed characteristics: "When life options are tied to racial categories we call it racism at best and apartheid at worst. When life options are tied to gender categories we call it marriage" (p. 36). Women did find that they were expected, because they were women, to perform certain responsibilities in the home, including the maintenance and re-creation of domestic culture. The women's desire to re-create their homes, and their senses of self along with them, may have stemmed from socialization (they were taught to want that) or from cultural scripts (they were expected and rewarded for that). However, no matter the motive for taking on the responsibility to make their homes sacred, reestablish rituals, and preserve artifacts, the consequence was clear: it was important for the women's well-being and sense of identity.

Re-creating domestic culture is not a powerless role. Jacobs (1996) suggests that women may continue to maintain the culture within the home because the role can empower them and they can define and create "sacred spaces" (p. 107). Women's involvement in the private sphere is often associated with their lower status in society because domestic work is devalued. However, women's connection to the re-creation of domestic culture after a disaster can be both empowering and meaningful. They are reprivatizing their lives but also reclaiming a female-centered domain, the home, one site where women have some autonomy. Indeed, other research has claimed that the decoration of rooms, pots, and containers is a form of silent discourse conducted by women (Braithwaite 1982; Donley 1982; Hodder 1991). According to this research, the decoration silently marks out an area of female control and expresses female power.

By re-creating domestic culture, the women were also establishing a connection to their own families and to other generations. In *The Elementary Forms of Religious Life*, Durkheim ([1912] 1954) explained that rituals have a connective function. It was through rituals and other aspects of the domestic culture that the women of Grand Forks tried to connect with others. As Gilligan (1982) and Chodorow (1978) have articulated, women often have a need to connect, and they use many strategies to develop a connective culture. Gilligan (1982), for example, has found in her research that women often combine intimacy and identity. When asked to define themselves, female subjects discuss a relationship with someone who represents their identity. Thus, she argues, identity must include the notion of interconnectedness (Gilligan 1982). Chodorow (1978) posited that the most important feature of development is that it occurs in relation to another person, to a mother. As a result of mothers identifying more with girls, women are more open to and concerned with relational issues and search more for a connection to others. This is not to say that women have a natural connection to others or that some genetic maternal instinct exists. Rather, it acknowledges that whether we draw on psychoanalytic or sociological theories, there is evidence of women's need to connect to others and that their relationships are often a high priority.

In Grand Forks, the loss of homes was a loss of connective context for the women, and the rituals and artifacts were part of re-creating that connection to family and to their past. What could be mistaken for women's materialism, such as wanting to shop for items for the home, was actually a strategy by which they could build a connective context. This finding challenges the common stereotype of white, middle-class women being highly materialistic and of shopping as a shallow and self-centered exercise. The women of Grand Forks were merely finding ways to build connections to others, in this case family members and their shared domestic culture.

There were no clear differences by age, race, class, disability, or sexual orientation in terms of women filling this role and basing their identity on a connection to others. For all the women, family and home were priorities. Some women, due to a lack of resources, had less access to material means of re-creating domestic culture, but that does not mean their commitment to this role was any less. Rachel worked hard to reestablish the home as a consecrated place, despite having to "hide" her partner in her new apartment. Overall, all the women, no matter their differences, seemed to have a common experience with prioritizing the home, as it was critical to reestablishing bonds with family members and maintaining a sense of identity.

In sum, the study illuminates how in a crisis period, or a turning point moment, women experience both role and identity continuity, as well as role and identity shifts. We see these competitive realities working simultaneously, first in how the women managed accumulation of roles both traditional and nontraditional and how this led to a positive sense of self. Second, the study found that women took on the role of the other during downward mobility and the acceptance of charity, a situation that altered their ideologies and their identities. Finally, in their work to re-create domestic culture, women re-created their domestic roles and identities but simultaneously found autonomy, connection to others, and positive senses of self.

Policy Implications

Disaster research has long been committed to producing practical applications, in an effort to work towards minimizing losses and vulnerability.[2] Based on the insight gained from this study, I would like to offer several policy recommendations. First, I recommend that domestic violence services be increased during a disaster. The stories of Karen and Liz provided important illustrations of why we need to focus on the increased demand for domestic violence services. If we were to try to calculate the battering rates in disasters, we might say that Karen and Liz cancel each other out—the disaster pushed one woman into domestic violence and pushed one out of domestic violence—and thus, we could see how domestic violence rates remain stable. If we look only at statistics, however, we might miss the larger issue: both women desperately needed domestic violence services. In light of the demand for services, social service providers need to be better prepared and to be given more assistance from the larger community. The Community Violence Intervention Center found that in the flood aftermath the domestic violence services seemed peripheral to the rebuilding of the community. The federal, state, and city monies for flood recovery went to infrastructure and economic rebuilding, with almost nothing allocated for rebuilding the nonprofit service providers.

In addition, I suggest that women's service providers be better included in community disaster planning. Woman battering organizations need to be better prepared for disasters, and emergency management organizations need to be more aware and sensitive to woman battering issues. As Wilson et al. (1998) state, communities need to be aware of the domestic violence issue prior to the disaster event in order to be effective after a disaster. This points to the need for domestic violence organizations to be represented in disaster planning and to be included as an important component of the disaster recovery community. Finally, I propose that we view disasters as a window of opportunity for the community to address woman battering. Disasters are often a time of change and possibility, thus an opportune time to acknowledge and assist women in battering situations. I argue that communities should take disasters as an opportunity to make long-lasting changes to their policies and structures so that domestic violence organizations and shelters receive sufficient support and that women receive the help they need in both disaster and nondisaster times.

My second policy recommendation concerns the issue of childcare. This study found a lack of safe, affordable childcare during and after the disaster. Nationwide, the availability of safe, affordable childcare is a significant problem for many American families, especially poor ones, during nondisaster times. Research has found that childcare is a large problem for single mothers and women on welfare who are now being required to work. Even in households with both a male and female parent present, the woman, regardless of her paid work status, typically has primary responsibility for childcare duties. Thus, childcare is a large concern for women. It is no surprise, therefore, that after a natural disaster the need is even greater when family and community resources are strained.

Staples (2000) found that in Grand Forks after the flood, childcare was a major concern for many families. Approximately 47 percent of eligible households in Grand Forks use childcare, while approximately 42 percent of American households use childcare.[3] In addition, households in Grand Forks with young children were more likely to have two adults in the labor force and more likely to work more hours than households without young children. This points to the great need for childcare programs. In Grand Forks, approximately half of the childcare was located in the homes of private providers, usually women with small children of their own. Many of these home-based childcare facilities were destroyed in the flood because they were located in the basement level. Several churches in Grand Forks set up free daycare programs for about two months after the flood. While this helped ameliorate the problem to a small extent, some women expressed fears about using new, temporary daycares because they feared that they were not licensed or safe and that the workers there had no experience. Thus, even when the childcare is free, the children's safety was the women's main concern. The childcare situation was exacerbated for women because they needed to work because of the financial demands on them after the flood and the threat of being fired if they did not return to work.

Federal, state, and local agencies need to include childcare issues in disaster recovery plans so that the community can have a proposed strategy and resources in place when a disaster strikes.

Disaster managers and employers should anticipate and plan for the need for childcare after a disaster. In some cases, a disaster provider has lost her location, and if another location could be found, she and her staff could continue operations. As parents are already enduring anxiety, the availability of safe, affordable childcare in the disaster aftermath is a necessity. State authorities should work with local churches that set up temporary childcare centers by helping to make sure they meet federal and state safety requirements.

My third recommendation concerns the availability of safe and affordable housing for disaster victims, especially for poor families and the growing number of single mothers and their children. Options are limited after a disaster, and as we saw in Grand Forks, women had many housing problems. FEMA brought in hundreds of trailers, and these did an adequate job of housing families temporarily, despite complaints of rodents, windows and doors that frequently froze open or shut, and walls and ceilings that amplified every wind or rain storm so much that it was nearly unbearable to be indoors.[4] The FEMA trailers, however, were temporary, and the need remained for affordable permanent housing. As housing prices skyrocketed, women had few options. Thus, state and local agencies should work with the private sector postdisaster to create a supply of affordable homes, perhaps by offering incentives to builders, developers, and sellers of homes. Again, these plans should be drawn up prior to any unforeseen disaster so that strategies are ready to be implemented when the disaster strikes.

I also recommend rethinking public and private assistance after a disaster. The findings of this study concerning the stigma of charity illustrated the discomfort that women felt in receiving both public and private assistance. Indeed, for some women accepting disaster assistance was so unpleasant and degrading that they opted to forgo the assistance. This clearly is a large issue, and to deal with it fully, we would need to change the societal beliefs and ideologies that stigmatize the poor and those on welfare. As that may be an unwieldy first step, we could take smaller steps to alleviate the discomfort. Many women were most uncomfortable at the large giveaway centers, where hundreds of people came to collect free items. While they needed the food vouchers or the cleaning supplies, the experience was too humiliating. Charities and agencies like the Red Cross could attempt to have various neighborhood days, where they open centers to smaller groups of residents. In addition, more training could be given to officials with FEMA and SBA, as well as the Red Cross and the Salvation Army, educating them on the stigma of charity after a disaster, instructing them to be cognizant of those reactions, and to be more sympathetic to the disaster victims' ideologies concerning assistance.

One final issue regarding public and private assistance addresses difference and accessibility. Several women in my study spoke of how standing in line for some types of assistance, such as gas vouchers or paper towels, could take hours. Elderly women and women with physical disabilities were forced to stand in the same lines, despite the obvious hardship on them to do so. One straightforward change that could be made in future disaster situations is to make assistance more accessible to those with special needs. The Salvation Army, SBA, FEMA, and the Red Cross should establish a system whereby the agencies first assist the elderly and the disabled.

Women's voices should be included in disaster planning and management. Grand Forks had a female mayor, still a rarity in most American cities, and her leadership appeared to be important to most of the women in the study. However, it is also important to have more women included at other levels of planning and response. Research has shown that women are markedly absent in the decision-making positions, leadership roles, and higher levels of emergency response organizations (Noel 1990; League of the Red Cross and Red Crescent Societies 1991). In Australia, for example, of those trained in emergency management through the Australian Emergency Management Institute in 1994, only 5 percent were women (Wraith 1997). Therefore, long before a disaster hits a community, women need to be recruited into emergency response planning organizations, and barriers should be removed so that they can pursue leadership roles.

Past research found that when women's grassroots groups tried to bring their disaster concerns to the planning table, they were regarded as "hysterical housewives," and their disaster work was trivialized and not seen as legitimate (Neal and Phillips 1990). Phillips (1990) notes that women in this field face many obstacles, such as the "old boys' network" and gender stereotyping. These same issues emerged in my study. Many argue that women's vulnerability in disasters would decrease tremendously if they were given a voice in how disasters are managed in their communities.

In Grand Forks, for example, women's perspectives could have contributed to alleviating the problems of childcare, housing, domestic violence, and the stigma of charity. Women had experiences in the disaster that were particular to them as women. For example, most women were responsible for childcare duties, and many women expressed feelings of vulnerability and emotional loss due to painful memories of past sexual and physical abuse. If women were involved in disaster planning, they could prepare local mental health services agencies for some of these female-specific issues, so counselors could look for signs of these situations and be able to help. In addition, women were more sensitive to the threat of risk, resulting in gender differences in preparation activities and evacuation. Women's perspectives on risk and response to risk could be well utilized in disaster planning and management.

Research Recommendations

The women's experiences in the disaster were shaped by certain characteristics of who they were—factors such as disability, race, age, social class, and sexual orientation—and the politics of difference. In the debate on the concept of "woman," feminist theorists argue that it is problematic to conceptualize woman in universal terms. Many feminist theorists strive for a balance in recognizing differences among women and acknowledging some shared experiences. I found in my data both commonalities of experience and instances of difference. I think future research should continue to examine how difference and vulnerability intersect in disasters.

Class, power, status, and money all played a role in how the women experienced the disaster. Resources were critical during the evacuation period, as they determined where families were evacuated and the degree of comfort that they lived in during evacuation. Middle-class families with relatives or friends in homes large enough to accommodate additional families obviously fared better than those women with no resources who had to stay in evacuation shelters. Resources were also critical during the economic upheaval, as individuals struggled to cope with enormous and devastating financial losses and having to abandon future goals, such as returning to school or adopting a child. Future research could continue to test the idea that women's experiences in disaster are affected by their access to resources and examine more women at both ends of the resource continuum.

Research should also address the effect of mental and physical disabilities, sexual orientation, and age on women's disaster experiences. In my research, women with physical and mental disabilities faced greater challenges during the flood than women without disabilities. Thus, it would be worthwhile to explore that topic further. Research should also address how homophobic ideologies affect lesbians and gays in a disaster. Sexual orientation was found to be important in my study, but I only had one lesbian in my sample. I found that, for her, vulnerability from the disaster was added to a previous vulnerability, living in a homophobic society. She and her partner had to hide in their own home, as their temporary housing only allowed married couples. I found that older age also contributed to a greater vulnerability to emotional, physical, and financial pressures. While they would deny it and claim they were luckier than younger families, the elderly women often had to cope with more emotionally, physically, and financially. They had fewer options to pick up and start over.

The intersection of race, ethnicity, and gender in the disaster context should be explored further in future research. As the Grand Forks region is predominantly white, my sample is not diverse in terms of race and ethnicity. The two Latina women in the study were of middle-class and working-class backgrounds and did not seem to be more vulnerable or marginalized due to race or ethnicity.[5] As they spoke English, they faced no language barriers, an issue that has surfaced in other disasters. Future research could also look for the ways in which the patterns discovered in this study, such as women's complex relationships to their families and their religion or their experiences with threats to their emotional and physical well-being, differ by race and ethnicity.

Second, I recommend more research on the issue of domestic violence. Domestic violence is acknowledged as a social problem, but the experience of being battered is still not well understood. Examining intimate violence within the context of a natural disaster provides insight into domestic violence behaviors in general. For example, we can begin to understand how batterers use the disaster as an excuse and justification for the violence. Past research has found that some battered women also blame an external force, such as drug addiction or pressures at work, for the situation (Ferraro and Johnson 1983). In that way, the violence is seen as a temporary situation that can be overcome, and the women can deny that the abusers want to hurt them. Thus, battered women may frame disasters as an external force rationalization, as Karen did to some extent in her interview. Disasters are important research sites, and I believe domestic violence theories could be advanced by further research in the disaster context.

Future research needs to go beyond asking if woman battering rates increase. Research should help us to determine when in the disaster that battering is most severe. This study and the limited existing research on woman battering in the context of disasters indicate that increased demand for services may occur even months after the disaster. For example, in Enarson's (1998) survey of domestic violence organizations, many reported increases six months to a year later. Yet I learned that the Community Violence Intervention Center in Grand Forks, which had their hotline number forwarded to a cell phone so that evacuated staff scattered across Minnesota and North Dakota could continue to receive calls, received many calls for help in the acute period of the crisis. Thus, research could assess when the need for services is the greatest and why and how women at risk could be helped prior to the disaster.

Research should continue to test the universal risk theories that claim that all women are vulnerable to domestic violence, and that the risk of being battered is shared equally by women of all classes, ages, races, and abilities. In terms of social class and disability issues, my data challenge these theories of woman battering by showing that women's status does affect their vulnerability and exposure to risk. For example, the data show that disabled women are more vulnerable as they are more isolated and more likely to have to stay in the same location as the batterer, due to medical and housing needs. The experiences of violence for women with disabilities are not often heard (Chenoweth 1996), and the intersection of gender and disability in general is not well explored in research (Thomson 1994). Also, the data show that lower-class and middle-class women have different experiences as victims of domestic violence because resources may make a difference in the women's ability to move out and find new housing and locate support services. Future research could confirm these results about domestic violence, disability, and class, by studying these issues in even more depth with a larger sample.

My last research recommendation concerns the issue of women and social change. This study revealed that crisis situations and turning point moments may provide opportunities for positive changes in women's conceptions of themselves, and these in turn could lead to social change in regard to gender and economic equality. I believe future research should focus on this phenomenon. The extant literature has shown that men and women do not equally share the division of labor at home and that most women still occupy female-dominated occupations in the economic sector, which pay less than traditionally male occupations. The research on attitudes, however, shows that men's and women's attitudes about the division of labor at home and in the workplace are ahead of their behavior. In this research, women took on new roles because the situation demanded it, and they excelled in juggling multiple roles, including leadership roles usually occupied by men. I believe that research could help us understand how these moments of change could happen in nondisaster times and how women who have the capacity for positions in male-dominated fields could be presented with opportunities to enter these fields.

This study also found that women's changes in themselves also included shifts in their ideologies about the poor and people who accept welfare. Again, these shifts could lead to significant social change, and should be explored in future research. As the gap between rich and poor has continued to expand in the new century, and administrations cut funding for federal assistance programs for poor families and children, it is critical that we learn how the achievement ideology can be challenged. Future research should examine how crises provide opportunities for Americans to develop a greater empathy for those in poverty, as well as a greater understanding of how the economic system, and not individual factors such as hard work, determine one's economic standing. It may be overly optimistic, but I hope that the women's experiences present a hopeful account of social change: middle-class women from the heartland of America became empowered and more self-confident as women, and learned to sympathize with marginalized Americans who live in poverty.

In what used to be a neighborhood full of family homes now stands a new park (in the foreground) and a new floodwall (in the background) in East Grand Forks. Both Grand Forks and East Grand Forks demolished neighborhoods close to the river and created parks, picnic areas, and bike paths. Many believed that this was the best option for a long-term sustainable approach to the flooding of the Red River. In Grand Forks, hundreds of homes were removed from the 100-year floodplain. *Photo by Pattijean Hooper.*

* * *

In all, the women's stories are about continuity and change, about loss and discovery. The book opened with the story of Elaine, a story that illustrated the hardship of the event but also the appreciation that was nurtured for neighbors, family, and a hometown that was hit by two disasters, flood and fire. The residents of Grand Forks did not give up on their city; they worked for years—sometimes with great conflict—after the flood to rebuild the homes, businesses, and schools in a manner that was meaningful and would work for them. Some residents left Grand Forks for good, but not as many as originally feared. Elaine was not the same person she was before the winter and spring of 1997. She is sad about things she lost, but she does not think about it as much now. Occasionally she walks through the park that was once her neighborhood and is overwhelmed simply by the profound change of the landscape—where the homes of her neighbors stood are now trees and grass. Elaine and the women of Grand Forks are not alone in their ordeal. Thousands of Americans survive the devastating effects of natural, technological, and environmental disasters each year, and hundreds of thousands more endure crises related to joblessness, illness, poverty, divorce, and homelessness. My findings suggest that for all of these survivors, their stories should be heard with compassion, remembering that their plight is not due to a flaw in character or a lapse in judgment but most often due to forces and structures out of their control.

Appendix

Notes on Methodology

This book began as my dissertation. I was a graduate student research assistant for many years at the Natural Hazard Center at the Institute for Behavioral Sciences at the University of Colorado and thus was prepared to do my doctoral research on a natural disaster. One morning in April 1997, my advisor, Dennis Mileti, called me into his office and told me that I should pack my bags, grab my tape recorder, and head for Grand Forks, North Dakota, a place I had never been before. Several years later, my longitudinal, qualitative study was complete. This appendix briefly outlines some of the methodological issues of the project. The final project was based on data from a longitudinal, qualitative study undertaken over a period of several years.

The benefits of utilizing qualitative methods for this project were numerous. I considered qualitative methods to be an appropriate methodology for my project because qualitative methods are useful to study a previously unexplored topic, and there is a recognized dearth of qualitative research in disaster studies, especially in terms of studying women in disasters. Within the disaster community, qualitative research is now highly recommended as the way to study topics in disaster about which the database is weak. As with all qualitative research, the goal is to seek in-depth and intimate information about a smaller group of persons and to focus on the context of discovery rather than verification (Ambert et al. 1995).

The qualitative methods did, in fact, allow for the emergence of the unexpected as the in-depth interviews revealed issues not found in the literature. As I collected and analyzed the data, I realized that the information was rich and new to the literature. The interviews were longer, more complex, and more in-depth than anticipated. My final research design included sixty in-depth interviews with forty women as the primary method of data collection, some limited observation as a secondary method, and, finally, document analysis as a tertiary or supplementary method. To protect the privacy of the participants, pseudonyms have been used for all participants throughout the project.

My research design was longitudinal. I collected forty interviews with forty women and then returned to Grand Forks one year later and reinterviewed twenty of the same women. A longitudinal design is considered particularly valuable for disaster research as it allows the researcher to examine the recovery phase of the disaster. While the recovery phase is considered the least researched and least understood disaster phase, some attention has been paid to it in the past few years. The follow-up site visits were scheduled for fifteen months after the initial flooding, as disaster recovery researchers have found that examining the first twelve to twenty-four months after a major disaster provides a good perspective on long-term recovery.[1] In disasters, "recovery" covers a variety of complex activities, so it is important to revisit a disaster site during this time to research how individuals, families, and communities have fared during this phase of disaster. I visited Grand Forks in June, July, August, and September of 1997 and again for follow-up interviews in February and June through July of 1998.

In addition to the goals of qualitative research to acquire rich, meaningful data, I also worked toward the goals of feminist research in my project. This research project was designed in an effort to make women's lives visible and their voices audible, goals that Shulamit Reinharz (1992) posits are important objectives of feminist ethnography. I used fieldwork to get closer to women's realities, and in alignment with feminist research in general, I worked toward three goals in this research: "(1) to document the lives and activities of women, (2) to understand the experience of women from their own point of view, and (3) to conceptualize women's behavior as an expression of social contexts" (Reinharz 1992, p. 51). I set out on this project with the hope that I could improve the lives of women by understanding and writing about their experiences and challenges in the disaster.

My role in the setting involved several dimensions. First, I took on an observer-as-participant role,[2] as my study began with one-visit interviews and involved meeting a wide variety of people

over short periods of time. As an observer-as-participant, I identified myself as a researcher immediately, and I made no pretense of
being a member of the group that I was researching. As this role
dictates, I participated in group activities only in a superficial manner. I was not a member of the group at this point. The "group" in
my research was not a cohesive group as in some studies, but rather
they were women living in one geographical area who all experienced the same natural disaster. Thus, I identified myself as a researcher to each individual woman I met, as well as more publicly in
an article about my study that appeared in July 1997 in the local
newspaper, *The Grand Forks Herald*.

Over time, however, I took on a participant-as-observer role, as
I developed in-depth relationships, made formal and informal observations, and established relationships with informants who trusted
me and interacted with me as friends. As an observer-as-participant,
I participated in the activities of the group that I was studying, but
unlike the complete participant, everyone understood that I was
conducting research. After "breaking into the setting," I fulfilled the
roles of observer-as-participant and participant-as-observer simultaneously for the year-long data collection process. I was continuously
conducting new interviews as well as visiting and spending time with
women I had initially interviewed months before. For example, in a
single day I took on the observer-as-participant role in the morning
as I interviewed a woman for the first time and then became a
participant-as-observer in the evening to attend a barbecue and relax
with a former interviewee and current informant. Taken as a whole,
my researcher role could be classified as that of a peripheral group
member; such a classification captures aspects of both participating
and observing. With a peripheral membership role, I interacted
closely and frequently enough to be an insider without taking on the
role of a central or full member. One barrier to more central membership was that I did not live in or near my setting, thereby limit-
ing my contact and relegating me to being "with" but not "part of"
the group (Adler and Adler 1994).

One other aspect of my entree into the setting deserves men-
tion. Several members of the Sociology Department at the University of North Dakota assisted me in becoming more integrated into
the community of Grand Forks. These faculty members invited me
to local events, gave me names for leads, spent time giving me background information on the setting, and took phone calls for me

from potential interviewees when I was not in Grand Forks. Indeed, one professor even let me stay in her home during one of my site visits, a gesture that was most helpful as it placed me right in the middle of a neighborhood undergoing a difficult recovery: half the neighborhood was going to be demolished, the other half preserved. By staying there, and not at my usual motel on the other side of town, I felt more immersed in the community.

In the sample, my goal was to achieve as much diversity as possible, considering the restrictions within the population. I hoped, especially, to have diversity in the areas of amount of flood damage, age, class, marital status, and family composition, and I was able to achieve this sample diversity. I understood that the area was racially homogenous, so it would be difficult to achieve diversity in terms of race and ethnicity.

The sample was generated from two sources. First, more than half of the respondents were found through a snowball sample technique (Biernacki and Waldorf 1982). A work colleague in Boulder, a native of Grand Forks, provided the names of two women as my initial contacts. From these women, I got the names of two more women to interview, and thus my sample "snowballed." At the end of each interview, I asked my respondents to recommend someone "different from themselves" for my next interview, in order to increase the diversity of the sample, a strategy that worked well. Women often suggested someone of a different age, marital status, occupation, or degree of flood damage from themselves. There were some challenges finding some of the women suggested because many women were not in their original homes or reachable at their old phone numbers. Most women agreed without hesitation to meet me for an interview the first time I called; usually when they heard that their friend or work colleague had given me their name, they felt comfortable agreeing to the interview. Myrna, an eighty-year-old woman who lost her house, was surprised that I wanted to hear her story and not her husband's, as "he's the talker in the family," but she was happy to oblige. One woman needed some persuasion, and two women, unfortunately, for reasons unknown to me, declined to be interviewed. I made a judgment call when talking with these three women. The first one hesitated but seemed interested. I did not feel as if I was persuading someone to participate who did not want to, and as a result I did not feel this was unethical. The other two women, however, declined outright, and I did not feel it would be ethical to try to persuade them to participate if they did not feel comfortable doing so.

The second half of my sample was self-selected. During a field visit in July 1997, I received a telephone call from a reporter at the *Grand Forks Herald* who wanted to interview me. This reporter had heard through the grapevine that I was in town interviewing women, and the gender piece of my research caught her attention. She convinced her (male) editor that this story was worth pursuing, and her story included a phone number for women to call if they were interested in participating in my study. I received dozens of phone calls. Interestingly, the North Dakota Museum of Art in Grand Forks conducted an oral history project (at the same time as my research), recruiting participants with radio ads and newspaper articles, but had few volunteers. This contrasted sharply with the response to my study. It may have been a status issue, as I was doing a student project, as opposed to the high-status museum with the high-status oral history project. It may have also been that in addition to having the low status of a student, I was also fairly young and a woman, all of which may have been perceived as less intimidating than the more official researchers at the museum. As Warren (1988) has argued, one advantage to being a female researcher is that you are seen as harmless.

The women who telephoned offered a wide variety of reasons for volunteering, some wanting to help out and others worrying that no one else would call. One woman said, "I think people need to do these things for each other." One woman felt that her story was "not very exciting," but she thought I might need extra people, while another woman felt that she was coming at the flood "from different angle" so she thought I might be interested in her story. Many of them seemed pleased that a researcher was interested in women's experiences, and a few noted that they felt that women's stories are often overlooked. While these women were self-selected for the study, they were diverse in their experiences, backgrounds, and demographics.

The final sample of forty women represented a suitable amount of diversity. The women ranged in age from eighteen to eighty years old, with a majority falling into the range of thirty to sixty years old. Marital statuses were also varied, including married, divorced, widowed, single (never married), and cohabitating with a significant other. Most of the women had completed high school, many of them had gone to college, and a few had postgraduate degrees. The women were a mixture of upper-middle class, middle class, working class, and lower class, although most fell into the middle- and working-class categories, and almost all self-identified as middle class, as most Americans do. In terms of occupations and professions, many were in nursing or teaching, a few in food service, postal service, and department store sales, and several were homemakers. Three were unemployed and looking for work, and one was unable to work and received disability assistance. Religious affiliations included Lutheran, Catholic, agnostic, Jewish, Methodist, Evangelical, and Baptist. Thirty-nine of the women were heterosexual, one was a lesbian. Thirty-eight of the women were white, and two were Latina. Nineteen had children under the age of eighteen living at home, several had adult children, and others had no children. The backgrounds of these women reflected the larger demographics of Grand Forks, which is predominantly white, middle class, heterosexual, and a mixture of religions, although largely Lutheran.

The sample was also diverse in the degree of flood damage they experienced. Thirty-six of the women had significant damage to their homes, and thirteen of those had homes that could not be salvaged. Most of the damaged houses were flooded on one floor, so the women lost the belongings, appliances, and furniture on that floor. During the reconstruction period, the women and their families were forced to live in half their normal living space. The women who lost their homes often lost all their belongings, furniture, clothes, and appliances; most of them had painstakingly had moved all of those items to the second floor of their homes, only to have the flood waters reach the roof. The four undamaged residences were in the western part of Grand Forks, the only area the flood waters did not reach. Those four women, however, were affected greatly by the problems and stresses associated with evacuation, child care, and employment during and after the disaster.

I used three methods of data collection: sixty in-depth interviews, analysis of documentary data, and observation. I collected data over a thirteen-month period from 1997 to 1998. My primary data collection method was in-depth interviews. I conducted sixty in-depth interviews with forty women during six site visits, each lasting one to two weeks, between July 1997 and July 1998. I began the interviews in July 1997, having received approval from the University of Colorado's Human Research Committee to conduct the research. I arranged the interviews during the initial phone conversation with each woman; often I called from Colorado before I left for the site visit. I conducted the majority of the interviews in the participants' homes, but a few were held in my hotel room, local coffee shops or restaurants, or at the participants' place of work. While coffee shops were noisy and thus made it more difficult to transcribe the interviews later, some women chose this option so that they did not have to worry about family members interrupting the interview or be concerned that I saw the state of their homes. During one interview on a woman's deck, we were interrupted a few times by a crop duster plane, as her house backed onto a potato field. When I met them at cafes or restaurants, I always paid for the interviewees' meals or coffee during interviews, as I felt this was a reasonable expense to take on considering the time and effort they were giving me by doing the interview. When I conducted interviews in the women's homes, I was almost always served refreshments.

All interviewees were given a written consent form to read and sign. This form explained the project and informed the participants that the interviews were voluntary and they had the right to discontinue participation at any time. The form also articulated that the interviews would be tape recorded but that their privacy would be maintained; tapes would be erased after transcription, and their identity would remain confidential. None of the women seemed to have any hesitation or reluctance to sign the form. Some had trouble filling out the address section as they did not know how long they would be in their temporary housing. I took the signed interviews back to Colorado, photocopied them, and then sent a copy back to the interviewee, as I had promised them. Every interviewee received a thank-you note from me after each interview. Interviews lasted from one to five hours, with most interviews taking approximately two hours. For longer interviews, we took breaks in the middle (we walked the dog or had lunch), or we arranged to meet another day to complete the interviews.

During the interviews, I asked the women to tell me the story of their entire flood experience. I began with "Tell me what happened" and continued with "And what happened next?" as we progressed. As with all unstructured interviews, my goal was understanding. By asking for the entire story, listening carefully, and prompting for details and explanation, I was able to help each participant touch on all the subjects that were relevant and important for her. I strove to make the interviews conversations with give-and-take, as that makes an interview "more honest, morally sound, and reliable" by treating the participant as an equal (Fontana and Frey 1994, p. 371). I offered support throughout the interviews, and I shared any information I could that would help. As Oakley (1981) found in her research, the women looked to me to "not only reassure but inform" (p. 43). The women often asked me questions on a wide variety of topics, such as my own experiences with disaster,[3] if I had children, what other women were going through, and what my preliminary findings were. For example, when asked if anyone else was "falling apart," I reassured women that other women and their families were having similar troubles.

As Oakley found in her research (1975, 1981), the women were curious about what kind of person I was and how I became interested in this subject matter. I always answered any questions. I also provided any information I had about disaster resources or advice I had heard from other women. For instance, one woman told me that her minister told the congregation to think of flood recovery as a marathon, not a sprint, so go slowly, breathe, and acknowledge that it will take a long time. I repeated this line to other women who were frustrated by the length of recovery, and they later told me that this one piece of advice helped them more than any other. In alignment with Oakley, I refused to "parry" or avoid the women's questions, because the interview was not a one-way process but rather a conversation with give-and-take between interviewer and participant. I followed Oakley's principle that an interview should be nonhierarchical, and the interviewer should be willing to invest his or her own personal identity in the relationship. Indeed, I found that Oakley's belief that in longitudinal, in-depth interviewing, there is "no intimacy without reciprocity" to be especially accurate in my interviews (1981, p. 49).

In some cases my relationships with the interviewees were ongoing. In between the site visits, I kept in touch with many of the women, exchanging phone calls and correspondence, such as Christmas letters and baby announcements. For example, I called one woman after a site visit to talk more about her domestic violence situation because I could tell she could use the support. Another woman expressed interest in moving to Colorado, where I lived at the time, so I periodically sent her the classifieds from the

Colorado newspapers, and I offered to host her at my house when she arrived. At one time I mailed a magazine article on a little-known disease afflicting one of the participants, as we had discussed her disability and the lack of knowledge surrounding her illness. Keeping in touch with the forty women was a logistical challenge; during my study most of the women moved at least once. I felt very close to many of the women and continued to correspond with many of them for many years (three of them even six years) after the flood.

As mentioned above, twenty of the women were formally interviewed a second time, for a total of sixty interviews. The sample for follow-up interviews was chosen for its diversity, just as the original sample of forty was chosen. In order to achieve diversity, I sought to speak with women who represented different backgrounds and circumstances: I chose women from the original sample of forty who represented a range of class backgrounds, different ages, religions, and marital statuses, and who experienced various flood damage levels. In addition, I made an effort to include in the follow-up interviews a balance of those women who at the first interview had felt powerless, those who had been empowered, those who felt negatively about the future, and those who were more optimistic. Finally, I arranged to interview women a second time if they had circumstances that especially needed follow-up, such as the women in domestic violence situations. In these interviews, because background information had already been collected, I focused on the period of time between the first and second interviews. Sometimes, however, the participant wanted to return to an issue that we had previously discussed, or she brought up a subject that had occurred prior to the first interview but that she had not discussed then. For the follow-up interviews I brought a loosely structured interview guide that I had prepared, for covering issues that I wanted to make sure we followed up on in our talk. Usually I did not need to refer to that sheet as the topics came up more naturally.

While the in-depth interviews were my primary data collection method, I also used observation as a secondary method. Observation is an important method, although rarely used solely on its own, that involves looking, listening, watching, and asking. Unlike other members of society, who also observe in their everyday life, social scientists have a more systematic and purposive approach to observation, studying their surroundings repeatedly and regularly, motivated by theoretical questions (Adler and Adler 1994; Lofland and Lofland 1984).

I observed both the interviewees as well as other women and men in the community throughout the thirteen months of the data collection period, witnessing a wide variety of activities and settings. For example, I attended community potluck meals, family barbecues and dinners, chamber of commerce town meetings, and museum gatherings. I visited the town's family violence prevention center and Fourth of July celebration, and spent time with women, and sometimes also with their children or partners, at diners, parks, coffee shops, recreation centers, shopping malls, and family homes. I attended church with one participant and her family.[4] I also went to a women-only workout center and took long walks through neighborhoods. I gained a good sense of family and gender relations in the community by watching and observing; for example, at the local shopping malls, men waited in cars, with the engine running, smoking, while the women went into the mall and shopped, a phenomenon I had not observed to such an extent in other places I had lived. I recorded significant information from these observations and informal interactions in my field notes.

In addition, I listened in on official FEMA conference calls on the Grand Forks flood from April through June 1997. Each conference call had a wide range of participants, such as FEMA officials in Washington, representatives from the Salvation Army and the Humane Society, and Grand Forks emergency managers, and the goal was to have an "information exchange opportunity." In these calls, the participants discussed various problems, such as volunteer managers becoming burnt out or how produce from California had gone bad, and analyzed strategies for recovery, such as having a telethon to raise money or how to improve communication between agencies. These calls helped to keep me on the pulse of what was happening day to day when I was not there doing fieldwork. The calls were once a week for three months, and each lasted several hours. I also attended "The Flood of the Century" conference at the University of Manitoba in September 1997, and sessions on the Grand Forks flood at the Natural Hazard Center workshop in July 1998 for more information gathering.

The tertiary method of data collection was the analysis of documentary data. Analysis of any type of documents, including newspapers, graffiti, essays, songs, and pictures, tells us a great deal about how humans live because a person's conscious or unconscious beliefs, attitudes, values, and ideas are often revealed in their communications (Fraenkel and Wallen 1996). Quarantelli (1994) posited that these types of documentation are significant for sociological research on disasters but often ignored. I analyzed documentary data, which I placed into three categories: (1) official, such as newspapers or agency files, (2) personal, such as journals, and (3) cultural, such as graffiti. This analysis was intended to be supplementary data to the in-depth interviews.

Most of the official documents that I analyzed were from two sources. First, I examined hundreds of issues of the *Grand Forks Herald* newspaper to better understand the event from the media's perspective and to keep in touch with human interest stories while I was in Colorado. The newspaper was useful to verify information I gathered more casually and to learn about the events prior to my arrival. Second, I analyzed documents from the Community Violence Intervention Center. These documents provided information on the domestic violence situation during the disaster, such as the number of protection orders filed during the recovery period.

I also collected, read, and analyzed many personal documents given to me by women in Grand Forks. The most common items shared were diaries, photo albums, and calendars. Diaries were the most personal item to share, and many women chose to read me passages during our interviews, while others gave me copies of certain pages. Photo albums were also very personal and cherished items for the women. They shared both albums of their life before the flood and the albums they had made with photographs from the flood. Some of the women also showed me photographs that had been damaged in the flood, a moment that was often very emotional. The photographs of their old lives were especially important in terms of impression management and dealing with downward mobility. For many of the women, the calendar was a treasured item after the flood, as it documented the event for them. On these wall calendars, the women had written items such as "Browns left for Bemidji today" (neighbors evacuating to a town in Minnesota named Bemidji, a common evacuation destination) or "Last dinner at home" or "First night back in house." Some of the women felt they could not participate in the interview with me until they found their calendars and had them in front of them. They often remarked that they would forget something without the calendar to serve as a guide because of their "flood brain."

In addition to diaries, calendars, and photo albums, the women also shared personal letters and e-mails. Most of these items were written to, or by, close friends or family. For example, one woman gave me a copy of a church newsletter that had printed a letter she had written to the church to express thanks for a donation to flood victims. E-mails were an interesting way to see how the women presented their situation to their friends and family in other parts of the state or country, and unlike handwritten letters, the author generally retained a copy. While most of these items were given to me by interviewees, usually during an interview, at times I gathered these documents from women who were not in my interview sample. For example, one interviewee brought a friend with her to our breakfast date at Denny's, and the friend brought a list of her thoughts on the flood to share with me.

Cultural artifacts were also important documents for content analysis. One such artifact was the emergent graffiti in the town, such as the angry "49 Feet My Ass!" message. I observed numerous other examples, including the sentimental "Home Sweet Home" on the front door of a destroyed house and the tongue-in-cheek "Wipe Your Feet" on the side of a house that was full of mud, silt, and sewage. The graffiti helped me to get a good sense of how the community was coping, and because the comments were anonymous, I felt that the graffiti artists were able to express their true feelings about the disaster. Other researchers termed the Grand Forks graffiti messages "catastroffiti," and found that they show a mixture of humor, frustration, and political commentary (Hagen et al. 1999).

Other cultural artifacts included the town's "flood songs," Bruce Springsteen's "My Hometown," Bette Midler's "You're the Wind Beneath my Wings," and "In the Middle of the Night" by Billy Joel. The local radio stations dubbed these three songs the official songs of the flood and played them continuously. Numerous flood videos created by local radio stations and hospitals often included the three flood songs as background music. I also took note of various "flood art products" such as colorful, optimistic posters showing community members holding hands, and observed the special art exhibit on the flood, which displayed flood photographs. Finally, I also documented and analyzed the local flood humor, which included jokes about having a "flood moment," a joking, self-deprecating comment made when an individual went totally blank while talking, and other nascent expressions, such as "Silt Happens," the disaster version of the common expression "Shit Happens."

The interview process was designed to generate rich, detailed descriptions of the women's experience in the disaster to lay the groundwork for inductive theory construction. In other words, I did not enter the research setting to test a theory or model but rather to create a theoretical model based on what I found. I analyzed the interviews, the observations, and the documentary data in order to find patterns, create conceptual categories, and develop a model with high validity.

I transcribed all sixty interviews in their entirety. I began to analyze the transcribed data immediately, during the summer that I began interviewing. In the initial stages of data collection, I identified patterns in the data, and these patterns were then tested each time I collected more data. In this type of research, the data collection process and the data analysis process are interwoven, cyclical, and dynamic processes (Glaser and Strauss 1967; Lofland and Lofland 1984; Ambert et al. 1995). In other words, the interviews and the interpretation and analysis of the data were ongoing and simultaneous. Such a structure allows the researcher to take control of the data, as the early analytic work leads to data collection around emerging themes and questions (Charmaz 1995, p. 31).

As the research progressed, I continued to code my field notes and interview transcriptions according to the different conceptual categories that emerged from the interviews, following the grounded theory approach (Glaser and Strauss 1967). I began to see how the women's experiences followed similar patterns, and I explored the variations in each additional interview. This method allowed me to test the strength and validity of my model with each additional interview, a process known as "constant comparative analysis" (Glaser 1978). Once the initial pattern emerged, I could then probe for more details to hone in on the concept or pattern in later interviews. This method permits the preliminary findings to influence the subsequent data gathering and analysis, while always allowing the women to tell the stories of their own experiences.

The analysis was ongoing, but I focused particularly on my theoretical models after the first forty interviews and before I began the follow-up interviews. I felt that understanding the patterns that emerged from the first wave of data would help me determine the direction of the follow-up interviews and identify concepts requiring further verification. After each interview, I would return to my model and see whether the new data challenged, confirmed, or expanded it. When I finished my sixtieth interview, I felt that my data gathering was complete. I felt I had reached "theoretical saturation" (Glaser and Strauss 1967), meaning I was no longer finding new information with which to expand or change my theoretical model, and the major trends were repeating. The goal of this analysis was to develop a theoretical framework that was grounded in the empirical events being studied (Glaser and Strauss 1967; Lofland and Lofland 1984). The emerging concepts and theories were then linked to the existing research literature.

There are some positive and negative aspects to being an outsider in the research setting. The clear disadvantage is that by not living in or near my research setting, I could not become a full member of the setting, which would allow for the most intimate data to be collected. I lived thousands of miles away and could only collect data firsthand when I made my site visits. In addition, I collected most of my data through interviews with people I had never met before, thereby raising concerns that I might not be able to gain trust and respect from the participants. Often, participant observation researchers find that only from continuous, immersed contact did they find the richest data (Adler and Adler 1987).

While being an outsider may have had some drawbacks, ultimately it was a beneficial role for me. Most residents were open and hospitable to me, even though I was an outsider, and in many cases they were more hospitable, due to the norms of their culture, which included hospitality and generosity. Often, I felt that I got a more complete story from women, as they realized that I needed more background information. For example, on numerous occasions women would say, "You know what I mean?" and then would catch themselves and say, "Oh, probably not! Let me explain." This was extremely valuable for my data collection. As Lofland and Lofland (1984) point out, there are some advantages for the investigator in being the "socially acceptable incompetent" in the research setting, as it allows people to teach things to the investigator, and the subjects believe that it will not offend the investigator to be told "obvious" things. In this situation, the "ignorant" investigator is in a good position to keep "the flow of information coming smoothly"

(Lofland and Lofland 1984, p. 38). Lewis (1978) refers to the outside investigator as a "greenhorn," and believes that greenhorns are more sensitive to things in the new environment that others might miss: "As one trying to become familiar with an unfamiliar social setting, the newcomer has to be a learner, and as such is more likely than anyone else to be a conscious assimilator of local styles, practices, and beliefs" (p. 93).

Clearly, not living in Grand Forks restricted my contact with the women, but it also facilitated my greater involvement in their lives. During my site visits I was thoroughly disengaged from my own family, friends, job, and practical matters of everyday life and completely immersed in the lives of the residents. In addition, being an out-of-towner aided my peripheral membership role in that it allowed me to enter and leave the setting freely, protecting me against overinvolvement. Yet, at the same time it promoted more intimate relationships with my informants as they would include me, sympathetically, in their daily lives because I had no family or home when I was visiting their town.

I would like to add a few words on the subject of emotions in the interviews. In almost every interview that I conducted, the respondent would cry at some point in telling her story. I was concerned about upsetting my interviewees, and I always apologized to the women for upsetting them and let them know that we did not have to continue the conversation. In all cases, the women wanted to continue telling their stories, and they often noted that they felt that it was good for them to cry. Some of the women even told me that it was "therapy" for them, as well as "cathartic" and "helpful." Some women were surprised when they cried, having believed that they were over it. Many of the participants acknowledged the emotional benefits they felt they received by telling their story. Indeed, several of the women asked me if I would be willing to talk with their friends or family members in other places who had gone through disasters and wanted to talk with me about their experiences. One participant in my self-selected sample joked that she called me because she thought, "Here was someone who will listen to my story!"

A few weeks after the flood, most residents admitted that they were sick of hearing everyone's flood stories. Indeed, there was a T-shirt sold in town with the words "Thank-you for not telling me your flood story" printed on the front. The general feeling was, while people were sympathetic, they had gone through the disaster themselves and had no emotional reserves left to help, or even listen to, others. In light of this, I felt it was particularly important to give the women a space in which to tell their stories and to have me, the outsider, listen to them and sympathize. Some of the women even admitted that this was the first time they had ever told some parts of their stories. North Dakota culture generally is not receptive to seeking professional help for mental health problems. Many of the residents of Grand Forks would have benefited from speaking with a therapist about their losses but did not consider that an option. In light of that, I felt that as an objective, uninvolved, impartial, but very sympathetic listener, I could provide some assistance just by listening to their stories.

Notes

Chapter 1

1. In Grand Forks, the "berm" referred to the area of grass between the street and the sidewalk, sometimes called a "tree lawn" in other areas.

2. According to the 1999 report submitted by the International Joint Commission's International Red River Basin Task Force, the 1997 flood in the Red River Basin was the worst disaster per capita in the United States.

3. A worthwhile future study would be to examine males in a disaster outside of these official roles and look at their experiences as husbands, fathers, and sons, and their conflicts with family, work, and community demands.

4. The model I use to make sense of the data is an inductive theoretical model, as the issues, concepts, and themes that are presented in this study emerged from the women's stories. Overall, however, the analysis of my data is rooted in the theoretical frameworks of, primarily, gender studies and an interactionist perspective.

5. For a more detailed discussion of this debate see Spelman (1988), Collins (1990), Grant (1993), and Smith (1987).

6. For example, see Fordham and Ketteridge's (1996) study of floods in Europe. They acknowledge that retaining the public/private dichotomy conceals the complexity of women's lives and that including the community sphere is important, but they utilize it nonetheless because they argue that the dichotomy illuminates social and economic relations under a capitalist patriarchy.

7. Simmel (1965) posited that individuals are only "poor" when they receive assistance. According to Simmel, the main issue is not the

actual deprivation but the social response to such deprivation. The poor are not defined by their socioeconomic status, as one might presume, but by the receipt of charity. As Simmel stated:

> No one is socially poor until he has been assisted. . . . A person is called poor who receives assistance or should receive it. . . . The poor, as a sociological category, are not those who suffer specific deficiencies and deprivations, but those who receive assistance or should receive it according to social norms. Consequently, in this sense, poverty cannot be defined in itself as a quantitative state, but only in terms of the social reaction resulting from a specific situation. . . . The binding function which the poor person performs within an existing society is not generated by the sole fact of being poor; only when society—the totality or particular individuals—reacts towards him with assistance, only then does he play his specific social role. . . . It is only from the moment they are assisted . . . that they become part of a group characterized by poverty. (p. 138–139)

Thus, extending Simmel's argument, the women of Grand Forks, therefore, did not become poor in their own eyes and in the eyes of others when they lost their homes, belongings, and financial standing. Instead, the women took on the status of the poor the moment they went to stand in line for assistance or when they spent a night in a shelter. The poor, according to Simmel, are not united by the interaction of their members but by the collective attitude which society as a whole adopts towards them. While I cannot accept his argument entirely—I believe individuals can suffer from extreme poverty without receiving any assistance—I think his argument is worthwhile to consider since it illustrates the profound impact of collecting assistance.

    8. For a complete discussion of the self and identity, see Mead (1934), Cooley (1902), and Goffman (1959).

Chapter 2

    1. Some ethnographies use pseudonyms for the city, state, or region where the research takes place. Disaster research, however, usually identifies the actual location of the research because much can be learned by knowing the very specifics of the location, terrain, hazard risk, and population. In this study, I use the term "Grand Forks" to refer to both East Grand Forks, Minnesota, and Grand Forks, North Dakota.

2. Disaster sociologists have been writing and talking about the myth of panic in disasters for decades. Despite popular opinion, there is no research evidence that panic is anything but a rare phenomenon in disasters. See Quarantelli (1999a) for a discussion on this point.

3. See Pielke (1999) for more discussion on the problems with the forecasts and other details of the flood. Some of the details presented here were confirmed by his article.

4. In a 1998 study, researchers found that suicides increased 63 percent in the year following earthquakes and then they quickly dropped back to normal. They were 31 percent higher after hurricanes, but returned to normal in two years. For floods, the rates were 14 percent higher, but stayed elevated for four years. In general, approximately 2 out of every 100,000 people who survive disasters commit suicide as a result (Associated Press article, "Suicide rise after natural disasters," by Daniel Q. Haney *The Denver Post*, Feb. 5, 1998.)

5. For a discussion on the issue of blame in disasters, see Phillips and Ephraim (1992).

6. Rochford and Blocker (1991) found in their study that flood survivors placed blame on the U.S. Army Corps of Engineers.

7. For a comprehensive discussion on the issue of marginalized groups and disaster vulnerability, see Blaikie et al. (1994).

8. At one time, this was a somewhat controversial debate in the disaster field: to reduce losses, should the focus be on physical approaches or social ones? See Mileti (1999) and Blaikie et al. (1994) for more discussion on this issue.

9. Some of the early sociological writings discuss this point most clearly. Classic articulations of the benefits of social science research in disasters are Barton (1969) and Merton (1969).

10. Quarantelli (1994), often regarded as the grandfather of the field of disaster sociology, hoped to see disaster researchers go beyond the theories of social psychology and collective behavior in order to understand disasters.

11. For more details and discussion about my methodology, see the appendix in this book.

12. These portraits are constructed from a combination of my field notes, the interviews, and letters, e-mails, and phone calls for several years after the flood.

13. Because the other children from the school lived on the other side of the bridge, no other families from that school faced this particular problem.

14. Many of the parents of the women in my study died during the flood and recovery. It is unclear to me if this is just a coincidence in my sample or if the number of deaths among older residents was incredibly high during the year after the flood. There is no doubt that grieving the death of one's parent contributed to the trauma of the flood, and vice versa.

15. Despite its name, the Small Business Administration provides loans for homes as well as businesses.

Chapter 3

1. Discussing traditional and nontraditional gender roles, as I do in this book, is tricky. Sociologists, who do not use the terms "class role" or "race role," are beginning to steer away from overusing the term "gender role" to explain gender in our society. The term is seen as simplifying gender and hiding gender stratification. In light of this, it is important—in this book and in our conversations on gender in general—that we understand that roles are gendered, but gender is much more than a role.

2. Some scholars prefer the term "role stress" to "role conflict" as the latter may imply that an individual is in an "either or" situation. By using "role conflict" I do not mean that women always had to give up one role to perform the other. Sometimes that was the case, but most times the women devised a way to perform all roles.

3. See, for example, Leik et al. (1982) and Turner, Nigg, and Paz (1986) for data on risk perception and preparedness activities.

4. For more on the gendered division of labor in disasters, see Morrow and Enarson (1996), Alway et al. (1998), Dann and Wilson (1993), and Wenger and James (1994.)

5. Morrow and Enarson (1996) also found that these tasks were performed by women after Hurricane Andrew.

6. Alway et al. (1998) found after Hurricane Andrew that husbands often returned to work sooner than their wives.

Chapter 4

1. Newman states in her preface that in the ten years from when her book was first published (1989) until its 1999 edition, there have been

"no other ethnographic studies of middle class Americans who have lost everything they have worked for" (p. ix).

2. Interestingly, this situation emerged more often than one might expect. Many residents did not evacuate with credit cards, an interesting phenomenon given that most of the country uses credit cards for many of their daily financial transactions. Many of the Grand Forks residents spoke of using only cash or checks in their everyday lives, so evacuating with their wallets did not necessarily mean having credit cards. In addition, the local banks closed during the mandatory evacuation, so residents could not withdraw money. Again, many residents did not have, or did not carry, bank cards.

3. For more discussion on the issue of low-income disaster victims and problems with affordable housing, see Bolin (1993), Peacock, Morrow, and Gladwin (1997), and Bolin and Stanford (1998).

4. Quarantelli (1984) reported that higher-income evacuees obtain any surplus housing in a community, and there is almost always a problem finding rental housing for low-income victims. Comerio, Lardis, and Rofe (1994) found that a year after a California quake the single family homes were rebuilt, but the multifamily rental units rented by low-income families were not.

5. Section 8 refers to a federal program that provides assistance to low-income renters, and in this case, Liz qualified because of her domestic violence situation and her low-income status.

6. For example, food stamp recipients are not allowed to use their food stamps for many items, such as alcohol or cooked chickens.

7. Newman (1989) found that many families in her study had a similar situation. All their money was invested in their house, and they had to forgo many other amenities and "make considerable sacrifices in other domains" to retain their middle-class homes (p. 98). For these families, "food, appliances, vacations, clothes, and cars," the basics of a middle-class existence, were sacrificed in order to place all their economic resources in their houses (Newman 1989, p. 102). Unlike Newman's study, however, women in Grand Forks were more likely to experience being "house poor" as a result of forced upward mobility. The families in Newman's study became house poor to be able to stay in affluent areas so they would not face social isolation in poorer neighborhoods, whereas families in Grand Forks were forced to move to wealthier areas where they faced social isolation, a loss of connection, and alienation, and they felt like outsiders.

8. It is important to note that many of these working-class and middle-class families had second homes and cabins "at the lake," which could mean any one of over a thousand lakes in Minnesota and North Dakota that are within driving distance of Grand Forks. Most of these cabins were modest, unweatherized, and inexpensive, and had been in families for years, often inherited by these women, and not purchased. Unlike some areas of the United States, having a second home was not solely the luxury of the upper-middle or upper class in Grand Forks; instead, having a lake house was a fairly common phenomenon of the working and middle classes. Thus, it was common to be relatively financially desperate while still owning a lake house.

9. An anonymous donor, later named by a local newspaper against her wishes, donated millions of dollars to the City of Grand Forks for recovery. The city dubbed this money the "Angel Funds" and tried to distribute a portion of the money to all residents. Unfortunately, the residents were widely displeased with how the city determined who deserved the money, and the rumor was that they miscalculated the amount for each household, so that they ran out of money before they distributed to all neighborhoods.

10. In a study on suicide after natural disasters, the researchers found that the rates of suicide lasted longer after floods—an average of four years—than after earthquakes and hurricanes because of the wide availability of loans—leaving families in debt for years (Krug et al., reported by the *Associated Press* 1998).

11. A basement does not sound at first like a large loss. In many regions of the United States, the basement is solely a crawl space or a laundry room with exposed pipes and cement floors. In Grand Forks, hundreds of families lost basements, which were the main living areas of their homes. These were finished basements with carpeting, bedrooms, fireplaces, offices, and family rooms with entertainment systems. For example, in Lorna's house, the basement consisted of eight rooms: an enormous family room, three bedrooms, a hot tub room, a bathroom, a laundry room, and a storage room. Thus, the basement is for many the center of the home, and for some, the site of most economic home investments.

12. The City of Grand Forks instituted a buyout program to move people out of the floodplain. The logic was that the value of a home would be assessed, the owners would be given a buyout check for that amount, and the City would demolish the home and prohibit building on that site.

13. See, for example, Kai Erickson's *Everything in Its Path* (1976), about the Buffalo Creek dam disaster.

14. Financial problems and conflicts lasted for many years. For example, more than six years after the flood, FEMA gave the city of Grand Forks a bill for $7.9 million, stating that the city had used FEMA funds for work that was not flood related (*Grand Forks Herald*, May 16, 2003).

15. This was a common expression used in Grand Forks to convey that in their culture people are courteous, considerate, and nice to each other.

16. Past research found that in one California earthquake, for very low-income disaster victims a government trailer was a step up in quality of living, and the trailer recipients wanted to stay in the trailers permanently (Bolin and Standford 1991).

17. Peacock et al. (1997) found some of these problems in Florida after Hurricane Andrew.

18. For research illustrating this see Peacock et al. (1997), Bolin and Stanford (1998), and Enarson and Fordham (2001), as well as a literature review on poverty and disasters by Fothergill and Peek (2004).

19. Such a program has been put in place after other disasters as well. For example, after the May 2003 tornadoes in the Midwest, high school students were able to pick out free prom dresses when theirs had been lost in the storm damage.

20. Other research has found that lower-income individuals are more likely to use public evacuation centers in a disaster than higher-income individuals (Yelvington 1997).

21. Enarson and Fordham (2001) found that status, based on gender, race, and class, played a large role in vulnerability in a disaster and in the ability to recover fully.

22. Past research has documented how more marginalized groups, such as poor people of color, often have trouble negotiating the bureaucracies of disaster recovery, including insurance companies, local, state, and federal agencies, and various grant offices (Aptekar 1990).

Chapter 5

1. For more on the hardships of public assistance, the sexism and racism in the social welfare system, and the stereotypes of those who receive welfare, see Wyers (1977), Rank (1994), Sidel (1986), Gordon (1990), Day (1977), Piven (1990), Abramovitz (1994), and Edin (1997).

2. See Collins (1990) and Zinn (1989) for more discussion on race, ethnicity, poverty, and welfare.

3. See Rank (1994) and Kozol (1988, 1995) for a discussion of just how close—often one paycheck—Americans are to poverty, welfare, and homelessness, and see Arendell (1986) and Newman (1989) for more discussion on the effect of divorce on women's fall down the economic ladder.

4. Some of these six techniques are similar to what Goffman (1963) described as efforts by the stigmatized individual to learn and participate in the activities ordinarily not available to someone with that stigma in order to "correct his condition indirectly" (p. 10).

Chapter 6

1. While I discuss the physical and emotional issues the women faced separately for organizational purposes in the chapter, the two areas of their lives have considerable overlap.

2. Rittner and Roth (1993) found that women spoke of these issues and how these areas of their lives were compromised during their experiences in the Holocaust. In concentration camps, for example, women ate moldy bread, wore dirty clothing, and had no privacy when going to the bathroom (Hillesum 1993). Clearly, their experiences were far more traumatic and extreme than those of the women of Grand Forks.

3. This comment was made during her remarks at the Natural Hazard Center annual workshop in Boulder, Colorado, in July 1998.

4. There has been quite a bit written on the issue of women and weight, how women are judged by their appearance, and how young girls are taught in our culture that they must be thin at all costs, even if this means suffering from eating disorders. See, for example, Cunningham (1997).

5. Research on Hurricane Andrew revealed that feelings of being unsafe and threatened were commonplace, as residents felt scared of men from other cities coming in to do construction work (Peacock et al. 1997).

6. A T-shirt worn in Grand Forks reads, "Grand Forks is a rotten place to visit, but I sure would want to live there."

7. It is possible, of course, that like any sensitive and stigmatizing subject matter, the women did not want to tell me about their substance abuse. However, my finding that very few women used substances (other than cigarettes) is consistent with the literature.

8. Research has shown that alcohol abuse is common after a natural disaster, although it has been found to be more common among males than females (Green 1993). Preliminary data from research conducted on the Grand Forks flood showed a rise in alcoholism ( ). ("For Disaster Survivors, a Storm Can Reignite Terror," by J.C. Conklin p. B1, Jan. 18, 1999, *Wall Street Journal*).

9. While I heard several negative comments about the mayor from men, I did not study the issue enough to draw any conclusions about men's overall perceptions of, experiences with, and feelings about the flood. Thus, I cannot comment on whether or not the female mayor got more or less support from women than men.

10. For my purposes in this analysis, both a woman's self-diagnosis and a doctor's diagnosis of depression count as depression.

11. See, for example, Hochschild (1989) and Lopata (1994) for more discussion of the link between women who are full-time homemakers and depression.

12. The American Psychiatric Association includes sexual assault and physical attack in its description of traumas that may result in PTSD.

Chapter 7

1. Some scholars warn of interchanging the concepts of religion and spirituality (Bellah 1970), as they are not the same. While I discuss them together here, I do not use them interchangeably, unless the women did when they told their stories. I let the women use their own voices to describe what they mean by either religion or spirituality in their lives.

2. In order to determine if divorce rates went up after the flood, I went to the Grand Forks's clerk's office to collect data on the number of divorces in Grand Forks in the 1990s. Unfortunately, I was told that all of the city's records on divorces in the years prior to the flood had been destroyed in the flood.

3. Kitson's (1992) work is relevant here. She found that divorces are part of a longer process, not something decided on quickly or on a whim. The average length of time that a marriage is bad before people divorce is four years. Contrary to public opinion, Kitson found that people were often cautious and tentative about the divorce decision process.

4. One exception is the research by Mitchell (1998) on religion and hazard perception. Almost no research has been done on religion as a coping strategy in disasters.

Chapter 8

1. See, for example, Dobash and Dobash (1979), Walker (1979), and Gelles (1997) for more discussion on violence in the home.

2. One limitation in these case studies is that both women are white, so there are no racial implications, but these women do represent the racial demographics of Grand Forks and differed in their class status. Future research should keep in mind that the experiences of battered women of color are likely confounded by race (e.g., Miller 1989; Abraham 1996; Belknap 1996).

3. This quote is from a personal conversation with Faye, a staff member of the center, on June 2, 2003. In addition to the new shelter, the center also has a new office and a new visitation center set up for abusers to visit with their children and to provide a safe place for parents to turn over children for home visits. It was perhaps due to their extensive losses in the flood that they were able to prioritize their needs, gain community support, and run a successful capital campaign. It may be that the flood provided them with the opportunity to grow and meet more needs in the community. They are now able to serve approximately two-thousand clients a year.

4. To date, only two studies focus on the issue of woman battering in the context of disasters. First, Wilson, Phillips, and Neal (1998) studied community organizations' perceptions of and responses to domestic violence in Santa Cruz, California, after the Loma Prieta earthquake; in Lancaster, Texas, after a tornado; and in Dade County, Florida, following Hurricane Andrew. Second, Enarson (1998) surveyed seventy-seven domestic violence organizations in the United States and Canada, fourty-one of which had some disaster experience, to learn about their disaster planning and experience. Other disaster studies have mentioned the issue of woman battering in tangential, less focused ways.

5. Wilson and her colleagues (1998) found that Santa Cruz reported large increases in domestic violence, the city of Lancaster, Texas, reported no noticeable increase, and in Dade County, Florida, the data were mixed, although they suggested an increase. Enarson (1988) found that those domestic violence programs that experienced a disaster indicated declining service demand during the impact period, as women could not access the services, but an increased demand after that, which was complicated by a decrease in organizational resources. For many domestic violence programs the demand for services was mostly from existing clients, not from women seeking help for the first time. Morrow and Enarson (1996), in their research on women in Hurricane Andrew, did not focus specifically on the topic of domestic violence but reported that social

service providers felt strongly that family violence had increased. Morrow (1997) reported that there was initially a drop in domestic violence injunctions after Hurricane Andrew, perhaps due to the inaccessibility of government services, but that subsequently the number of injunctions increased substantially. Based on their experiences in disasters in Australia, several social service providers reported that increases in domestic violence rates are "repeatedly found" during disasters and their aftermaths (Honeycombe 1993, p. 29; Dobson 1994). While evidence is limited, the common perception, based on increased demand for services, is that battering rates increase. It is difficult to know if the battered women seeking assistance are mostly existing clients, meaning they sought help for their battering situations prior to the disaster, or new clients, implying that the disaster brought on physical violence in relationships that were not abusive before the event. If indeed all the clients are existing ones, then technically the number of battered women does not increase, and the increased demand is indicative of the clients all needing help at the same time. Another scenario may be that many women were in domestic violence relationships prior to the disaster but had never gone for assistance, so they count as new clients but are actually not new victims.

6. See, for example, Dobash and Dobash (1979), Belknap (1995), and Gelles (1997).

7. Morrow and Enarson (1996), in their study of women in Hurricane Andrew, found that poor women had a difficult time recovering from the disaster.

8. Davis's results are in alignment with many in the disaster research community who believe that disasters speed up or exaggerate, but do not drastically alter, social processes, structures, and relationships.

Chapter 9

1. After the Buffalo Creek dam disaster, Kai Erikson (1976) observed, "To lose a home or the sum of one's belongings is to lose evidence as to who one is and where one belongs in the world" (p. 177).

2. Erikson (1976) found the same results in the Buffalo Creek flood, as one resident there stated, "I have a new home right now, and I would say that it is a much nicer home than what I had before. But it is a house, it is not a home."

3. Bolin (1982) asserts that despite the importance of these rituals, disaster researchers have long ignored the postdisaster process of reestablishing the daily routine.

4. Smith and Belgrave (1995) explain that after Hurricane Andrew there was a need to reinstate "approximate versions" of the old routines in the transition to normality (p. 247), and that these new routines of everyday life were being continuously shaped and negotiated (p. 259).

5. Ronn (1998) found that Swedish women in the United States also preserved familial and cultural Christmas foods in order to feel connected to home.

6. Coulees are waterways that run throughout the city and are designed to help with flood control. See the map in this book showing the location of several coulees in Grand Forks and East Grand Forks.

7. Erikson (1976) also found that flood survivors were traumatized over the loss of their belongings, which they said were a sign of their hard work over many years.

Chapter 10

The title of this chapter is adapted from the title of Kai Erickson's book, *Everything in Its Path*.

1. While the women represented other classes, such as lower, working, and upper-middle classes, the majority of the women self-identified as middle class, and it is their perception of their class standing that is most important to this analysis, for that is the basis of their class identity.

2. While some argue that the disaster field is too applied and policyoriented and does not engage in enough analysis of structure and inequality, I believe that sociological research on disasters can make significant contributions to both theory and policy.

3. Staples (2000) defined eligible households as those with children under the age of twelve years.

4. Erickson (1976) found some of the same problems with temporary trailers for the flood victims in his study.

5. Enarson and Fordham (2001) found that female Latina, migrant workers suffered from job and housing discrimination after disasters.

Appendix

1. For a more detailed discussion of the disaster recovery process, see the work of Rubin (1985) and Quarantelli (1999b).

2. This terminology on research roles was originally introduced by Raymond Gold (1969).

3. I shared with them my experience in the 1989 Loma Prieta earthquake in San Francisco, but I made sure to tell them that my apartment suffered minimal damage in that earthquake and that the disasters were different in many ways. I wanted to share my experience because they asked but also make it clear that I had a lot to learn about their loss and humanity.

4. Unfortunately, I was never given an opportunity to attend services at the synagogue.

Bibliography

Abraham, Margaret. 1996. "Ethnicity, Gender, and Marital Violence." *Gender and Society* 9(4):450–468.

Abramovitz, Mimi. 1994. "Is the Social Welfare System Inherently Sexist and Racist?" In *Controversial Issues in Social Policy,* edited by H. J. Karger and J. Midgley. Boston, MA: Allyn and Bacon.

Adler, Patricia A., and Peter Adler. 1987. *Membership Roles in Field Research.* Newbury Park, CA: Sage Publications.

———. 1991. *Backboards & Blackboards: College Athletes and Role Engulfment.* New York: Columbia University Press.

———. 1994. "Observational Techniques" Pp. 377–392 in *Handbook of Qualitative Research,* edited by N. K. Denzin and Y. S. Lincoln. Thousand Oaks, CA: Sage.

Alexander, David. 1997. "The Study of Natural Disasters, 1977–1997: Some Reflections on a Changing Field of Knowledge." *Disasters* 21(4):284–304.

Alway, Joan, Linda Liska Belgrave, and Kenneth J. Smith. 1998. "Back to Normal: Gender and Disaster." *Symbolic Interaction* 21(2):175–195.

Ambert, Anne-Marie, Patricia A. Adler, Peter Adler, and Daniel F. Detzner. 1995. "Understanding and Evaluating Qualitative Research." *Journal of Marriage and the Family* 57:879–893.

Anderson, William A. 1996. "The Underserved in Natural Disaster Reduction." Unpublished paper. Washington, DC: Hazard Mitigation Section, National Science Foundation.

Aptekar, L. 1990. "A Comparison of the Bicoastal Disasters of 1989." *Behavior Science Research* 24(1–4):73–104.

Arendell, Terry. 1986. *Mothers and Divorce: Legal, Economic, and Social Dilemmas.* Berkeley: University of California Press.

Arendt, Hannah. 1958. *The Human Condition.* Chicago: University of Chicago Press.

Barton, Allen H. 1969. *Communities in Disaster.* Garden City, NY: Anchor Books, Doubleday.

Baruch, Grace, Rosalind Barnett, and Caryl Rivers. 1983. *Lifeprints: New Patterns of Love and Work for Today's Women.* New York: McGraw-Hill.

Belknap, Joanne. 1995. "Law Enforcement Officers' Attitudes about the Appropriate Responses to Woman Battering." *International Review of Victimology* 4(1):47–62.

———. 1996. *The Invisible Woman: Gender, Crime, and Justice.* Belmont, CA: Wadsworth.

Bellah, Robert N. 1970. *Beyond Belief: Essays on Religion in a Post-Traditional World.* New York: Harper & Row.

Bellah, Robert N., R. Madsen, W. M. Sullivan, and S. M. Tipton. 1985. *Habits of the Heart: Individualism and Commitment in American Life.* Berkeley: University of California Press.

Biernacki, Patrick, and Dan Waldorf. 1981. "Snowball Sampling: Problems and Techniques of Chain Referral Sampling." *Sociological Methods and Research* 10:141–163.

Blaikie, Piers, Terry Cannon, Ian Davis, and Ben Wisner. 1994. *At Risk: Natural Hazards, People's Vulnerability, and Disasters.* New York: Routledge.

Blumer, Herbert. 1969. *Symbolic Interactionism.* Berkeley: University of California Press.

Bolin, Robert. 1993. "Household and Community Recovery After Earthquakes." Monograph #56, Program on Environment and Behavior. Boulder, CO: University of Colorado, Institute for Behavioral Sciences, Natural Hazards Research and Applications Information Center.

Bolin, Robert, and Patricia Bolton. 1986. *Race, Religion, and Ethnicity in Disaster Recovery.* Boulder, CO: University of Colorado Institute for Behavioral Science.

Bolin, Robert, and Lois Stanford. 1991. "Shelter, Housing, and Recovery: A Comparison of U.S. Disasters." *Disasters* 15(1):24–34.

———. 1998. "The Northridge Earthquake: Community-based Approaches to Unmet Recovery Needs." *Disasters* 22(1):21–38.

Braithwaite, M. 1982. "Decoration as Ritual Symbol." In *Symbolic and Structural Archaeology,* edited by I. Hodder. Cambridge, England: Cambridge University Press.

Bullock, Heather E. 1995. "Class Acts: Middle-Class Responses to the Poor." Pp. 118–159 in *The Social Psychology of Interpersonal Discrimination,* edited by B. Lott and D. Maluso. New York: Guilford Press.

Burke, Peter J., and Donald Reitzes. 1981. "The Link between Identity and Role Performance." *Social Psychology Quarterly* 44(2):83–92.

Caputi, Jane, and Diana E. H. Russell. 1997. "'Femicide': Speaking the Unspeakable." Pp. 421–426 in *Feminist Frontiers,* edited by L. Richardson, V. Taylor, and N. Whittier. New York: McGraw-Hill.

Chafetz, Janet Saltzman, 1990. *Gender Equity.* London: Sage.

Chafetz, Janet Saltzman.1998. "From Sex/Gender Roles to Gender Stratification: From Victim Blame to System Blame." Pp. 159–164 in *Feminist Foundations,* edited by K. A. Myers, C. D. Anderson, and B. J. Risman. Thousand Oaks, CA. Sage.

Charmaz, Kathy 1995. "Grounded Theory." Pp. 27–49 in *Rethinking Methods in Psychology,* edited by J. A. Smith, R. Harre, and L. Van Langenhove. London: Sage.

Chenoweth, Lesley. 1996. "Violence and Women with Disabilities." *Violence Against Women.* 2(4):391–411.

Chodorow, Nancy. 1978. *The Reproduction of Mothering: Psychoanalysis and the Sociology of Gender.* Berkeley: University of California Press.

Collins, Patricia Hill. 1990. *Black Feminist Thought.* Boston: Unwin Hyman.

Collins, Randall. 1988. *Theoretical Sociology.* New York: Harcourt Brace Jovanovich.

Coltrane, Scott. 1998. *Gender and Families.* Thousand Oaks, CA: Pine Forge Press.

Comerio, Mary C., John D. Landis, and Yodan Rofe. 1994. "Post-Disaster Residential Rebuilding." Working Paper #608. Berkeley, CA: University of California Institute of Urban and Regional Development.

Cooley, Charles Horton. [1902] 1964. *Human Nature and the Social Order.* New York: Schocken Books.

Coser, Lewis A. 1965. "The Sociology of Poverty." *Social Problems* 13(2):140–148.

———. 1974. *Greedy Institutions: Patterns of Undivided Commitment.* New York: Free Press.

Cuba, Lee, and David Hummon. 1993. "Constructing a Sense of Home: Place Affiliation and Migration Across the Life Cycle." *Sociological Forum* 8(4): 547-572.

Cunningham, Kamy. 1997. "Barbie Doll Culture and the American Waistland." Pp. 122–125 in *Feminist Frontiers,* edited by L. Richardson, V. Taylor, and N. Whittier. New York: McGraw-Hill.

Dann, Susan, and Paul Wilson. 1993. "Women and Emergency Services." *Symposium: Women in Emergencies and Disasters.* Brisbane, Australia: Queensland Bureau of Emergency Services.

Davis, Karen, and Morten G. Ender. 1999. "The 1997 Red River Valley Flood: Impact on Marital Relationships." *Applied Behavioral Science Review* 7(2):181–188.

Day, Phyllis. 1977. "The Scarlet 'W': Public Welfare as Sexual Stigma for Women." *Journal of Sociology and Social Welfare* 4(6): 872–881.

Denzin, Norman K. 1997. *Interpretive Ethnography: Ethnographic Practices for the 21st Century.* Thousand Oaks, CA: Sage Publications.

DeVault, Marjorie. 1991. *Feeding the Family.* Chicago: University of Chicago Press.

Dobash, R. Emerson, and Russell Dobash. 1979. *Violence Against Wives.* New York: Free Press.

Dobson, Narelle. 1994. "From Under the Mud-Pack: Women and the Charleville Floods." *Australian Journal of Emergency Management* 9(2):11–13.

Donley, L. 1982. "House Power: Swahili Space and Symbolic Markers." In *Symbolic and Structural Archaeology,* edited by I. Hodder. Cambridge, England: Cambridge University Press.

Durkheim, Emile. [1893] 1964. *The Division of Labor in Society.* New York: Free Press.

———. [1912] 1954. *The Elementary Forms of Religious Life.* New York: Free Press.

Dutton, Donald G. 1988. *The Domestic Assault of Women.* Boston: Allyn and Bacon, Inc.

Dutton, Mary Ann. 1996. "Battered Women's Strategic Response to Violence: The Role of Context." In *Future Interventions with Battered Women and the Families,* edited by J. Edleson and Z. Eisikovits. Thousand Oaks, CA Sage Publications.

Dynes, Russell R., and Enrico L. Quarantelli. 1976. "Community Conflict: Its Absence and Its Presence in Natural Disasters." *International Journal of Mass Emergencies and Disasters* 1:139–152.

Enarson, Elaine. 1998. "Battered Women in Disaster: A Case Study of Gendered Vulnerability." Presented at the meeting of the American Sociological Association, August, San Francisco, CA.

Enarson, Elaine, and Betty Hearn Morrow. 1997. "A Gendered Perspective: The Voices of Women." In *Hurricane Andrew: Ethnicity, Gender, and the Sociology of Disasters,* edited by W. G. Peacock, B. H. Morrow, and H. Gladwin. New York: Routledge.

Enarson, Elaine, and Maureen Fordham. 2001. "Lines that Divide, Ties that Bind: Race, Class, and Gender in Women's Flood Recovery in the U.S. and U.K." *The Australian Journal of Emergency Management* 15(4): 43–52.

Erez, Edna, and Joanne Belknap. 1998. "In Their Own Words: Battered Women's Assessment of the Criminal Processing System's Responses." *Violence and Victims* 13(3):3–20.

Erikson, Kai T. 1976. *Everything in Its Path: Destruction of Community in the Buffalo Creek Flood.* New York: Simon and Schuster.

Feagin, J. 1975. *Subordinating the Poor: Welfare and American Beliefs.* Englewood Cliffs, NJ: Prentice-Hall.

Ferraro, Kathleen J., and John M. Johnson. 1983. "How Women Experience Battering: The Process of Victimization." *Social Problems* 30(3):325–337.

Fontana, Andrea, and James H. Frey. 1994. "Interviewing: The Art of Science." Pp. 361–376 in *Handbook of Qualitative Research,* edited by N. K. Denzin and Y. S. Lincoln. Thousand Oaks, CA: Sage.

Fordham, Maureen, and Anne-Michelle Ketteridge. 1996. "Men Must Work and Women Must Weep: Examining Gender Stereotypes in Disasters." Pp. 81–94 in *The Gendered Terrain of Disaster,* edited by E. Enarson and B. H. Morrow. Westport, CT: Greenwood Publishing.

Forrest, Thomas R. 1978. "Group Emergence in Disaster." Pp. 105–125 in *Disasters: Theory and Research,* edited by E. L. Quarantelli. Beverly Hills, CA: Sage.

Fothergill, Alice, and Lori Peek. 2004. "Poverty and Disasters in the United States: A Review of Recent Sociological Findings." *Natural Hazards* 32(1): 89–110.

Fraenkel, Jack R., and Norman E. Wallen. 1996. *How to Design and Evaluate Research in Education.* New York: McGraw-Hill, Inc.

Frankenberg, Ruth. 1993. *White Women, Race Matters: The Social Construction of Whiteness.* Minneapolis: University of Minnesota Press.

Fritz, Charles. 1961. "Disaster." Pp. 651–694 in *Contemporary Social Problems,* edited by R. K. Merton and R. A. Nesbit. New York: Harcourt, Brace, & World, Inc.

Gelles, Richard J. 1997. *Intimate Violence in Families.* Thousand Oaks, CA: Sage Publications.

Gilligan, Carol. 1982. *In a Different Voice: Psychological Theory and Women's Development.* Cambridge, MA: Harvard University Press.

Glaser, Barney. 1978. *Theoretical Sensitivity.* Mill Valley, CA: Sociology Press.

Glaser, Barney, and Anselm Strauss. 1967. *The Discovery of Grounded Theory.* Chicago: Aldine.

———. 1959. *The Presentation of Self in Everyday Life.* New York: Doubleday.

Goffman, Erving. 1963. *Stigma: Notes on the Management of Spoiled Identity.* Englewood Cliffs, NJ: Prentice-Hall, Inc.

Gold, Raymond L. 1969. "Roles in Sociological Field Observations." In *Issues in Participant Observation,* edited by G. J. McCall and J. L. Simmons. Reading, MA: Addison-Wesley Publishing Company.

Gordon, Linda. 1990. *Women, the State, and Welfare.* Madison, WI: University of Wisconsin Press.

Grant, Judith. 1993. *Fundamental Feminism: Contesting the Core Concepts of Feminist Theory.* New York: Routledge.

Green, Bonnie L. 1996. "Traumatic Stress and Disaster: Mental Health Effects and Factors Influencing Adaption." *International Review of Psychiatry.* 2:177–210.

Hagen, Carol A., Morten G. Ender, Kathleen A. Tiemann, and Clifford O. Hagen, Jr. 1999. "Graffiti on the Great Plains: A Social Reaction to the Red River Valley Flood of 1997." *Applied Behavioral Science Review* 7(2):145–158.

Hansen, Karen V. 1987. "Feminist Conceptions of Public and Private: A Critical Analysis." *Berkeley Journal of Sociology* 32:105–128.

Hansen, Karen, and Anita Ilta Garey. 1998. *Families in the United States: Kinship and Domestic Politics.* Philadelphia, PA: Temple University Press.

Hatty, Suzanne E. 1996. "The Violence of Displacement: The Problematics of Survival for Homeless Young Women." *Violence Against Women* 2(4):412–428.

Hays, Sharon. 1996. *The Cultural Contradictions of Motherhood.* New Haven, CT: Yale University Press.

Herman, Judith Lewis. 1992. *Trauma and Recovery.* New York: Basic Books.

Hillesum, Etty. 1993. "A Letter from Westerbork." Pp. 46–57 in *Different Voices: Women and the Holocaust,* edited by C. Rittner and J. K. Roth. New York: Paragon House.

Hochschild, Arlie Russell. 1983. *The Managed Heart: Commercialization of Human Feeling.* Berkeley, CA: University of California Press.

———. 1989. *The Second Shift: Working Parents and the Revolution at Home.* New York: Viking.

———. 1997. *The Time Bind: When Work Becomes Home and Home Becomes Work.* New York: Henry Holt and Company.

Hodder, Ian. 1991. *Reading the Past.* Cambridge: Cambridge University Press.

———. 1994. "The Interpretation of Documents and Material Culture." Pp. 393–402 in *Handbook of Qualitative Research,* edited by N. K. Denzin and Y. S. Lincoln. Thousand Oaks, CA: Sage.

Hoffman, Susanna M. 1998. "Eve and Adam among the Embers: Gender Patterns after the Oakland Berkeley Firestorm." Pp. 55–61 in *The Gendered Terrain of Disasters,* edited by E. Enarson and B. H. Morrow. Westport, CT: Greenwood Publishing Group.

Hollander, Jocelyn A., and Judith A. Howard. 2000. "Social Psychological Theories on Social Inequalities." *Social Psychology Quarterly* 63(4):338–351.

Honeycombe, Beth. 1993. "Special Needs of Women in Emergency Situations." *Symposium: Women in Emergencies and Disasters.* Queensland Bureau of Emergency Services. Brisbane, Queensland, Australia.

hooks, bell. 1981. *Ain't I a Woman: Black Women and Feminism.* Boston: South End Press.

Hughes, Everett C. 1945. "Dilemmas and Contradictions in Status." *American Journal of Sociology* 50:353–5.

International Red River Basin Task Force. 1999. "An Assessment of Recovery Assistance Provided in Canada and the United States after the 1997 Floods in the Red River Basin." Report prepared by the Natural Hazards Center, University of Colorado, and the Disaster Research Institute, University of Manitoba, and submitted to the International Joint Commission, Ottawa, Ontario.

Jacobs, Janet. 1996. "Women, Ritual, and Secrecy: The Creation of Crypto Jewish Culture," *Journal for the Scientific Study of Religion* 35(2):97–108.

Kanter, Rosabeth Moss. 1977. *Men and Women of the Corporation.* New York: Basic Book, Inc.

Kantor, Glenda K., and Murray A. Straus. 1987. "The 'Drunken Bum' Theory of Wife Beating." *Social Problems* 34(3):213–230.

Ketteridge, Anne-Michelle, and Maureen Fordham. 1998. "Flood Evacuation in Two Communities in Scotland: Lessons from European Research." *International Journal of Mass Emergencies and Disasters* 16(2):119–143.

Kimmel, Michael S. 2000. *The Gendered Society.* New York: Oxford University Press.

Lamphere, Louise. 1993. "The Domestic Sphere of Women and the Public World of Men: The Strengths and Limitations of an Anthropological Dichotomy." Pp.67–77 in *Gender in Cross-Cultural Perspective,* edited by C. B. Brettell and C. F. Sargent. Englewood Cliffs, NJ: Prentice Hall.

Larson, Reed, and Maryse H. Richards. 1997. "Healthy Families: Toward Convergent Realities." Pp.214–220 in *Family in Transition,* edited by A. S. Skolnick and J. H. Skolnick. New York: Longman.

League of the Red Cross and Red Crescent Societies. 1991. "Working with Women in Emergency Relief and Rehabilitation Programmes." Field Studies Paper No. 2. Geneva, Switzerland: League of Red Cross.

Leik, Robert K., Sheila A. Leik, Knut Ekker, and Gregory A. Gifford. 1982. *Under the Threat of Mount St. Helens: A Study of Chronic Family Stress.* Minneapolis: University of Minnesota Family Study Center.

Leonardo, Micaela di 1987. "The Female World of Cards and Holidays: Women, Families, and the Work of Kinship" *Signs.* 12 (3): 440–453.

Levitin, Teresa A. 1975. "Deviants as Active Participants in the Labeling Process: The Visibly Handicapped." *Social Problems* 22 (4): 548–557.

Lewis, Michael. 1978. *The Culture of Inequality.* New York: Meridian Books.

Liebow, Elliot. 1993. *Tell Them Who I Am: The Lives of Homeless Women.* New York: Penguin Books.

Lindesmith, Alfred R., Anselm L. Strauss, and Norman K. Denzin. 1975. *Social Psychology.* Hinsdale, IL: The Dryden Press.

Lipstadt, Deborah E. 1993. "Facing the Void." Pp. 349–354 in *Different Voices: Women and the Holocaust,* edited by C. Rittner and J. K. Roth. New York: Paragon House.

Loewenberg, Frank M. 1981. "The Destigmatization of Public Dependency." *Social Service Review* 55(3) 434–452.

Lofland, John, and Lyn H. Lofland. 1984. *Analyzing Social Settings: A Guide to Qualitative Observation and Analysis.* Belmont, CA: Wadsworth.

Lois, Jennifer. 2003. *Heroic Efforts: The Emotional Culture of Search and Rescue Volunteers.* New York: New York University Press.

Lopata, Helena Znaniecka. 1994. *Circles and Settings: Role Changes of American Women.* Albany, NY: State University of New York Press.

MacLeod, Jay. 1995. *Ain't No Makin' It.* Boulder, CO: Westview Press.

Marks, Stephen R. 1977. "Multiple Roles and Role Strain: Some Notes on Human Energy, Time and Commitment." *American Sociological Review,* 42: 921–936.

Mead, George Herbert. 1934. *Mind, Self, and Society.* Chicago: University of Chicago Press.

Merton, Robert K. 1969. Foreward in *Communities in Disaster* by A. H. Barton. New York: Doubleday.

Mileti, Dennis S. 1999. *Disasters by Design: A Reassessment of Natural Hazards in the United States.* Washington, DC: Joseph Henry Press.

Miller, Susan L. 1989. "Unintended Side Effects of Pro-arrest Policies and their Race and Class Implications for Battered Women." *Criminal Justice Policy Review* 3:299–317.

Milroy, Beth Moore, and Susan Wismer. 1994. "Communities, Work and Public/Private Sphere Models." *Gender, Place, and Culture* 1(1):71–90.

Mitchell, Jerry Tyrone. 1998. "Hazards, Religion, and Place: Prayer and Peril in South Carolina." Ph.D. Dissertation, Department of Geography, University of South Carolina.

Morrow, Betty Hearn. 1997. "Stretching the Bonds: The Families of Andrew." In *Hurricane Andrew: Ethnicity, Gender, and the Sociology of Disasters,* edited by W. G. Peacock, B. H. Morrow, and H. Gladwin. New York: Routledge.

Morrow, Betty Hearn, and Elaine Enarson. 1996. "Hurricane Andrew Through Women's Eyes: Issues and Recommendations." *International Journal of Mass Emergencies and Disasters* 14(1):5–22.

Neal, David M., and Brenda Phillips. 1990. "Female-Dominated Local Social Movement Organizations in Disaster-Threat Situations." Pp. 243–255 in *Women and Social Protest,* edited by G. West and R. L. Blumberg. New York: Oxford University Press.

Newman, Katherine. 1989. *Falling From Grace: The Experience of Downward Mobility in the American Middle Class.* New York: Vintage Books.

———. 1999. *Falling From Grace: Downward Mobility in the Age of Affluence.* Berkeley: University of California Press.

Nielsen, Joyce McCarl. 1984. "Sex and Gender in Disaster Research." Unpublished report. Boulder, CO: Department of Sociology, University of Colorado.

———. 1990. *Sex and Gender in Society: Perspectives on Stratification.* Prospect Heights, IL: Waveland Press, Inc.

Nigg, Joanne. 1994. "Influences of Symbolic Interaction on Disaster Research." Pp. 33–50 in *Self, Collective Behavior, and Society,* edited by G. M. Platt and C. Gordon. Greenwich, CT: JAI Press, Inc.

Noel, Gloria. 1990. "The Role of Women in Disaster Management." Paper presented at the 17th Biennial Conference of the Caribbean Nurses' Organization, Castries, Saint Lucia, July 24.

Oakley, Ann. 1975. *The Sociology of Housework.* New York: Pantheon Books.

———. 1981. "Interviewing Women: A Contradiction in Terms." Pp. 30–61 in *Doing Feminist Research,* edited by H. Roberts. London: Routledge & Kegan Paul.

Okun, Lewis. 1986. *Woman Abuse: Facts Replacing Myths.* Albany: State University of New York Press.

Olesen, Virginia L. 1992. "Extraordinary Events and Mundane Ailments: The Contextual Dialectics of the Embodied Self." Pp. 205–220 in *Investigating Subjectivity: Research on Lived Experience,* edited by C. Ellis and M. G. Flaherty.

———. 2000. "Feminisms and Models of Qualitative Research." Pp. 215–255 in *Handbook of Qualitative Research,* edited by N. K. Denzin and Y. S. Lincoln. Thousand Oaks, CA: Sage.

Parsons, Talcott. 1951. *The Social System.* New York: Free Press.

Peacock, Walt, Betty Hearn Morrow, and Hugh Gladwin. 1997. *Hurricane Andrew: Ethnicity, Gender, and the Sociology of Disasters.* New York: Routledge.

Phillips, Brenda. 1990. "Gender as a Variable in Emergency Response." pp. 84–90 In *The Loma Prieta Earthquake: Studies of Short-Term Impacts.* edited by R. C. Bolin. Boulder: Institute of Behavior Science, University of Colorado.

Phillips, Brenda, and Mindy Ephraim. 1992. "Living in the Aftermath: Blaming Processes in the Loma Prieta Earthquake." Working Paper #80. Boulder, CO: Institute for Behavioral Science, Natural Hazard Research and Applications Information Center, University of Colorado.

Pielke, Roger A. 1999. "Who Decides? Forecasts and Responsibilities in the 1997 Red River Flood." *Applied Behavioral Science Review* 7(2):83–102.

Piven, Frances Fox. 1990. "Ideology and the State: Women, Power, and the Welfare State." In *Women, the State, and Welfare,* edited by L. Gordon. Madison, WI: University of Wisconsin Press.

Pleck, Elizabeth. 1987. *Domestic Tyranny: The Making of American Social Policy Against Family Violence from Colonial Times to the Present.* New York: Oxford.

Quarantelli, Enrico L. 1984. "Organizational Behavior in Disasters and Implications for Disaster Planning." Emmitsburg, MD: National Training Center, Federal Emergency Management Agency.

———. 1994. "Draft of a Sociological Disaster Research Agenda for the Future: Theoretical, Methodological, and Empirical Issues." Preliminary Paper #228. Newark: Disaster Research Center, University of Delaware.

———. 1999a. "The Sociology of Panic." Preliminary Paper #283. Newark: Disaster Research Center, University of Delaware.

———. 1999b. "The Disaster Recovery Process: What We Know and Do Not Know from Research." Preliminary Paper #286. Newark: Disaster Research Center, University of Delaware.

Rank, Mark. 1994. *Living on the Edge: The Realities of Welfare in America.* New York: Columbia University Press.

Reinharz, Shulamit. 1992. *Feminist Methods in Social Research.* New York: Oxford University Press.

Ridgeway, Cecilia. 1997. "Interaction and the Conservation of Gender Inequality: Considering Employment." *American Sociological Review* 47:76–88.

Risman, Barbara. 1998. *Gender Vertigo.* New Haven, CT: Yale University Press.

Rittner, Carol, and John K. Roth. 1993. *Different Voices: Women and the Holocaust.* New York: Paragon House.

Robinson, Elwyn. 1966. *History of North Dakota.* Lincoln: University of Nebraska Press.

Rochford, E. Burke Jr., and T. Jean Blocker. 1991. "Coping with 'Natural' Hazards as Stressors: The Predictors of Activism in a Flood Disaster." *Environment and Behavior* 23:171–194.

Rollins, Judith. 1985. *Between Women: Domestics and their Employers.* Philadelphia: Temple University Press.

Ronn, Sara. 1998. "Kaldolmar I Colorado" ("Kaldolmar in Colorado"). Unpublished report (in Swedish). Sweden: Etnologiska Instutionen, Uppsala: Uppsala University, Department of Cultural Anthropology and Ethnology.

Rosaldo, Michelle Zimbalist. 1980. "The Use and Abuse of Anthropology: Reflections on Feminism and Cross-Cultural Understanding." *Signs* 5(3):389–417.

Rubin, Claire B. 1985. "Community Recovery from a Major Natural Disaster." Monograph #41. Boulder, CO: University of Colorado Institute of Behavioral Science.

Sarup, M. 1994. "Home and Identity." In *Travellers' Tales: Narratives of Home and Displacement*, edited by G. Robertson, M. Mash, L. Tickner, J. Bird, B. Curtis, and T. Putnam. London: Routledge.

Schor, Juliet. 1988. *The Overspent American: Upscaling, Downshifting, and the New Consumer.* New York: Basic Books.

Schwartz, Martin. 1988. "Ain't Got No Class: Universal Risk Theories of Battering." *Contemporary Crises* 12:373–392.

Sennett, Richard, and Jonathan Cobb. 1972. *The Hidden Injuries of Class.* New York: Vintage Books.

Sidel, Ruth. 1986. *Women and Children Last: The Plight of Poor Women in Affluent America.* New York: Viking Penguin, Inc.

Sieber, Sam D. 1974. "Toward a Theory of Role Accumulation." *American Sociological Review* 39:567–78.

Simmel, Georg. 1965. "The Poor." *Social Problems* 13(2):118–140.

Sims, John H., and Duane D. Baumann. 1972. "The Tornado Threat: Coping Styles of the North and South." *Science* 176: 1386–1392.

Smith, Dorothy E. 1987. *The Everyday World as Problematic: A Feminist Sociology.* Boston: Northeastern University Press.

Smith, Kenneth J., and Linda Liska Belgrave. 1995. "The Reconstruction of Everyday Life: Experiencing Hurricane Andrew." *Journal of Contemporary Ethnography* 24(3):244–269.

Sobsey, R. 1994. *Violence in the Lives of People with Disabilities: The End of Silent Acceptance?* Baltimore, MD: Brookes.

Spelman, Elizabeth. 1988. *Inessential Woman: Problems of Exclusion in Feminist Thought.* Boston: Beacon Press.

Staples, Clifford L. 2000. "Child Care Arrangements in Grand Forks." Grand Forks, ND: Unpublished research report. Department of Sociology, University of North Dakota.

Strauss, Anselm. 1959. *Mirrors and Masks.* Mill Valley, CA: Sociology Press.

Stryker, Sheldon. 1968. "Identity Salience and Role Performance." *Journal of Marriage and the Family* 30:558–564.

Taylor, James B. 1972. "An Approach to the Analysis of Emergent Phenomena." Pp. 110–129 in *Proceedings of the Japan-United States Disaster Research Seminar: Organizational and Community Responses to Disasters.* Columbus, OH: Disaster Research Center, Ohio State University.

Thomson, R. G. 1994. "Redrawing the Boundaries of Feminist Disability Studies." *Feminist Studies* 20:583–595.

Tiemann, Kathleen, A., and Clifford L. Staples. 1999. "From the Editors." *Applied Behavioral Science Review* 7(2):8.

Tong, Rosemarie. 1984. *Women, Sex, and the Law.* Totawa, NJ: Rowman & Allanheld.

Tuana, Nancy. 1993. "With Many Voices: Feminism and Theoretical Pluralism." Pp. 281–289 in *Theory on Gender/Feminism on Theory*, edited by P. England. New York: Aldine de Gruyter.

Turner, Ralph H. 1976. "The Real Self: From Institution to Impulse." *American Journal of Sociology* 81(5):989–1016.

———. 1978. "The Role and the Person." *American Journal of Sociology* 84:1–23.

Turner, Ralph H., Joanne M. Nigg, and Denise Heller Paz. 1986. *Waiting for Disaster: Earthquake Watch in California.* Berkeley, CA: University of California Press.

Walker, Alice. 1983. *In Search of Our Mothers' Gardens: Womanist Prose.* San Diego, CA: Harcourt Brace Jovanovich.

Walker, Lenore E. 1979. *The Battered Woman.* New York: Harper & Row.

Warner, Susan, and Kathryn M. Feltey. 1999. "From Victim to Survivor: Recovered Memories and Identity Transformation." Pp. 161–174 in *Trauma and Memory*, edited by L. M. Williams and V. L. Banyard. Thousand Oaks, CA: Sage.

Warren, Carol A. B. 1988. *Gender Issues in Field Research.* Newbury Park, CA: Sage.

Wenger, Dennis E. and Thomas F. James. 1994. "The Convergence of Volunteers in a Consensus Crisis: The Case of the 1985 Mexico City Earthquake." Pp. 229–243 in *Disasters, Collective Behavior, and Social Organization*, edited by R. R. Dynes and K. J. Tierney. Newark, NJ: University of Delaware Press.

West, Candace, and Don. H. Zimmerman. 1987. "Doing Gender." *Gender and Society* 1(2):125–151.

Wilson, Jennifer, Brenda D. Phillips, and David M. Neal. 1998. "Domestic Violence after Disaster." Pp. 115–122 in *The Gendered Terrain of Disaster: Through Women's Eyes*, edited by E. Enarson and B. H. Morrow. Westport, CT: Praeger.

Wraith, Ruth. 1997. "Women in Emergency Management: Where are They?" *Australian Journal of Emergency Management*, January: 9–11.

Wyers, Norman L. 1977. "Shame and Public Dependency: A Literature Review." *Journal of Sociology and Social Welfare* 4(6):955–966.

Yelvington, K.A. 1997. "Coping in a Temporary Way: The Tent Cities." Pp. 92–115 in *Hurricane Andrew: Ethnicity, Gender, and the Sociology of Disasters*, edited by W. G. Peacock, B. H. Morrow, and H. Gladwin. New York: Routledge.

Zinn, Maxine Baca. 1989. "Family, Race, and Poverty in the Eighties." *Signs: Journal of Women in Culture and Society* 14(4): 856–874.

Index

Achievement ideology, 12, 79, 80, 81, 208
  need to challenge, 219
Alcohol, use of, 116–17
Angel Fund, 60, 67, 77, 82, 83, 98
  creation of, 244 n. 9
Anger
  at being taken advantage of, 122
  breaking gender norms of, 121
  toward family, 121, 143–44
  toward government, representatives of, 121
Artifacts
  belonging to children, loss of, 199
  belonging to husband, loss of, 199
  Christmas decorations, loss of, 197
  furniture of the self, 192
  hard work represented by 200–1
  possessions, loss of, 193, 194
  preserving from flood, 192–97, 202
  and sense of self, 196

Between Women (Rollins), 58
Blame, 23–24
Blizzard "Hannah," 18
Buffalo Creek disaster, 181
  survivors of, 192

Charity, accepting of, 13. *See also* Public assistance
  at odds with caregiving role, 86
  different perspectives on, 85
  people undeserving of, 84
  status, causing loss of, 91
  temporary, 95–96
Childcare, during and fater disaster
  lack of, 42
  need for, 213–14
Church. *See also* Religion
  attachment to, 153
  attendance after flood, 150–53
  creation of by evacuees, 154
  relationship with, 137, 155
  sermon, topics of, 154–55
Cigarettes, use of, 116–17
Class, 10, 75, 78, 97
  classism, 103–4
  entitlements of, 77–78
  return to divisions of, 73–74, 75
  role of in disaster experience, 216
  and trailer, link to, 95
Community Violence Intervention Center, 158, 162, 165, 212, 218
  effect of flood on, 168
  services of, increase in, 167–68
Conflict, after flood
  in family, 138, 141, 155
  from financial problems, 65
  with government, 67, 68
  living space, lack of, 140, 143
  in marriage, 138
  from work, changing demands of, 139–40